Reconstructing the Dreamland

The Dreamland Theatre had been a meeting place for Greenwood residents, talking about the ideas of the renaissance. The shell, with its marquee falling, suggests the trajectory of the Greenwood community. The theater also represents the vitality of the community, for in 1922 the Williams family had it rebuilt; the art deco structure was better than the one that had been destroyed.

RECONSTRUCTING THE DREAMLAND

The Tulsa Riot of 1921

Race, Reparations, and Reconciliation

Alfred L. Brophy

OXFORD

UNIVERSITY PRESS

2002

OXFORD
UNIVERSITY PRESS

Oxford   New York
Athens   Auckland   Bangkok   Bogotá   Buenos Aires   Cape Town
Chennai   Dar es Salaam   Delhi   Florence   Hong Kong   Istanbul   Karachi
Kolkata   Kuala Lumpur   Madrid   Melbourne   Mexico City   Mumbai
Nairobi   Paris   São Paulo   Shanghai   Singapore   Taipei   Tokyo
Toronto   Warsaw

and associated companies in
Berlin   Ibadan

Library of Congress Cataloging-in-Publication Data
Brophy, Alfred L.
Reconstructing the dreamlamd: the Tulsa riot of 1921:
race, reparations, and reconciliation / Alfred L. Brophy.
p. cm.   Includes bibliographical references and index.
ISBN 978-0-19-516103-8
1. African Americans—Oklahoma—Tulsa—History—20th century.
2. African American neighborhoods—Oklahoma—Tulsa—History—20th century.
3. Riots—Oklahoma—Tulsa—History—20th century.
4. Violence—Oklahoma—Tulsa—History—20th century.
5. Tulsa (Okla.)—Race rellations.
6. African Americans—Oklahoma—Tulsa—Claims.
7. Racism—Oklahoma—Tulsa—History—20th century.
I. Title.

F704.T92 B76 2002
976.6'86—dc21   2001036770

Printed in the United States of America
on acid-free paper

For the journalists and historians who have preserved the remembrance of the riot, especially Brent, Don, Ellie, Bob, Arnold, Dick, Valerie, and Scott

Contents

Contents

Preface

On June 1, 1921, white mobs, abetted by state and local law enforcement authorities, destroyed the Greenwood section of Tulsa, Oklahoma, a vibrant African American community whose entrepreneurial verve led some to call its main thoroughfare "the black Wall Street." Resentful of the evident ambitiousness and affluence of Greenwood's upper class, fearful of the assertiveness displayed by black veterans of World War I who insistently demanded for themselves the democracy for which they had risked their lives abroad in the Great War, animated by the idea that Negroes must be made to stay in their "place" at the bottom of the social totem pole, habituated to the use of vigilante violence, and angered by (false) news reports and rumors about the rape of a white woman by a black man, white Tulsans killed at least twenty-five of their black neighbors—and probably dozens more—and torched thirty-five city blocks, rendering more than a thousand families homeless.

Brophy reveals fascinating facts about the Tulsa riot, its antecedents, and its aftermath that will enlighten specialists as well as novices in the study of race relations. He details the initial acknowledgment by some prominent whites that white Tulsa had committed a terrible crime against black Tulsa, the superseding effort (largely successful) to blame the riot on the victimized black community, and the layers of deceit, prejudice, and indifference that have, until recently, enshrouded this baleful episode.

Reconstructing the Dreamland is a timely contribution to a variety of important and contentious discussions involving American history, African American culture, and the problems encountered in attempting to right past wrongs. Professor Brophy's study rightly emphasizes the centrality of racially motivated violence to the American experience. Nowadays when Americans use the term "race riot," many

immediately conjure up images of Los Angeles in 1992 (following the
infamous acquittals of the police officers who assaulted Rodney King)
or the disturbances in Detroit, Newark, and elsewhere during the
long, hot summers of the late 1960s. In those riots, people of color
comprised the bulk of the looters and arsonists, targeting the businesses of "whiteys" and others perceived to be exploitative outsiders.
Reconstructing the Dreamland recalls an older tradition of race rioting in which whites targeted blacks and their property for destruction,
a tradition in which police, national guards, and other ostensible
guardians of law and order invariably sided with the perpetrators of
mayhem against vulnerable racial minorities.

Despite a recent outpouring of scholarship about lynching and
resistance, many Americans remain ignorant of the extent to which
anti-black, racially motivated violence has significantly shaped
African American political culture. The National Association for the
Advancement of Colored People (NAACP) was created in direct
response to the Springfield, Illinois riot of 1908—an anti-black eruption eerily similar to that which engulfed Greenwood. For the first
twenty years of the NAACP's existence, its primary activity consisted
of publicizing the truth about racially motivated lynching and riots.
To this day, past and present failures by police to extend to blacks the
equal protection of the law (including, of course, protection against
police misconduct) seed a conspicuous cynicism toward police
authority that is discernible within many black communities. For
those who want to know more about the etiology of this cynicism—
or, perhaps, it is better termed realism—*Reconstructing the Dreamland* offers sobering detail.

Professor Brophy goes to considerable lengths to tell the story of
the Tulsa riot "from the Greenwood perspective." Appropriately dissatisfied with the sanitized and distorted version of events bequeathed
to the public by an all-white grand jury that blamed blacks predom-
inantly for the violence, Brophy carefully scrutinizes sources that have
often been slighted: the observations of black journalists, reminis-
cences by African American witnesses, briefs written by black
lawyers, and impressions penned by black poets. By doing so, he
unveils corrective facts and forgotten interpretations. He also uncovers a spectrum of views that contended for primacy within black
Tulsa, thus showing that even under exigent circumstances responses
are never dictated solely by surrounding circumstances but are, to

some extent, the result of choices for which people, even cruelly oppressed people, can appropriately be held responsible. Professor Brophy introduces readers to blacks who were willing to resort to arms to thwart lynching and to little known black litigants and attorneys who displayed far more faith in the administration of justice than state and federal tribunals deserved.

Brophy's explorations of litigation arising from the Tulsa riots are especially noteworthy insofar as they contribute substantially to an important development in legal academia: the reconsideration of what well-educated lawyers are expected to know (or at least to know about). Even the most comprehensive treatises and casebooks on race relations law typically omit references to state statutes that provided money damages to persons injured by mobs when police authorities neglected their duty. Similarly overlooked have been lawsuits that attempted (typically unsuccessfully) to obtain relief for victims in jurisdictions, like Oklahoma, which failed to enact legislation specifically aimed at punishing nonfeasance or malfeasance by police in the context of nonviolence. Professor Brophy explains carefully why such statutes were enacted, why they remained largely unenforced, the circumstances in which a few victims were able to invoke these statutes to obtain relief, and the staunch refusal of courts to grant relief to victims in the absence of such laws. In the course of doing so, he shows that there is a tradition of debate over rectifying communal racial crimes in America that is more developed than has been generally recognized.

In the concluding chapter of *Reconstructing the Dreamland*, Professor Brophy changes roles. He takes off the garb of a historian primarily interested in dissecting and explaining the past and dons that of a policy analyst who openly and candidly argues in favor of the proposition that survivors of the attack on Greenwood ought now to receive an apology from municipal and state officials in Tulsa as well as financial reparations. Carefully attending to the fear that granting reparations to one group of claimants for one egregious injustice will open the way to a flood of claims generated by countless injustices, Brophy stipulates four criteria by which demands for reparations could be limited. Using those criteria, he compares the case for reparations in Tulsa to those in which reparations have been granted to others and concludes, among other things, that Greenwood's survivors have an even stronger argument for reparations than already-successful claimants in analogous circumstances.

Finally, Professor Brophy situates the ongoing debate over the proper way to make amends in Tulsa within larger national and international conversations regarding the moral, political, and legal difficulties encountered when governments are called upon to acknowledge and rectify wrongs that they or their predecessors have committed. This broad, comparative perspective is a useful antidote to the smug triumphalism that massively afflicts American culture, particularly its historiography. Professor Brophy reminds us that deadly, cruel, racial violence is not something that only happens "out there" in the rest of the world but is something that has also happened here in the United States on a massive scale and that just as others out there have fallen short in reckoning with their pasts, so too have Americans have largely failed to honestly and honorably face daunting problems tragically bequeathed to them.

Randall Kennedy

Acknowledgments

If, as Ralph Ellison said, geography is fate, it has been my great good fortune to spend the first six years of my teaching career at Oklahoma City University (OCU) School of Law. It was there that I was able to work on reparations for the Tulsa riot, which has given me more pleasure than anything else I have ever done. I have made many friends through the Riot Commission—people who are interested in understanding the issues of history, race, law, and property that intersected on May 31, 1921.

I owe an especially large debt to two colleagues at OCU, Arthur LeFrancois and Richard Coulson, who convinced the faculty to hire me to teach property and legal history. Over the years Art and Richard, along with many other colleagues, have helped me make a home in Oklahoma City. They—and particularly Fran Deathe, Judy Morgan, and John Perkins in the library—have tolerated my odd research interests, which have wandered from seventeenth-century German law, to antebellum property law, to the Tulsa riot, and have provided the financial and scholarly support that has made my writing possible. (Whether their confidence in me was misplaced is a question best answered by my students!) My friends and colleagues at OCU, including Fiona Smith, Donna Greggory, Vicki Canady, Phyllis Bernard, Charlie Cantrell, Dan Morgan, Norwood Beveridge, and Michael Gibson, have helped this project in many ways. Dana Jim first alerted me to the Riot Commission by sending me an article from the *New York Times* about it; Von Creel convinced Bob Blackburn, the chair of the Riot Commission, to give me a piece of the puzzle to work on.

More recently, my colleagues at Boston College Law School have aided this project immensely. Phyllis Goldfarb, Sharon Beckman, Aviam Soifer, Dean Hashimoto, Zygmunt Plater, Ruth-Arlene Howe, Judy McMurrow, Reginald Alleyne, Mark Brodin, Sanford Katz, Bob

Bloom, and Anthony Farley have helped me formulate the case for reparations. Mary Sarah Bilder helped enormously with this project and so many others. Dean Ken Randall of the University of Alabama School of Law financed a final summer of work on this project.

Before I ever set foot in Oklahoma, I was the beneficiary of a great many teachers, who took time away from their work and their families to help me. I owe them all much more than I can repay—or even express. But perhaps I can help some other aspiring scholars somewhere down the road and thus keep the circle going. And when I do I will be thinking of them. I begin with my parents, my two most important teachers. Then, at the University of Pennsylvania, Walter Licht, Richard S. Dunn, and Bruce Kuklick all took me under their tutelage and taught me much about doing history—and loving it. At Columbia Law School Eben Moglen taught me about property and legal history—and a great many other things as well. It is because of Eben that I am a legal historian. In the History of American Civilization Program at Harvard I had the honor of studying with Morton J. Horwitz, Bernard Bailyn, Charlie Donahue, Alan Heimert, and Werner Sollors. I owe them deeply for expanding my universe and teaching me about writing history.

The people who have worked on the Tulsa riot with me—scholars all—have contributed in enormous ways to my understanding of the riot. The journalists who have worked on this project, Brent Staples, Eleanor Beardsley, Terry Gross, Arnold Hamilton, Valerie Malone, Randy Krehbiel, James Hirsch, V. Dion Haynes, Doug Bukowski, Ben Fenwick, Rik Espinosa, Samm Brown, Jim Brown, Lois Romano, Oralandar Brand-Williams, and Claudia Kolker, have asked questions—and shared their own insights into the riot with me. With their help—and especially with Brent Staples' help and questions—I have learned about many people and events I would not have otherwise known about. They have taught me much, but, above all, they are responsible for telling the story of the riot. They are some of the modern heroes of this story.

Professor Kenneth W. Mack and Randall Kennedy both read and commented on the manuscript, and I am particularly grateful for their criticisms and for making me believe in the rule of law as a key theme. I have been the beneficiary of a great many lawyers and historians who have taken an interest in this project, including Robert Westley, Christine Desan, William W. Fisher, Martha Minow, Carlos Ball, Daniel

Filler, Wythe Holt, Daniel Hulsebosch, Richard Storrow, Joseph Kennedy, Daniel Hamilton, Andrew R. Klein, John Schlegel, Angela Kupenda, Rebecca J. Huss, Jennifer S. Byram, Jack Chin, Peter Hoffer, Stephen Siegel, Calvin Massey, and John Nowak. And most important, my editor at Oxford, Dedi Felman, has been amazingly helpful. She took in my wayward project, helped me formulate and then reformulate it, told me lots of things I needed to hear, rewrote numerous drafts—in short, made the manuscript into what it is now. She is simply wonderful. I cannot thank her enough.

Everyone who works on the Tulsa riot owes an enormous debt to Scott Ellsworth. It is odd, it seems to me, that his magnificent book, *Death in the Promised Land*, which is one of the first books I read when I started teaching in Oklahoma, should now occupy such an important place in my life. (Although, as Ralph Ellison said, perhaps it is not. Find out enough about a given event and the unexpected becomes commonplace.) Scott has taught me a great deal about the riot and although I disagree with him on some areas, I am indebted to him for his generosity and the role he has played in preserving the story of the riot.

I have also learned from a dedicated group of Tulsa historians. Although Bob Norris and I disagree on many aspects of the riot, he is, nevertheless, a lovable rouge, a scholar, and one of the most knowledgeable and generous people I have met while working on this project. Plus, Bob shows the detachment of a scholar drawn from the ranks of hard-drinking fraternity men. Beryl Ford, like Bob, will disagree with much (maybe most) of what I have to say. Beryl's warmth and generosity led him to help me, as he has helped so many other Tulsa historians, and I am grateful to him, as I am to Coni Williams and Michelle Powell at the Tulsa Historical Society, to Dick Warner, of the Riot Commission, and to my friend Bruce Fisher of the Oklahoma Historical Society. (Coni, I bet you never thought you'd be in the same sentence with Beryl!) In addition, Larry O'Dell, Sally Howe Smith, and especially Lee Conner have helped me on many occasions. Lee's help was indispensable in locating key grand jury and other court records.

The politicians and commission members have been unfailingly kind to me. Eddie Faye Gates has shared her knowledge and research, as have Currie Ballard, Jimmy White, and Major Madison. I appreciate the kindness of Vivian Clark and Senator Maxine Horner. Jim Lloyd assisted me with research when I have been out of town and has discussed legal issues with me at length. Bob Blackburn, the first chair of the Riot Commission, was kind enough to take me onto his project. The cause of truth owes a debt to Dr. Blackburn and his successor as chair, T.D. "Pete" Churchwell. They guided the commission through rough political waters.

Everyone owes Representative Don Ross their warmest thanks for his decades-long commitment to preserving the memory of the riot—and for his tireless efforts on behalf of the Riot Commission. I remember the first time I heard Representative Ross speak. I thought he was leading a graduate seminar in American social history. He spoke the language of the scholar—the importance of recovering the true story of Greenwood and the riot—and mixed it with the passion and enthusiasm of an Ivy League history professor. "In memory of those who will never read it, I want the report to have the true story," I think was how he began. Don, those of us interested in race in American history owe you a debt.

Alfred L. Brophy
Cambridge, Massachusetts

Prologue

"[T]he silence and neglect of science can let truth utterly disappear or even be unconsciously distorted."—W.E.B. DuBois, *Black Folk Then and Now*[1]

This book tells the story of what many believe to be the worst and most deadly American race riot of the twentieth century. It is the story of an event that tore apart a city and scarred a state, that saw white police officers deputizing and arming a bloodthirsty mob, and later National Guardsmen firing on American citizens. The race riot that devastated Greenwood, the black section of Tulsa, offers one of the most searing examples of racial violence in American history and chilling evidence of government complicity in the destruction.

Reconstructing the Dreamland does more than simply tell Tulsa's tale, however. The attempt to "run the Negro out of Tulsa," as contemporaries referred to the riot, speaks directly to current struggles to make sense of America's racial past and to agree on ways to reconcile this past with the present. In 1997 the Oklahoma legislature established the Tulsa Race Riot Commission to investigate the riot—and to make recommendations on reparations. I learned about this effort to make something positive out of Oklahoma's sad history from an article in the *New York Times* and volunteered to research legal issues for the commission. Thus began my journey into the heart of an event whose dark complexities we had not even begun to fathom.

At the time I volunteered, I knew a little about the riot. I had stumbled upon Scott Ellsworth's wonderful book, *Death in a Promised Land*, shortly after I began teaching in Oklahoma. One thing that stuck out in my mind was Ellsworth's account of the failure of the police to stem the violence and the role of special police deputies in looting. That memory was central to my case for reparations, since it suggested the government's role in the riot. At the time I started working, I thought I would spend a few weeks reading the (white) newspapers and other well-known sources, then write a short paper detailing the government's liability—if any—under federal civil rights laws. I suspected there would be no way of filing a lawsuit today, so many years after the riot, so my idea was to use federal law as a framework for figuring out whether the city and state would have any culpability if the riot occurred in the same way today. Using that framework I hoped to explore the government's moral culpability.

A search of the Oklahoma Supreme Court's decisions, however, convinced me that there was much more to the story. The Oklahoma Supreme Court's 1926 decision in *Redfearn v. American Central Insurance Company*[2] contains an account of the riot that pointed to greater government involvement than the mere failure to protect Greenwood. The briefs in the case have several hundred pages of eyewitness testimony, which no previous historian had used. Blacks and whites told the Court how people on each side of the railroad tracks perceived the other, how the riot unfolded, and what the role of the police and special deputies was in the riot. So I began to see a different, richer story emerging than we had previously had—and the more I looked, the more the government seemed to be involved in the riot. The police department had deputized hundreds of men to put down what they believed was a "negro uprising." In the process of putting down that uprising, blacks were systematically taken into custody. Then, once the Greenwood population was in custody or had fled, their homes were looted and burned. A bleak picture was emerging from official sources.

Black newspapers elaborated on those accounts of police misconduct. An alternative view of the riot was there, waiting to be brought back to light lo' these many years later. That account appeared in two important black papers: the Oklahoma City *Black Dispatch* and the *Chicago Defender*. Together with the court cases—the *Redfearn* case from the Oklahoma Supreme Court and a lawsuit filed in Chicago by J.B. Stradford, a black man who fled Tulsa after the riot to avoid prosecution[3]—many important details were emerging. Soon it was apparent that there was a new story to be told, the story of one of the deadliest riots in human history—but from the perspective of those whose homes had been lost, from the *Greenwood* perspective.

That story has always been there, sitting on the pages of black newspapers and in the minds of survivors. As Ralph Ellison, author of *Invisible Man* and an Oklahoma City native, has said, we Americans have two versions of our history: "one which is written and as neatly stylized as ancient myth, and the other unwritten and as chaotic and full of contradictions, changes of pace and surprises as life itself."[4] But we rarely heard the black story. Meanwhile, white Tulsa presented its sanitized version of the story, which was captured in the headline of the *Tulsa Tribune* when the all-white grand jury investigating the riot returned its report: "Grand Jury Blames Negroes for Inciting Race Rioting; Whites Clearly Exonerated."[5]

At the same time I began to see the alternative, black version of the riot, I wrote a series of short papers for Brent Staples, who was writing an article on the riot and what it means for us today for the *New York Times Magazine*.[6] The papers addressed the ideas of Oklahoma blacks in the 1910s and 1920s about what the Constitution's equal protection clause should mean and how those ideas of equality were central to key civil rights decisions in the United States Supreme Court in the 1910s and later; about the government's culpability for the riot; about the failure of the city to rebuild; and about the possibility of a lawsuit today. I expanded those papers into a report to the Tulsa Riot Commission in February 2000. (My report, which has more technical detail than this book, especially on the possibility of lawsuits today, is available at: www.law.ua.edu/abrophy. There are also key documents from the riot, as well as links to photographs, historians' interpretations, and even jazz music played in Oklahoma around the time of the riot.)

As I continued to read the *Black Dispatch* I came to understand that it offered more than an alternative interpretation of the riot. Its editorials presented a new way of thinking about law. They taught that there should be equal access to the ballot, equal funding of segregated schools, equal accommodations on railroads; that blacks should sit on juries; and that lynchers and rioters should be punished. There was a sophisticated alternative vision of law promulgated in the pages of the *Black Dispatch*. The distinction between white law and black ideas about justice was great on the southwestern plains.

As the Riot Commission pursued its work, it became apparent to me that the "true" story of the riot was not being adequately heard and that the case for reparations was not being adequately made. The scholars' report, prepared by Scott Ellsworth and John Hope Franklin, tells the unfolding of events in the riot and does important work to correct the biased interpretation of the riot that white Tulsa had told.[7] But there is still more to be said. And so I present this book as an alternative account of the riot's origins in the conflicting attitudes of blacks and whites toward law. Blacks searched for the "rule of law"—equal treatment under law. Whites, however, pursued a different law—a law that often devolved into control through terror and subordination of black citizens.

The chapters that follow tell that story: how blacks' search for justice and opposition to violence and discrimination clashed with the attitudes of white Tulsans to spark the riot; how the police and white mobs, in conjunction with the local units of the National Guard, "ran the Negro out of Tulsa"; and finally, how the city responded to the riot by attempting to prevent rebuilding. Relying on previously unknown court records and unstudied black newspapers, we can have a richer understanding of the riot itself and of race in Progressive-era Oklahoma.

This story also says something about reparations. We are hearing a great deal these days about the case for reparations—for slavery, for Nazi atrocities, for deprivation of land from native people from Europe to the Americas, Australia, and New Zealand, for apartheid in South Africa, for war crimes in China and the Balkans. Tulsa provides the opportunity to ground claims for reparations in a very specific historical context. The question of reparations in Tulsa provides a concrete context for analyzing claims about reparations throughout American society. Much as the Tulsa riot illustrates larger issues in race, history, and law in the early part of the twentieth century, Tulsa speaks to reparations claims generally. It is a laboratory in which to test ideas about reparations, to ask the question, can justice be done? What are the benefits and what are the costs?

The epilogue takes up the case for reparations. It establishes a framework for discussing reparations, and then fits the Tulsa riot into that framework. I conclude with suggestions of what reparations might look like in Tulsa and what one might reasonably ask of reparations. But even if—as appears likely—Oklahoma never provides a penny of reparations, the process of understanding the riot has already advanced the cause of justice, for we are closer to understanding the truth of the riot and the culpability of the city in it. And truth is very difficult to purchase. One hopes that by understanding the riot's causes and consequences it might be "transformed into something deeper and more meaningful than its surface violence."[8]

Chapter One

Seeking Justice and the Origins of the Riot

Well, many things have happened this week to black folk, yet
through it all we have exercised a fortitude almost unexplainable.
One could stand anywhere in the black section of this city and
say as is said in "Revelation": "Here is the patience of the Saints."
We have stood this week and looked at the naked passions of the
barbarians that rule us. We have seen the venom of the reptile
gush from his loins; we have seen down in the bottom of what he
calls law and still we have been patient.

And this is the white man's law?
—*Oklahoma City Black Dispatch*, September 3, 1920

At the beginning of May 1921, 8,000 people lived in Greenwood, the
black section of Tulsa, which was situated just north of the center of
the "magic city," as Tulsa called itself. Greenwood residents frequently worked in white Tulsa, across the railroad tracks, but they
returned home at night. "Little Africa," as Greenwood was called,
was largely a self-sufficient community, with a school, a hospital,
hotels, grocery, drug, and clothing stores, two newspapers, and two
movie theaters. One of the theaters was called the Dreamland. Greenwood itself could easily have passed for a dreamland. It was a place
where fewer than sixty years after slavery ended, black people lived
in relative freedom. Veterans of the World War, men who had traveled the world, lived there and discussed great ideas of equality. The
economic prosperity of the community fostered the ideas of equality,
which mixed with a new music, called jazz. Alcohol, drugs, and dancing were readily available, and sometimes at night the strict line separating black and white broke down in the dance halls, the choc joints
(where Choctow beer was sold), and the juke joints.

1

Greenwood was a vibrant, proud community. It built upon the Oklahoma tradition that promised cheap land and opportunity to both blacks and whites in the aftermath of the Civil War. "Geography was fate," as former slaves understood.[1] So freed slaves headed for the Indian Territory, which later became the state of Oklahoma, as slaves had once headed for the Mason-Dixon Line and the freedom that it promised. Even though Oklahoma had once been slave territory, it held out the promise of a better life. It drew, as Ralph Ellison, author of *Invisible Man,* told an audience at Brown University, "many of the descendants of the freed slaves, who considered it a territory of hope, and a place where they could create their own opportunities. . . . [F]or Negroes it had a traditional association with freedom which had entered their folklore."[2] Life was better in Oklahoma, for it "lacked the intensities of custom, tradition and manners which 'colored' the institutions of the Old South."[3]

Greenwood's residents spoke about the need to prevent lynchings, to protect voting rights, to develop the community. Central to their thinking was the idea of the rule of law: that the government should establish impartial rules and apply them equally to whites and blacks. The principles that made up the rule of law were simple. Blacks—even if segregated—should receive the same treatment as whites on railroads; black schools should be equal in funding and quality to white schools; blacks should be allowed to register to vote and serve on juries on the same terms as whites; police officers should treat blacks with the same respect they accorded whites. Those ideas about law were promulgated in the pages of the black newspapers. Sometimes they appeared in more formal arenas, like the federal courts, where blacks filed suits to protect their right to equal treatment. They won two cases in the United States Supreme Court in the 1910s. One struck down Oklahoma's grandfather clause; the other, Oklahoma's railroad segregation statute, which allowed railroads to provide unequal treatment to blacks.[4]

Oklahoma's blacks in the early part of the twentieth century were full of hope, with increasing faith in law and optimism for the future. Like the first immigrants to Oklahoma, they had a renewed sense of the possibility of freedom. That optimism was nurtured in large part by the promises of the First World War and by the cosmopolitan ideas spread by the Harlem renaissance.

The ideas of the renaissance were brought to Greenwood in many ways. The most important vehicle was the *Tulsa Star*, published weekly by editor A.J. Smitherman. Greenwood residents also read the great vehicles of the renaissance: the *Crisis*, published by the NAACP; the *Chicago Defender*; and such now forgotten but important newspapers as the *Indianapolis Freeman*.[5] Together these periodicals alerted Greenwood residents to their legal rights and informed them of recent victories—and setbacks—in the courts and legislatures, as well as in literature and art. Some ideas were brought to Greenwood in the minds of the men and women who migrated there, like J.B. Stradford, a lawyer trained in Indianapolis, whose lifelong passion was equal treatment through law. Veterans also brought ideas to Greenwood. They had seen and lived in a world where blacks were asked to fight to defend freedom and where they were given more of it than white Oklahomans would generally allow.[6]

A key theme of the renaissance was the promise of the World War to remake American society. President Woodrow Wilson harnessed images of democracy during the war. As the black press fondly pointed out, Wilson said in 1918 that "I can never accept any man as a champion of liberty either for ourselves or for the world who does not reverence and obey the laws of our own beloved land."[7] That appeal to law had important implications for civil rights at home.

In a speech in January 1918 in Bristow, Oklahoma, on the fifty-fifth anniversary of the emancipation proclamation, Roscoe Dunjee, the editor of Oklahoma City's weekly black newspaper, the *Black Dispatch*, drew upon Wilson's ideals. Dunjee outlined the freedom and equality that the war effort promised for Oklahoma blacks: "President Wilson says we go out to make the world safe for democracy. . . . Democracy in Bristow means that black men as well as white men shall set in jury boxes and everywhere. Democracy means, if we would breathe the 'pure air' of which Wilson speaks, that spoilation and exploitation of black men's property and labor shall cease, it means that segregation, Jim Crowism and mob violence must die, and that in its stead there must rise justice, equity and fairness. For these are the cornerstone of democracy."[8] By 1921, Greenwood residents who had served in the war, as well as those who looked proudly on as their friends and relatives participated in it, were ready to demand the freedom and equality that had been promised.

The power of patriotism promised to demolish "every plank in the fence separating blacks from democracy," Dunjee told his readers. A

THE MAUL OF PATRIOTISM

Black Dispatch (May 10, 1918)

cartoon in the *Black Dispatch* graphically depicted that lesson. It showed the power of the maul (hammer) of patriotism. Already patriotism had pushed down municipal segregation ordinances and disfranchisement.[9] Soon to fall were mob violence, segregation on railroad cars, bans from military units, exploitation, and peonage.[10] The *Black Dispatch*'s cartoons portrayed the optimism of its editor. One, entitled "What Santa Claus Brings" and printed just before Christmas 1917, showed a black Santa with a "sack of opportunity," containing presents like "Race Love," "Education," and "Happy Homes." Santa Claus was climbing over a fence comprised of planks like "Segregation," "Mob Violence," and "Disfranchisement."[11]

So the imagery of America's role in the World War raised the hopes and expectations of blacks. The returning veterans expected a "new reconstruction."[12] Those rising expectations led W.E.B. DuBois to predict that lynch mobs would now meet armed opposition:

For three centuries we have suffered and cowered. No race ever gave Passive Resistance and Submission to Evil a longer, more piteous trial. Today we raise the terrible weapon of Self-Defense. When the murderer comes, he shall no longer strike us in the back. When the

What Santa Claus Brings

Black Dispatch (December 21, 1917)

armed lynchers gather, we too must gather armed. When the mob
moves, we propose to meet it with bricks and clubs and guns.[13]

Similarly, when President Wilson spoke about stopping pogroms in
Poland, where Jews were driven from their communities (and sometimes killed), blacks asked for a focus on race riots at home.[14]

We know through editorials buried in now-forgotten newspapers
that black communities in Oklahoma believed that the solution to
racial conflict was respect for law. Leaders urged their fellow citizens
to understand their fundamental rights of citizenship: "equality with
the white man to have his person, property and family protected from
every form of lawlessness."[15] In response to the KKK's call for segregation, the leaders of the black community in Oklahoma City asked
for equal treatment. Why not "One law for Americans," they asked.

Blacks, as well as whites, deserved life, liberty, and the pursuit of happiness promised to American citizens.[16] Generations before the United States Supreme Court decision in *Brown v. Board of Education* remade American law, Oklahoma's blacks were thinking about filing lawsuits as a way of undoing segregation.[17] The vision of justice espoused in Oklahoma's black community grew from the simple premise that the government should treat its citizens equally. Thus, there should be at least equal, even if separate, accommodations on railroads, there should be equal funding for segregated public schools, blacks should have equal access to the ballot and jury boxes, and blacks should receive protection from the police. Such principles, so easily stated, proved difficult to achieve.

Yet that hope for the future existed in conjunction with the knowledge that much work needed to be done. At the same time they were making optimistic predictions about the possibilities of the war to change America's attitudes toward them, the black community discussed the plight of black troops, who were kept in segregated railway cars and given inferior accommodations in Oklahoma camps.[18] White southerners, bothered by the increasing status and attitudes of blacks, tried to return to prewar race relations: "you found beneath the talk of assaults upon women and 'crime waves,' a determination TO PUT THE NEGRO BACK WHERE HE WAS BEFORE THE WAR, while workmen would tell you that Negroes were getting too high wages and were becoming independent and [were] no longer servile as the southern white man wished."[19] As white southerners attempted to "put the Negro back," blacks pointed to the disparity between Americans' rhetoric about freedom and their actions at home. Such disparity led many to wonder whether the United States could claim moral leadership of the world.[20]

Ideals did not match reality. Despite all the optimism and faith in the future, Greenwood residents knew the law had limits. They also knew that in the most extreme cases, much more than equal protection was at stake. Throughout the southwest, breakdowns of law cast a shadow over the dreamland. Unregulated violence was common; often life itself was at stake.

Cartoons of the period depicted those breakdowns of law threatening Oklahoma's blacks. In the spring of 1920, one cartoon showed two black children innocently walking down the street. Four white men (with names like "Mobs" and "Segregation") lay in wait around

The Future

Tulsa Star (February 21, 1920)

the corner. The caption asked, "Shall These Horrors Await our Future Generations?"[21] The implication was that much work needed to be done to protect these future generations—and that the work actually could be done. Other cartoons portrayed the hurdles that had to be overcome. One showed a black woman doing some laundry, which was labeled "lynchings, hatred, mobs, riot, and prejudice." A white man (who was also a Communist) was dumping more dirty laundry for her to clean, labeled "10,000 Kansans mob negro" and "A U.S. Court upholds Jim Crow law."[22]

Tulsa Star (May 1, 1920)

There was a lot of work for Greenwood residents to do. Although the colorations of life in many Oklahoma towns lacked the taints of injustice found in the states of the Old South, whites sometimes used violence to drive out blacks or to control them. Oklahomans spoke of "negro drives"—the use of violence to drive out blacks from a town or county. Law enforcement officers did little to prevent violence and courts refused claims for relief. For example, in July 1898 a mob of twenty-five men in Norman (now the home of the University of Oklahoma) attacked a white man, J.J. Wallace. He had come to town to supervise some construction work and brought along a young black man to help with the construction. The mob, angry that the black youth was working in Norman, knocked Wallace unconscious; he lost his sight in one eye, and spent weeks recuperating.

Wallace filed a lawsuit against the city. He claimed that the mayor and other city officials had participated in the riot and that over the past three years many blacks who had tried to live or work in the city had been attacked and driven out. The Oklahoma Territory's Supreme Court refused any compensation. Even if "the conspiracy existed as described," the Supreme Court explained, there was simply prejudice "in the minds of the inhabitants of that locality" against blacks. Such prejudice "was a condition of the public mind, over which the corporate authorities of Norman could exercise no rightful jurisdiction."[23] The court effectively insulated municipalities from liability for crimes committed within their borders, even for acts committed by government officers. In the early 1900s, there was an unofficial law, which was placed on signs in prominent places around Norman: "nigger, don't let the sun go down on you in this town."[24]

Attacks on both individuals and black communities were common. A few months after the Norman riot, David Fitch, described in the *Norman Transcript* as "comparatively an inoffensive negro," was murdered in the eastern part of the county. Later reports indicated that his murder might have been part of a more general effort to scare blacks from the county. Because large numbers of blacks had recently settled in Pottawatomie County, Fitch's murder was interpreted by a white newspaper as part of a larger, organized effort to drive out the blacks.[25] The social norm that blacks could not live in the same town as whites, enforced by violence and unregulated by the courts, set the stage for the violence against blacks throughout the state. In 1918 twenty families were burned out of Dewey in northeastern Oklahoma.[26] Following the Dewey riot, there was a small, unsuccessful movement to obtain compensation from the state for the families who had lost property.[27] As the Oklahoma courts retreated from holding the towns liable for the acts of their officials, it was common to hear of blacks being driven out of towns.[28]

But even more than "negro drives," lynchings threatened blacks in

Oklahoma and throughout the South in the 1910s and 1920s.[29] When Congress considered an antilynching bill in 1922, which would have allowed victims' families to sue the local governments where lynchings took place, many opponents of the bill explained the sentiments behind lynching. Lynchings were partially the response—and, in the minds of many southerners, a seemingly appropriate response—to the rising aspirations of blacks. "We are ofttimes forced to use extreme measures with the Negro. This is caused by the Negro getting the wrong idea of his relation to the white man. He gets this erroneous idea from improper propaganda generally originating in sections other than the South. The man who does not know the darkey and who would help him by persuading him that he is the equal of the white man works the destruction of the Negro race."[30]

Apparently, lynching maintained the line between blacks and whites.[31] As Representative Lamar Jeffers of Alabama explained, when blacks overstepped accepted social boundaries, such as consorting with whites, they were subject to violence:

> Some gentlemen present may feel that they are doing a wonderful thing for the entire colored race, but believe me when I tell you that you are only playing to some of the so-called "big Negroes" of the North, who are, in my opinion, the worst enemies that the mass of the colored people have. . . . But while the southern white man will treat the colored people right, he will never change the social dead line, well established and well understood, and whenever the Negro oversteps the white man's dead line he knows, and he is so informed by the right-thinking members of his own race, that he thereby takes his life in his own hands.[32]

The most disturbing crossing of the boundary to the white southern mind was the rape of a white woman by a black man. The outrage that led to lynching was often stirred by charges of rape. Representative Thomas Upton Sisson of Mississippi described the rape of a fourteen-year-old white girl by a "black brute." "I do not know what you are gentlemen. You are Republicans in politics, but, God knows, I believe you are men and I believe you are white men. There is not one of you worthy of the name of Anglo-Saxon who would not have been willing to join in the mob to vindicate the death of the little girl."[33] Many simply did not think the life of the lynch victim was worth saving.[34]

Representative Hatton Sumners of Texas explained the emotion
wrapped up with rape by "alien blood." He thought it futile to
attempt to prevent lynching in those circumstances:

> This is a fact, and we had just as well be candid about it, too: When a
> white woman is raped by a black man the call to the white man is from
> his two strongest, most primitive instincts. No doubt when men lived
> in caves the strongest instinct of the man was to protect his woman.
> The next strongest instinct is to protect his blood. When the call comes
> from the woman crying out from the depths of her outraged chastity,
> there comes to the man a call which reaches back to the days when he
> was a savage in the cave, and he goes. . . . The impulse is to kill, to kill
> as they would kill a wild beast.[35]

[handwritten margin note: hot, American nature]

Southern white men could not abide any crossings of the line
between black and white. Death would be preferable to any mixing
of the races. "I would rather know that our population would sink
into the grave with the death of this generation, and that this conti-
nent would again become a howling wilderness, to be later settled up
by the white races of other lands," said Representative Jeffers, "than
to see our people accept the Negroes on terms of social equality and
our country go down to the future inhabited by a degraded mongrel
race."[36] Mixing of the races not only suggested a mongrelization of
the race to prejudiced whites, but more fundamentally threatened
white hegemony. Even as southern representatives were telling themselves about their superiority, they feared equality with blacks. To the
white southern mind there was a natural order of hierarchy, and
southerners were determined to keep that hierarchy intact.[37] Lynching, although not sanctioned by law, kept both the hierarchy and the
separation in place. There was a "just" punishment for violations of
this order and that punishment was death by mob. Many people
received that punishment. More than fifty blacks were lynched in
1920 alone. The widespread threat of lynching tells us that it served
important purposes for the southern community.

The violence of lynching highlights the disjunction between what
the law promises and what steps society takes on its own. The written
laws of Oklahoma promised protection against harm, yet social norms
sanctioned violence against blacks and criminals. As in many other sit-
uations, when there is a gap between what the society believes and
what the law commands, both the law and social system tend to break

down. When Oklahoma's Governor Cruce, who opposed the death penalty, refused to execute anyone, one lynch mob left a sign hanging on its victim, "dedicating" its victim to the governor.[38] The mob was enforcing its own sense of justice, at odds with the law as written.

Greenwood residents spoke about the importance of justice through law, about the importance of having rules that apply equally to blacks as well as whites, but the Greenwood vision of law broke down in the case of lynching, as local law enforcement failed to protect against lynchers. Greenwood residents, concerned for the ideas of equality, were being driven to increased militancy. They predicted that there would be disastrous violence unless lynchings stopped and the law was followed.[39]

On the third weekend in August 1920, eight months before the riot, two lynchings took place in Oklahoma. A white man was lynched in Tulsa and a black man was lynched in Oklahoma City, ninety miles away. The lynching of the black man held special significance. On the evening of Sunday, August 23, 1920, three unmasked white men entered the Oklahoma City jail, overpowered the jailer, and a few minutes later took Claude Chandler, a young black man accused of killing a white police officer. Police had raided the Chandler home, where moonshine was being made. Both Chandler's father and an officer died during a subsequent gun battle. Two hours after Chandler's kidnapping, rumors began circulating in Oklahoma City's black community that Chandler had been taken from the jail. The community, knowing that a lynching was imminent, went into action. Perhaps a thousand heavily armed black men assembled along Second Street, wondering how they might rescue Chandler. The police in Oklahoma City heard about the assemblage, and headed off for Second Street, the heart of Oklahoma City's black district.

Black men in two cars sped off from the meeting point on Second Street; a third, still being filled with gasoline, was detained by the police. Fifty police surrounded the car, pointing riot guns at the men inside. One black man in the back seat moved to cock his gun, and it looked as though he might "turn bedlam loose."[40] But another man in the car, a cooler head, warned, "We are not fighting the police, hold a moment, let's submit, it will come out alright."

The first two cars realized that the third was not with them and returned. The police, in the company of the mayor, disarmed the men

[handwritten margin note: police respond when blacks are armed]

in all three cars. After a meeting with leaders of the black community and two black policemen, the mayor allowed the unarmed men to chase after Chandler, under the supervision of the two black officers. The mayor would allow the community to take some action to protect itself, but limited their ability to carry guns. They headed off, and searched all night north and west of the city, near Chandler's home of Arcadia, trying to find him. At some point they realized they would not find him alive. Still they searched, but found nothing. Around noon the next day, they came back.

About the time the searchers were coming back, Claude Chandler's body was found hanging from a tree ten miles west of the city. He had been lynched the evening before, beaten, and shot twice. An undertaker brought the body back to East Oklahoma City, the black section of town, where people gathered to view the body. The news of the viewing in Oklahoma City, a harsh reminder of the limits of the dreamland, traveled quickly back to Greenwood residents.

Oklahoma City's *Black Dispatch* seized on the Chandler case as an example of how far the realities of life in the black community were from the promises of equal justice and equal protection. It drew out the conflict between the breakdown of law represented by Chandler's lynching and the ideal of law held by Oklahoma's blacks. How could the jailer have been so easily overcome by three unmasked men? How could the sheriff have known where to go to find Chandler's body?

The *Black Dispatch* highlighted the illegal actions of Oklahoma law enforcement. "And this is the white man's law?" was the incredulous title of the *Black Dispatch* editorial immediately following the lynching. It implicated the jailer in the lynching:

> It does not even matter if Sheriff Johnson and his jailor, two spineless cowards, can show that they were overpowered. The public will want to know BY WHOM WERE THEY OVERPOWERED? Everyone knows that even after you have entered the jail door, one must be adept, one must certainly have intimate knowledge of the keys and the location of prisoners, to accomplish their purpose as quickly as Jailor Sanders says they consummated their work. THINK OF IT, in five minutes, unknown men can come to the jail, tie the jailor, cut the wires and then find the man whom they seek, from among the many cells, they can do all of this without any information or assistance, from the inside. THE PUBLIC IS ASKED TO BELIEVE THIS.[41]

(handwritten margin note) not focused on actions, blaming whole jail scene/door

The *Black Dispatch* also laid blame on the prosecutor, who had ordered Chandler transferred from Logan County, where the attack occurred and where the sheriff was known to protect prisoners, to Oklahoma County.

> LOGAN COUNTY? No! They did not want Claude Chandler to get to the jail in Logan County. The former sheriffs of Logan County have a record for protecting prisoners. One sheriff stood on the steps of the jail and held off a mob of one thousand, who were trying to reach a Negro prisoner. AND THEY DID NOT TAKE THAT PRISONER, EITHER.[42]

[handwritten margin note: more than mob had]

Given his previous actions, the prosecutor was unlikely to investigate the lynching. When Oklahoma City's blacks were told by Oklahoma's governor to "LEAVE THE WHOLE THING IN THE HANDS OF OUR CONSTITUTED AUTHORITIES," they heard "GO TRY YOUR CASE IN HELL."[43] The jailers' participation in turning Chandler over to the lynchers and the prosecutor's complicity in sending Chandler to a less secure jail all illustrated for Dunjee the failure of law enforcement officers to protect blacks from violence.

Chandler's lynching was only the most recent in a long series of nationwide examples of law enforcement denying equal protection to blacks. In the East St. Louis riot of 1917, instead of protecting blacks, the police disarmed them. Then, the disarmed blacks "GOT . . . A BULLET OUT OF THE RIFLE OF THE MAN IN UNIFORM WHO HAD FIRST DISARMED HIM."[44] Such unequal treatment made people suspicious of law enforcement officers—and taught blacks not to give up their arms.[45] It also taught them that law did not mean equal protection for blacks. Looking back on his childhood in Oklahoma in the 1910s and 1920s, Ralph Ellison recalled that law enforcement officers were called "laws." They did not follow the law, however.[46]

The problems of law enforcement went beyond the people on the street. Not only did police and prosecutors fail to protect blacks, but when cases reached the courts, judges failed to apply the law equally to blacks and whites. Judges failed to convict whites who attacked blacks, issued harsher sentences to blacks than whites, and sometimes interpreted statutes to allow continued unequal treatment in schools and in voting. Ellison told of a quip made by an Oklahoma judge from the bench, that "a Model T Ford full of Negroes ranging at large on the streets of the city was a more devastating piece of bad luck than having one's path crossed by thirteen howling jet-black cats."[47] Given such statements, the law as established by whites could have little legitimacy in the black community.

Blacks suffered more than denial of equal treatment on the streets and in the courts, however. There was a third way in which the law victimized them: statutes passed by the legislature were primary vehicles for discrimination. After the United States Supreme Court struck the Oklahoma grandfather clause in 1915, the Oklahoma legislature passed another voter registration law designed to keep blacks from registering.[48] The legislature's unfair and in some cases illegal treatment caught the attention of Oklahoma's black community. An editorial in the *Muskogee Cimeter*, Muskogee's weekly black newspaper, protested that Oklahoma statutes treated blacks as objects. Laws might be passed to control and punish blacks, but "[m]easures that would improve his mentality, encourage his industry and mold his morals are never thought of."[49] The pattern of using law to reinforce white superiority was common to all three. Law on the street as established by police, law in the courts as established by judges and prosecutors, and statutes enacted by the legislature all worked together to keep blacks in their place. "[L]aw and order methods," an NAACP official concluded, "absolutely insure 'white superiority' in every way in which that superiority is real."[50]

There was building tension between the black views of justice and white views of "law." Across years of editorials, the black press wrote about the myriad of ways that blacks received unequal treatment at the hands of police, in the arbitrary commands of police officers and in capricious arrests of blacks, while whites insulted and attacked blacks with immunity. The unequal treatment continued in the courts and in the legislature. Oklahoma's blacks, therefore, developed a systematic, although straightforward, interpretation of what "law" ought to mean. It ought to mean equal treatment. These ideas, what we call today the equal protection of the law, existed in an intellectual realm, distinct from the harsh reality of life in Oklahoma. For whites, talk of law too often meant black obedience to the white commands and capricious and unequal treatment by the government. Blacks asked whether such unequal treatment actually could be "law." They argued that something so different from justice and so different from the Constitution's promise of equal protection could not be law. There might be something called "law" by the Oklahoma courts; there might be something police officers called "laws." But those statutes and the dictates of the law enforcement officers were not law. Sometimes the black vision of law won, as when the United States Supreme Court struck down Oklahoma's discriminatory voter registration statute in 1915.[51] But mostly the black view of law had to wait for another time, and blacks and whites continued to hold different understandings of what the word "law" meant.

Frustration with law enforcement and laws that were not just (and therefore were not law) was building. Some of the actions following Chandler's murder can be understood in this context. Blacks were increasingly determined to make their interpretations of the law heard, particularly in the fight against lynching. Some wanted to change the world by urging whites to follow simple rules of equal protection. They sought change through the newspapers and by pointing to the hypocrisy and the unfairness of such action. Others were becoming more militant and more willing to take action to make sure that they received equal treatment, even if that meant facing arrest or maybe even facing down law enforcement officers.

With Chandler's case, however, blacks still held out some hope that the law might triumph. Oklahoma's governor, J.B.A. Robertson, promised to investigate and punish the lynchers. He thought there was collusion between the jailer and the lynchers.[52] The *Black Dispatch* thanked Robertson, but wondered why he was not doing more. "Think of it: A human being has been swung to a tree in this county, his tongue choked out of his head, his brains shot out and yet TWO WEEKS AFTER THE ORGE, WE HAVE THE JUDGES AND THE COUNTY ATTORNEY UNABLE TO DETERMINE WHAT PROCEDURE SHOULD BE FOLLOWED TO INVESTIGATE."[53] Even though the *Black Dispatch* was dissatisfied that the prosecutions were going so slowly, Governor Robertson was doing more than any previous governor had done to prosecute lynchers. He ordered the attorney general to investigate the sheriff's culpability, and an Oklahoma County grand jury returned an indictment against the jailers.[54] The *Black Dispatch* praised the governor's determination: "Let judgments run down as waters and righteousness as a mighty stream."[55]

The charges—supported by Governor Robertson—that law officers were involved in the lynching contributed to the feelings of helplessness Oklahoma City residents had in fighting lynching. If Oklahoma City's blacks had tried to stop the lynching, or if they had confronted the people who had kidnapped Chandler, those blacks would probably have been told that he was being taken to a place of safety.[56] Oklahoma officials who asked that blacks abide by such law were hypocritical. Perhaps worse was the way that, following a gruesome lynching, officials left little hope for justice, then expected blacks to believe that "THIS IS LAW."[57] "Law" had different meanings for blacks and whites. At the center of the black view was the belief, expressed in the title of a *Black Dispatch* editorial, that "*Respect for the Law Must be Supreme, Lynching Must Go.*"[58] Lynching led to important discussions of the nature of justice. It also galvanized some, causing them to band together to protect themselves.

Other members of Oklahoma's black community drew even more radical conclusions from the Chandler case than the *Black Dispatch* had. The *Tulsa Star*, edited by A.J. Smitherman, was even more strident in urging the community to protect itself. In a series of editorials, the *Tulsa Star* chastised Oklahoma City blacks for not defending Chandler. Smitherman's first editorial criticized the Oklahoma City blacks, who "got together AFTER CLAUDE CHANDLER had paid the penalty with his life, and as we are informed, permitted one lone policeman to take their guns away from them, and literally boot them off the street." That failure to take a more aggressive stance was a commentary on the courage (and wisdom) of Oklahoma City's black community. The *Tulsa Star* maintained that blacks should have taken action sooner: "[T]he proper time to afford protection to any prisoner is BEFORE and DURING the time he is being lynched, and certainly not after he is killed."[59]

Many black communities throughout the state had, indeed, been organized for years. In the wake of a lynching in Durant in 1911, for example, blacks in Bryan County organized "with a determination to protect their lives and property against the ravages of lawless whites."[60] There was the ominous warning that Bryan County blacks were prepared for violence and that they would not count on protection from law enforcement, but would take action to protect their lives and property.[61] Later, when there was talk of lynching in June 1917, the *Muskogee Cimeter* warned that Muskogee residents would not abide a lynching: "We serve notice that there are at least fifty men who will uphold the law and meet the cowardly slackers when they make their attempt."[62]

Arguments raged over the proper response to Chandler's lynching. Had the Oklahoma City black community acted with sufficient

bravery? Was it proper to give up their guns to the police? Had the
men taken the correct, measured steps?[63] Some were willing to advocate direct confrontation with the police, but others were not willing
to go so far. A split in opinion appeared, between those who would
use violence to protect the community members against lynchers and
those who would go even further and pitch battle with the police.

Some believed that the Oklahoma City black community *had* sent
a clear message. The manner in which Chandler was killed showed
that lynchers feared the community. The lynchers had turned off the
lights when they entered the jail and took Chandler off in secrecy.[64]
That was evidence of the power of the black community. "The very
stealth and secrecy with which these vicious reptiles, who hung
Claude Chandler, went about their orge, goes to show that they feared
to let the Negroes of this community know that they had any such
intention. There was no challenge to anybody's manhood. Every step
INCLUDING THE LIES THAT WE HEAR NOW, bears the ear marks and the
slink of hungry wolves, who fear the light and who feast only on dead
carcasses in the night."[65]

Others thought that Oklahoma City blacks should have mobilized
and gone to the jail to protect Chandler. Those radicals thought,
despite the protestations that cool heads were needed when a lynching was imminent, that community members should have been more
responsive to the danger to Chandler. Had they done something,
Chandler might still be alive. They made sarcastic references to "the
courageous 'race men' of Oklahoma City who armed themselves and
paraded the streets (in the Colored section of the city) *after the lynching had occurred.*"[66]

The *Tulsa Star* urged aggressive action to combat lynching. It told
of the legal right, even duty, to use violence to protect against lynching. "While the boy was in jail and while there was danger of mob
violence any set of citizens had a legal right—it was their duty—to
arm themselves and march in a body to the jail and apprize the sheriff or jailer of the purpose of their visit and to take life if need be to
uphold the law and protect the prisoner."[67] The *Star* further urged
that men could arm for self-protection or "to uphold the majesty
of the law."[68] In either of those cases, no officers had the right to disarm them and it would be cowardly to give up arms.[69] Those statements—so emphatic in their prescription—are central to understanding the psychology of the Greenwood veterans who went to the

courthouse on the evening of May 31 when they heard rumors of lynching.

The Greenwood community had experience with such aggressive action, designed to preserve life and—as some phrased it—the majesty of the law. In September 1919, when Jewel Davis, a black man, was arrested in Tulsa, leaders of the Greenwood community allegedly showed up at the courthouse and demanded assurances that he would be protected.[70] A few months later, in March 1920, Oklahoma blacks again took action to protect an accused man from a lynching. Some men from Shawnee armed themselves and stole a couple of cars to chase after the mob that was forming to take a prisoner, Chap Davis, who had recently been convicted of attempted assault on a white teacher, from law enforcement officers.[71] Under the heading "*Mob Rule and the Law*," the *Tulsa Star* praised the men who acted to avert a lynching as Davis was being transported to the state penitentiary:

> As to the Colored men of Shawnee who, it is alleged, stole an auto, armed themselves and went to protect the prisoner, aside from taking the auto which was manifestly wrong, but perhaps not without extenuating circumstances, since their intentions were to uphold the law of our state, they are the heroes of the story. If one set of men arm themselves and chase across the country to violate the law, certainly another set who arm themselves to uphold the supremacy of the law and prevent crime, must stand out prominently as the best citizens. Therefore the action of the Colored men in this case is to be commended. We need more citizens like them in every community and of both races.[72]

Oklahoma's blacks spoke of law as they justified their armed actions. If the government would uphold the law, there would be reason (or even justification) for the community to take action. But when the government failed to protect, Greenwood residents were telling themselves, they had the right—sometimes they even spoke about it as a duty—to take action.

The debate between the *Black Dispatch* and the *Tulsa Star* over Claude Chandler's lynching raised the consciousness of both communities about the need for vigilance. It also demonstrates the complex, sometimes conflicting, ideas that Oklahoma's blacks held about what it meant to uphold the law. Both papers agreed on the need for the community to take an active role in upholding the rule of law, but they disagreed on what steps to take.

The *Tulsa Star's* readers had an additional reason to fear that government officials would be even more extreme in their disregard of the law. The day before Claude Chandler was lynched in Oklahoma City, a white man, Roy Belton, was lynched in Tulsa. Belton was taken from the jail on Saturday evening, August 22, 1920, where he was being held awaiting arraignment on charges that he had murdered a taxi driver.[73] The attorney general's investigation of the lynching of Roy Belton demonstrated that Tulsa's law enforcement officers had an even more contemptible disregard of the law than did Oklahoma City's. Tulsa Police Chief John Gustafson witnessed Belton's lynching. Neither Gustafson nor any of the other officers there did anything to stop it.[74] That failure to uphold the law further pointed to the need for vigilance.

The lynchings of Chandler and Belton were events that were unfortunately common in the South and Southwest in the early part of the twentieth century. They held important lessons for blacks in Tulsa. Chandler's death sparked a community spirit, for his lynching taught that law enforcement officers would not protect blacks; Belton's death taught that no one was safe in the hands of Tulsa officials. If the rule of law was going to prevail in Oklahoma, it would be through the actions of blacks, not the law officers.

Events following the Chandler and Belton lynchings reconfirmed the effectiveness of mobilization, as well as the need for the black community to protect itself. In October 1920, two months after Chandler's lynching, Jim Adkison, a black man from Okmulgee, was accused of raping a white woman. More than a thousand blacks in Okmulgee armed to protect themselves, as Adkinson's home was looted.[75] There was even a rumor (of doubtful validity) that some black men had disarmed the mayor and police. The rumor itself—whatever its truth—showed the popularity of the idea of aggressive action in black culture. Meanwhile, the sheriff brought Adkinson from Okmulgee to Muskogee, where he would be safe, and from there to the state penitentiary at McAlister, where he would be even safer. On the way to Muskogee, the sheriff paraded Adkinson through a black neighborhood, to let the community know that he was alive and safe.[76] The next week, the importance of protecting Adkinson became clear, when it turned out that he was innocent.[77]

In mid-April 1921 a group of black men in Muskogee freed a prisoner from Muskogee law enforcement officers, shooting a police officer in the process. The prisoner, John McShane, had been taken into "protective custody" after he won a fist fight with a white man.[78] The white newspapers focused on the fact that a deputy sheriff was shot in the abdomen when McShane was freed.[79] But the black community, which was unrepentant, saw the violent freeing of the prisoner as a justifiable act. In their view, when the sheriff brought McShane to jail, he did so with the knowledge that he would be taken from the jail and lynched.[80] McShane's comrades were determined to prevent the lynching.

The McShane escape electrified the attention of Tulsa's black residents.[81] In a back room of the Dreamland Theater, leaders of Greenwood's renaissance discussed the event and what to do about it. A.J. Smitherman, editor of the *Tulsa Star,* spoke with lawyer and real estate developer J.B. Stradford, who had fought in the court for equal treatment. The thirty-six-year-old Smitherman was small in stature but was often described as fearless in demanding his rights. He had stood down a mob in Bristow, Oklahoma, in 1918, when there was talk of lynching there and had filed a lawsuit against a railroad in 1919 after it gave him inferior accommodations to those given whites.[82] Smitherman may have acquired his grit from working in the coal mines in Alabama, where he was born, and from his life in Chicago, when he attended Northwestern University. Stradford, often described as a large man, was just as aggressive in fighting for equal rights.

Stradford and Smitherman heatedly discussed an article they planned to write about the Muskogee event. Inspired by the success of the men who freed McShane, they wanted to spread the good news to the Greenwood community as soon as possible.[83] The men agreed that when a black man was in danger of being lynched, the community must fight. It should not sit passively and see a man led to his death. They saw such aggressive action as a way of seeking justice. The sense that the black community needed to protect itself against lynching was growing in Greenwood. The refrain was heard at the Dreamland's vaudeville shows, "Don't let any white man run it over you, but fight."[84]

The failure of the courts to punish lynchers—or to otherwise uphold the law—was a large part of the problem. The *Black Dispatch* frequently invoked a line from the Bible to illustrate the difference between the image of courts as houses of justice and the reality of

them as places that solidified oppression. It likened courts "unto
white sepulchers, which while beautiful on the outside, are full of
dead men's bones and all uncleanness."[85] Such a passage portrayed
well the quality of the Oklahoma courts. When a judge in the Oklahoma City police court failed to convict a white man for assaulting a
black minister, the *Black Dispatch* used the failure to characterize the
court as the "place where lynchers are born":

> Now we had just as well face the truth. HERE IS THE SHAMBLES IN WHICH
> THE MOB AND THE HELLISH LYNCHER IS BORN. The day when the white-
> faced hounds, who go out to torture and burn defenseless black men,
> know that they will be hunted down and meted out justice as they
> deserve, that day is the day that lynching will cease. The lyncher in the
> embryo is the white boys on the street and in public places who show
> their disregard for the feelings and sensibilities of a black man or
> woman by offering insults. This representative of white superiority
> usually carries a loaded gun and has his gang near; if some self respect-
> ing black man with spirit happens to resent such treatment, trouble
> starts.[86]

The courts licensed lawless behavior and could not be counted upon
to be fair. When a black man breaks the law, "he must submit his person before a court constituted entirely from white authority. THE
JUDGE IS WHITE, THE JURY IS WHITE and his JAILOR WHEN HE GOES BEHIND
THE BARS IS WHITE ALSO." Given such a scenario, one wondered, "how
could there be a chance for the white man's justice to slip a cog?"[87]
Yet there was hope that someday the rule of law would triumph—that
blacks would be treated equally with whites by statutes and by
courts.[88] For it appeared that black attitudes were changing and with
them white attitudes:

> Though we battle for justice, we must always keep uppermost in
> our minds the fact that we can get help for the struggle, help with which
> to win, right from among and in the ranks of the white people. In the
> language of "Sojorner Truth," "God is not dead, Justice will yet
> triumph."[89]

The old order would not stand much longer; blacks were breaking
down the walls of segregation. A new Reconstruction was coming.
The ideas of the renaissance had come to the territory and were gain-
ing adherents:

The New Negro, who stands today released in spirit, finds himself in America and in this state, physically bound and shackled by LAWS AND CUSTOMS THAT WERE MADE FOR SLAVES, and all of the unrest, all of the turbulence and all of the violence that now is charged to my people, IS THE BATTLE OF FREE MEN, POUNDING UPON WALLS THAT SURROUND THEM AND THAT WERE MADE FOR SLAVES.[90]

[handwritten marginalia: new world]

Such were the ideas being discussed in Greenwood. The culture of Greenwood, where blacks lived in relative prosperity and freedom, fostered those ideas. People were listening to jazz in the Greenwood juke joints, where on occasion the strict line separating blacks and whites broke down. There was alcohol in Greenwood as well, available at the choc joints, where whites and blacks bought "choc," a beer named after the Native American Choctaw tribe.[91] There were movies, vaudeville shows, prostitutes, newspapers, rootless veterans, and sometimes there was wealth. It was a culture that would not easily abide unequal treatment. I.H. Spears, a black Tulsa lawyer, captured the defiant spirit when he told a white man, "Every time I hear of a lynching, [it] makes me want to get some more ammunition."[92]

Men living in Greenwood were primed, because of the newspapers they were reading and because of the freedom they had experienced during the war, as well as the freedom they held in Greenwood, to take action to prevent lynching. Meanwhile, white Tulsans were themselves on guard against blacks seeking "social equality" and primed to respond to allegations that a black man had raped a white woman. So the stage was set—with editor A.J. Smitherman, lawyer and businessman J.B. Stradford, Police Chief John Gustafson, and countless black and white veterans. The Greenwood residents were well-schooled in the idea of equality under law and they were ready to take life if necessary to uphold that idea. Tulsa was ready to be swept away in an irresistible wave of public passion.

Chapter Two

"Thinking He Can Whip the World": The Riot

"The False Story which Set Tulsa on Fire"

Sometime during the afternoon of Memorial Day, Monday, May 30, 1921, Dick Rowland took the elevator in the Drexel Building in downtown Tulsa to the top, where he used the bathroom facilities. Nineteen-year-old Rowland worked in the building on the ground floor shining shoes. After using the restroom, he reentered the elevator and Sarah Page, a young woman who worked as the elevator operator, brought the car to the ground floor. It is unclear whether Dick and Sarah knew one another before that day. Some rumors persist that they were friends, maybe even lovers.[1]

As Rowland was leaving the elevator, Page screamed. The story that appeared in the *Tulsa Tribune* the next afternoon gave a sensational account of their encounter. Under the heading "Nab Negro for Attacking Girl in Elevator," it reported that "Diamond Dick" assaulted Sarah Page in the elevator. He tore her clothes, it said, and scratched her face. It then reported that Rowland had already been arrested by two black police officers. The story alluded to attempted rape, sure to set Tulsans on edge.

The article, which appeared on the front page of the *Tribune*, has since disappeared, as has part of the editorial page, where there may have been an editorial encouraging lynching.[2] But back in 1921 everyone was talking about the story and it was readily available. In fact, the *Black Dispatch* in Oklahoma City reprinted the story on its front page, under the heading, "The False Story which set Tulsa on Fire":

A Negro delivery boy who gave his name to the police as "Diamond Dick" but who has been identified as Dick Rowland, was arrested on South Greenwood Avenue this morning by Officers Carmichael and Pack, and charged with attempting to assault the 17-year old white elevator girl in the Drexel building early yesterday.

He will be tried in municipal court this afternoon on a state charge. This girl said she noticed the Negro a few minutes before the attempted assault looking up and down the hallway on the third floor of the Drexel building as if to see if there was anyone in sight but thought nothing of it at the time.

A few minutes later he entered the elevator she claimed, and attacked her, scratching her hands and face and tearing her clothes. Her screams brought a clerk from Renberg's store to her assistance and the Negro fled. He was captured and identified this morning by both the girl and clerk, police say.

Rowland denied that he tried to harm the girl, but admitted he put his hands on her arm in the elevator when she was alone.

Tenants of the Drexel building said the girl is an orphan who works as an elevator operator to pay her way through business college.[3]

The *Black Dispatch* blamed the riot on the *Tribune*'s article. "Inciting to riot comes in many forms, mostly THRU WHITE NEWSPAPERS," it said. The story turned even more tragic. A few days after the riot, the editor of the *Tribune* allegedly admitted that some of the details reported in the paper were untrue.[4] As best as we can now determine, Rowland may have slipped as he exited the elevator and grabbed Page to try to steady himself.[5] That spring afternoon, however, Tulsans did not hear this more measured account of Rowland and Page's encounter.

The *Tribune*, Tulsa's afternoon paper, hit the streets with its sensational story about 4:00 P.M. People all over Tulsa began talking about the story. At the courthouse, B.C. Franklin, one of the few black lawyers in Tulsa, heard several people dismissing talk that there might be a lynching—and he did not think anything more of it.[6]

Down in Greenwood, across the railroad tracks from white Tulsa, people were taking the threat of lynching more seriously. At the intersection of Greenwood and Archer, the social and business center of the community, men were discussing what their next move should be. Undoubtedly, they were thinking about the events of the past year—August 1920, when Tulsa Police Chief John Gustafson was present at the lynching of Roy Belton and refused to do anything to stop it; and that same weekend, when Claude Chandler was taken out of the Oklahoma City jail by three masked men and lynched. Again, there had been official complicity in the lynching, as a state-ordered investigation had shown. Greenwood residents knew—as their newspaper the *Tulsa Star* said—that the time to act was when there was a threat of lynching. All over Greenwood, in those tense hours following the publication of the *Tulsa Tribune*, there were discussions of what to do next.

There were serious reasons to fear that Dick Rowland would be lynched. The *Tribune* headline was certain to incite the racial hostilities of white Tulsans, for nothing attracted attention the way a rape charge did. Together with the campaign against lynching, waged at both local and state levels, the climate was ripe for a conflict between black and white Tulsa. Greenwood residents understood the emotions that talk of rape would set off, and they were preparing to take action.

We know that Greenwood residents were fearful for Dick Rowland from testimony given in lawsuits after the riot. One suit in particular, by William Redfearn, a Native American man who owned property in Greenwood, contains several hundred pages of testimony. Redfearn had fire insurance policies, but his insurance company refused compensation, citing a "riot exclusion clause" in the contract. His suit revolved around the question, Was there a "riot" and was the property destroyed by riot, or by some other cause, such as official police action? The testimony in the case preserves minute details about the events surrounding the riot. From that testimony—often given by Greenwood residents—we know they were worried that Dick Rowland would be lynched. We also know what they were doing to prevent it.

One person who testified was C.F. Gabe, a black man who worked as a police officer after the riot. Gabe began his story about 6:00 on the evening of May 31. He was visiting some of his friends around Greenwood. He met Ed Howard, who was later killed in the riot. Howard was worried about Dick Rowland's safety; he said, "C. F., they are going to lynch that boy, tonight." Howard had a plan: "Let's see about it, let's go up there." Gabe went home, put away a gun he was carrying for his job with the city, and then got in a Ford to go up to the courthouse to see what was happening. When he arrived around 6:00 P.M., there were already perhaps 800 men, women, and children at the courthouse. Gabe went into the courthouse and saw

Deputy Sheriff Barney Cleaver, one of the few blacks in law enforcement in Tulsa. Cleaver had been on the Tulsa police force until March 1921, when he was fired, allegedly for operating a private detective agency.[7] He was subsequently hired by the sheriff's department, where he aggressively opposed vice in Greenwood. Cleaver and Sheriff W.M. ("Bill") McCullough were talking with O.W. Gurley, one of the wealthiest Greenwood residents and owner of the Gurley Hotel. Gurley was doing his best to defuse the situation. He had a reputation for fighting crime and often sought the assistance of police officers in enforcing the law.[8]

Sheriff McCullough had already taken steps to protect Rowland, who was in the jail on the top floor of the courthouse. As he sent his deputies up to the jail to guard Rowland, he instructed them to "lock the doors and don't open them. [N]o matter what happens, don't open them." When one of the deputies asked, "Now Uncle Bill, suppose that they do come and they get you and bring you up the stairs ahead of them?" "It don't make no difference, because I will be dead as hell when they come and it won't make any difference. . . . We will never open them, it don't make any difference what happens."[9]

If McCullough's testimony is to be believed, he was adamant about preventing a lynching. Sometime in the early evening, when three white men came into the lobby of the courthouse, he confronted them: "Now there has been some talk about lynching a negro here tonight. . . . [Y]ou are all strangers to me and you haven't any business around here at this time of night. Now get out of here, get on away from here for there will not be anything doing." They snickered, then left the building and wandered back to their car. After the riot, McCullough told a reporter that the failure to stop those men was his only mistake that evening:

> I should have killed those first three men who came into the courthouse. If I had done that, there would have been no further trouble. The white mob had no leader. Many if not all the members of it were willing to follow one another, but none would lead. If there is ever another mob comes to this jail while I am Sheriff, I will kill the first man who comes inside the building, and keep on killing them as fast as they come.[10]

After the three men left the courthouse, they crossed the street and sat in a car. McCullough went over to their car and ordered, "Now you drive that car on out of here and get away." Then he told the others standing around, "Boys, there isn't going to be a lynching here tonight if that's what you're looking for—you just as well go on home; get away from here and stop this excitement, because there isn't going to be anything doing."[11]

McCullough continued to discourage talk of lynching. He went out to the courthouse steps and told the crowd he would kill the next man who came into the building. "It would be an easy matter for you boys to kill me, but you wouldn't get any further," for the deputies at the top had instructions to kill lynchers as they came up the stairs. "I was pretty mad and ready to fight," McCullough recalled. "I expect I talked a little insulting."[12]

Meanwhile, McCullough was giving assurances to O.W. Gurley that Rowland was safe. Gurley went back to Greenwood to spread the news. Gurley's report that Rowland was safe caused one man to exclaim, "You are a damn liar, . . . they had taken a white man out of jail a few weeks before that, and that they [are] going to take this negro out."[13] Gurley said, "Fellow, you ought to be put in jail now."[14] A man named Anderson pointed a rifle at Gurley and threatened to shoot his heart out. I.H. Spears, a lawyer who worked in Greenwood and who was destined to play a leading role in legal battles surrounding the reconstruction of Greenwood after the riot, pushed it away.[15]

Whence those sounds in all directions
Firearms cracking everywhere;
Men and women all excited,
Cries of rioting fill the air.

Men with guns acid ammunition,
Rushing 'madly to the fray,
Shooting, cursing, laughing, crying,
"Come on, boys, come on this way!

"They are trying to lynch our comrade,
Without cause in law defy;
Get your guns and help defend him;
Let's protect him, win or die."

'Twas the cry of Negro manhood,
Rallying to the cause of right,

Ready to suppress the lawless,
Anxious for a chance to fight.

So they marched against the mobbists,
Gathered now about the jail,
While the sheriff stood there pleading,
Law and order to prevail.

A.J. Smitherman,
The Tulsa Riot and Massacre[16]

As events were unfolding in downtown Tulsa, there was action in Greenwood. Men were meeting at the offices of the *Tulsa Star*, whose editor, A.J. Smitherman, had campaigned vigorously against lynching, debating their next moves. Smitherman, who later fled Tulsa to avoid prosecution for inciting riot, was at the center of the discussions. Smitherman had done more than provide the men with a place to meet. He provided the ideological leadership. In the fall of 1920 he had written about what should be done if there was a threat of lynching:

> While the boy was in jail and while there was danger of mob violence any set of citizens had a legal right—it was their duty—to arm themselves and march in a body to the jail and apprize the sheriff or jailer of the purpose of their visit and to take life if need be to uphold the law and protect the prisoner.[17]

Legal right—indeed duty—to march to the jail and take life if necessary to protect the prisoner . . . Ominous words. Some of the men at the *Star*'s offices decided to go home, get their guns, put on their uniforms, and head to the courthouse to prevent a lynching. Here the separate paths of Greenwood and white Tulsa began to cross again.

At 7:00 P.M., about the time O.W. Gurley was facing the armed crowd in Greenwood, a group of Greenwood men took more direct action. Maybe thirty black men made the journey south from Greenwood, across the railroad tracks, into white Tulsa. They appeared at the west end of the courthouse and offered to assist in protecting Dick Rowland. Barney Cleaver went to the men and encouraged them to leave. "Boys, you are not doing right," Cleaver told them. "There isn't anybody going to get that boy tonight. He is perfectly safe here. You shouldn't have done this thing for it only stirs up race trouble. Go on home and behave yourselves."[18] The men left; it looked as though the situation might calm down.

police doing job

But men kept coming from Greenwood to the courthouse. Shortly after Cleaver encouraged the men to go, a single car with nine black men in it approached the Courthouse. There was a lot of shouting. McCullough was standing on the steps at the south end of the courthouse, giving a speech to the whites gathered there, much like Barney Cleaver's. He told them he would not turn over Dick Rowland and that they should go home. Such advocacy brought forth jeers. "Somebody hollered [to McCullough] 'You must be a nigger lover.' McCullough cursed and said 'If you come up here I will show you.'"[19]

McCullough then called to C.F. Gabe to head off the approaching Greenwood residents. Gabe walked alongside the car, which held the nine men, for about a block, persuading them to drive away. But even as the car was leaving, whites were preparing for a more violent clash. "Let's go to the Armory," Gabe heard some in the jeering crowd say.

White men went to armory several times to ask for guns that night, but the armory never gave them any. Two men from the National Guard armory went to the home of Major Jason Bell, the man in charge of the Tulsa units of the National Guard, around 9:00 in the evening. They told him that there was talk of lynching a black man being held at the Tulsa courthouse and that the blacks were arming to prevent it. Major Bell was not initially worried, because he had heard similar rumors before. But he told the men to go back downtown, gather information, and report back to him at the armory. And Bell, who lived across the alley from the armory, went there himself. Soon there were perhaps 300 or 400 men in front of the armory, asking for weapons. When Bell told them they could not get weapons, one voice shouted, "We don't know about that, we guess we can." One person tried to break in a side window, but Bell chased him away and put up a guard around the building, to make sure that no one would have access to any weapons.[20] Those men drifted away—probably back to the courthouse. But passions did not subside.

In Greenwood, as in white Tulsa, passions were hot. Veterans, armed and ready to use force to prevent a lynching, were getting ready to make more trips to the courthouse. They were motivated in part by a rumor circulating in Greenwood that Sheriff McCullough had called the office of the *Tulsa Star*. Some had heard the improbable story that McCullough called to ask for assistance. Luther Jones, a white lawyer who was at the courthouse that night, said that some of the blacks at the courthouse claimed that McCullough had called for them. "They said you told them to come up here." McCullough said, " 'I did not' and a negro said 'you did tell us to come.'"[21]

A more plausible story is that McCullough called to calm down feelings—and added he would call upon residents if he needed help. J.B. Stradford claimed that McCullough had called the *Tulsa Star* and told the men there that he might need assistance: "If he found he could not cope with the situation, for us to get together and he would call us to help protect him." Stradford, who fled first to Kansas and then to Chicago to avoid prosecution, recorded in his memoirs his role in keeping the peace in Greenwood:

> I hesitated at first, for the situation was a perilous one; I advised the boys to be sober and wait until the sheriff called for us. I further said that I had expected something of that nature on account of the bitter feeling against our group and I said then as I had said before that, the day a member of our group was mobbed in Tulsa the streets would be bathed in blood.[22]

If there was going to be a lynching, though, Stradford was going to do everything in his power to stop it. He recalled that he told the crowd, "If I can't get anyone to go with me I will go single-handed and empty my automatic into the mob and then resign myself to my fate."[23] Getting people to go to the courthouse was not a problem that night.

With such encouragement, men from Greenwood continued to make trips to the courthouse that evening. Around 9:30, Gabe, who was on his way home from the courthouse, confronted three carloads of men. They were probably among the men who had been meeting at the *Tulsa Star*. Gabe recalled that he "got out in the street and throwed up my hands and told them to go back. I says, 'Go back boys, go back to the other side of town, go back where you belong, let's don't do that.'" But by then they were not going to be told what to do. "One man pointed his gun at me and told me to get out of the street, . . . I could see the gun, and I got out of the way and they went on."[24] As those cars headed for the courthouse, Gabe made his way back to Archer Street.

"All Hell Breaks Loose"

The three carloads of men, which Gabe had unsuccessfully tried to stop, were about to clash with white Tulsa. They circled the courthouse;

then the men got out and began marching, single file, toward it. They were reenacting scenes from the World War, in which many of them had served. Here were Peg Leg Taylor, O.B. Mann, Will Robinson, W.S. Weaver, Bud Bassett, Henry Van Dyke, Chester Ross, Jake Mayes, John Supplesox, Jack Scott, Lee Mable, and John Bowman, as well as people known only by nicknames, like Fattie, Chummy, and Big Fred.[25] We will never know the details of their lives, but we can reconstruct their collective actions on a night eighty years ago.

"Thinking He Can Whip the World": Greenwood Veterans Confront the Mob

Thus responding to their duty,
Like true soldiers that they were,
Black men face the lawless white men
Under duty's urgent spur.

Cries of "Let us have the nigger"
"Lynch him, kill him" came the shout.
And at once there came the answer
When a sharp report rang out.

"Stand back men, there'll be no lynching"
Black men cried, and not in fun
Bang! Bang! Bang! Three quick shots followed,
And the battle had begun.

In the fusilade that followed
Four white lynchers kissed the dust,
Many more fell badly wounded,
Victims of their hellish lust.

A.J. Smitherman,
The Tulsa Riot and Massacre[26]

The *Tulsa Tribune* made disdainful comments about those Greenwood men: "They were nearly all dope dealers or jake drinkers with police records. However, there were a few more intelligent in the lead."[27] O.W. Gurley blamed the riot on veterans of the World War who lived in Greenwood. "The real leader of the gang was a tall, brown-skinned negro named Mann. He and his brother ran two or three stores in the colored quarter and they stand well in the community. But this boy has come back from France with exaggerated ideas about equality and thinking he can whip the world."[28] Men with such backgrounds were not about to let the lawlessness of lynching take place in their city.

The white crowd at the courthouse was equally aggressive. Before he began walking home, Gabe saw "quite a crowd of folks, probably five or six thousand had gathered." One white man was speaking to the crowd, trying to disperse them. He told them that blacks were "riding around with high powered revolvers and guns down town" and he seemed to be making an impact. Just as he was talking, however, three cars drove up.

As the three cars were arriving at the courthouse, there were already other Greenwood men seeking assurances that Rowland was safe. Sheriff McCullough met thirty-five or forty black men who were marching alongside the courthouse. "They were all excited and all trying to talk at once, but some of them told me they would go if I would assure them that I would not let them take this boy." He marched them away from the courthouse and soon another group of black men came up. "When they came I went right out in the street again, just as I did the first time. Got right in with them and told them they must go home." Barney Cleaver and Pete Joyce, a former Tulsa police officer, were there too. They "got in the bunch also with the negroes, and we three kept talking to them and arguing with them." As they were trying to persuade these men to leave, they were about half a block from the courthouse.

At the courthouse, a man, perhaps wearing a police badge, confronted some of the black men and began disarming them. One man refused to give up his gun. There are unsubstantiated, perhaps apocryphal, stories, that the police officer asked, "Nigger, where you goin' with that gun?" "I'll use it if I have to," was the response. A struggle resulted in the gun going off and the riot starting.[29]

McCullough was maybe half a block away from the shooting, so he could not see who had fired the first shot. But he testified to the events nearby. When the shot was fired, "that was just like throwing a match in the powder can."[30] The street cleared quickly. "Every negro drew his gun and started shooting." McCullough, who was surrounded by blacks, recalled that "I didn't think anything else but that these other white people would commence to shoot right down that way." So McCullough dove for the sidewalk. When he looked around, the street was empty.[31]

As the streets cleared, it seems that at least one victim of the shooting lay dead in front of the courthouse. Little is known about that confrontation; the stories cannot even agree if the person who was killed was black or white. One report was that the first victim was a black man, who lay dying under a billboard with a picture of Mary Pickford, America's sweetheart, smiling winsomely.[32] After the shooting, Gurley headed home. When stopped and asked what was going on, he replied, "Hell has broke loose."[33]

"excuses to start fighting"

In the chaos following the initial violence, whites sought guns any way they could get them. Men broke into Dick Bardon's nearby pawn shop and a sporting goods store. A few dozen men from the National Guard who were based at the Tulsa armory quickly arrived and stopped the looting, but not before thousands of dollars of merchandise had been stolen.[34] One newspaper reported, "Armed men seemed to spring from everywhere. Within half an hour an army of about 500 men was being drilled for duty and coached for emergency. Practically all hardware stores were emptied of guns and ammunition. Some opened their doors voluntarily."[35] There was a crowd gathering to watch: "Thousands of persons, both the inquisitive including several hundred women, and men, armed with every available weapon in the city taken from every hardware and sporting goods store, swarmed on Second Street from Boulder to Boston Avenue, watching the gathering volunteer army or offering their services to the peace officers."[36]

> Quick they fled in all directions,
> Panic stricken, filled with fear,
> Leaving their intended victim
> As the news spread far and near.
>
> Scattered now in great confusion,
> Filled with vengeance all anew,
> Leaders of the lynching party
> Planned for something else to do.
>
> "Blacks Prevent a Negro's Lynching"
> Read a bold newspaper head,

In an extra night edition,
"Fifty Whites Reported Dead."

Rallied now with reinforcements,
Brave (?) white men five thousand strong
Marched upon the black defenders
With their usual battle song:

"Get the niggers" was their slogan
Kill them, burn them, set the pace,
Let them know that we are white men,
Teach them how to keep their place.
A.J. Smitherman,
The Tulsa Riot and Massacre[37]

As whites were arming themselves and volunteering their services at the police station, the blacks headed back to Greenwood. Gabe, who was partway home, also described what he observed from a distance:

> I heard a shot fired, and it wasn't more than a minute until somebody came down and said there was a man killed at the Court House, and then the shooting began. I could hear shooting in most places, but I came back to the Court House and . . . met one of the young lawyers, Mr. James, I think and I was going down Sixth Street, . . . and then came two fellows out of the alley, two colored fellows came up out of the alley . . . and one of them was trying his best to get by and one of them was not certain and the other said to shoot and I said to them 'Don't shoot Mr. James here' and the boys turned and ran back the other way and I went on down the street.

Gabe soon heard someone say "there was a nigger dead there." Jim Adkison, the police commissioner, warned Gabe to leave, or he would be hurt.[38] Gabe again started making his way home. As he entered Greenwood, at the corner of Cincinnati and Archer, just a block west from the center of the Greenwood business district at Greenwood and Archer, Gabe could hear the sounds of the riot in the distance—"I could hear them breaking glass over on Main Street." Then a black man came by, "said they was breaking into Dick Bardon's store and he said 'Let's go and get us some guns now.' I said, 'No, no, don't go there' and I begged the other fellows to go back, and then I went back but this other fellow kept going."[39]

Gabe then heard another shot: "they fired at this fellow and I think killed him, I know they shot him because he hollered." He started running for cover, as he later told the court:

> There was a boiler down there, with one of those round box boilers, and the rest of the niggers ran and I ran and tried to get in that boiler but I couldn't get in, my head would go in but my shoulders wouldn't, and I came out then and got around by the side of the boiler and the thing seemed to be going pretty well, and then the crowd . . . was shooting out the lights over at the Frisco depot. You could see one man from the depot run out and shoot and somebody from over in the colored crowd would shoot, and the "ting" come pretty often and every once in a while you could see somebody holler, see somebody pick up a man. And then I ran and tried to get over the other side of the tracks, and at that time a man came along, a white man and his wife, and the boys was scattering to let them pass, and the people let him pass and I got on the car and started back to town with him and he told me 'You better not go, you will get killed' and I turned around and went on home, I left for home right there.[40]

Gabe continued toward his house. Stopping near the border between white and black Tulsa, along Boston Avenue, Gabe saw an early skirmish—and the first torches being set to Greenwood property:

> I ran across the street and there was some white boys on Boston with a light in their hands going toward the old shack that used to be down in there and somebody shot the first one that started and he did not get to the house. Then I ran up the street and right on the corner of . . . Archer and Cincinnati and on the east side of the street I got behind a telephone pole and then the people began firing, shooting, and I started over there and a guy came back toward me on the street, I don't recall the man's name, but he said, 'Let's go in this house and go up stairs, and won't be bothered,' and I saw them coming out with another torch and something happened to him before he got there and a third man came out and set the little house afire.[41]

The shacks lining the border between white and black Tulsa were the first to fall to fire; they were signs of things to come. When the Fire Department appeared around midnight to put out the fires, the white mob would not let them. One firefighter recalled, "as I pulled up there they shouted, 'Don't put that fire out. Get away from here.'"[42] They came back about an hour later, when one shack was still left standing, but again were stopped from fighting the fire.[43]

Back in the heart of Greenwood, there were three or four hundred men, armed with whatever weapons were available—guns, sticks, bricks. In the words of O.W. Gurley, "They were just running around." Families were leaving in automobiles. Others used automobiles to go to the front. Gurley saw his friend Ed Howard in a car full of other black men and tried to persuade him to come with him. Howard did not listen.[44]

The battle lines were being drawn along the Frisco tracks, which separated Greenwood on the north and white Tulsa on the south.[45] Henry Sowders, one of the few whites who worked in Greenwood, saw the chaos on both sides of the divide. Sowders ran the motion picture machine in the Dreamland Theater. The Dreamland Theater was on Greenwood, in the block north of Archer, at the center of Greenwood's business district. Sowders noticed a crowd gathering on Greenwood about 7:30. When the second showing was starting about 10 P.M., Mr. Cotton, the manager, asked him to turn the lights back on. At that point, Sowders saw that Cotton was armed. Cotton told Sowders he was "protecting himself—looking out for number one." Sowders also saw guns at a side door; someone called, "Quick, come out and get your guns." A few black men came to get the guns, as others left the theater. The building was empty in a few minutes.

Meanwhile, Sowders went out to Greenwood. When Cotton told him there was fighting going on, Sowders prepared to leave. But he found his car "full of negroes; that they had turned the top back and *mayhem* were standing up in the back seat, there being about nine in all."[46] When Sowders asked for his car, "a big husky negro picked him up and set him over on a Ford truck and told him to stay there." The man then paid the Ford's driver to take Sowders to the railroad station. On the way to the station, Sowers saw the street filled with men carrying guns. Upon crossing the tracks, Sowders saw Police Officer H.C. Pack holding back three black men, while others were crossing the tracks.[47] As they approached Cincinnati, "they nearly ran over a negro standing in the middle of the street shooting, and . . . he noticed two others lying in the street; he didn't know whether they were wounded or dead." Then, by himself at this point, he went to Main Street, where he saw men taking arms from a pawn shop. "[H]e made inquiry as to what was going on, and was told he had better get on home to his family, if he had one, or else get some arms, for the thing was coming on."[48]

"Stop at All Hazards These Armed Men": The White Response to the "Negro Uprising"

"Forward! March!" command was given,
And the tread of feet was heard,
Marching on the Colored district,
In protest there came no word.

In the meantime rabid hoodlums
Now turned loose without restraint.
Helped themselves to things of value,
More than useless to complain.

Guns were taken by the hundreds.
Ammunition all in sight.
Reign of murder, theft and plunder
Was the order of the night.

A.J. Smitherman,
The Tulsa Riot and Massacre[49]

[handwritten: Whites burning buildings] The response of the Tulsa Police Department to the "thing coming on" was to commission about 250 men, to help in putting down what they viewed as a "negro uprising." Soon after the riot began, cars flooded into downtown Tulsa, filled with armed men. "Little conversation was indulged in, but all wore an expression of determination to put down the uprising of the negroes. Old men carrying shotguns walked or marched side by side with youths in white flannels, carrying the largest rifles or small-bore shotguns."[50] Rumors fed mob fears. In response to a rumor that someone in Greenwood had called Muskogee and received assurances that 500 black men were coming as reinforcements, the Tulsa police ordered a machine gun crew put out on the road from Muskogee. They were instructed to "stop at all hazards these armed men."[51]

Soon Tulsa-based units of the National Guard appeared at the courthouse. The crowd believed that the Guard was going to protect white Tulsa. When those soldiers arrived at the courthouse, the crowd cheered, "now let the niggers come, if they dare."[52] The crowd saw the National Guard as an ally against Tulsa's blacks, for they thought there was a "negro uprising" in progress. The Guard units helped to stop looting near the courthouse, although the police were apparently issuing weapons taken from downtown stores.[53] The National Guard began working in conjunction with local authorities to try to quell the riot.

Some evidence of white Tulsa's response to the riot comes from Wesley Bush, the fire marshal. He arrived at the police station sometime after 10:00 P.M. Throughout the night he saw people standing around the station; the street was full of armed people. Many of them were going into the police station. He saw "bunches of men go out of the police station, but he didn't know where they would go; that they would leave the police station and go out, and come back."[54] By itself, Bush's testimony merely establishes that the police station was a gathering point for men planning their next moves.

Deputizing the Mob

What was happening inside the station is important. During the July 1921 trial of Police Chief John A. Gustafson for neglect of duty during the riot, Police Commissioner Jim Adkison discussed what had occurred. Inside the police station, men came to offer their services, and, "after a conference with the chief," they decided to "muster in the men as special officers." The commissions as deputies were handed out without sufficient discretion. In response to a question whether Adkison believed that police officers had engaged in arson, he admitted that he did not know. He protested:

> There was no testimony that uniformed men were bearing the torch. It was all about men wearing stars. Many of the men who were commissioned that night were given old police stars. We were unable to limit the commissions to our choice. I usually talked to the men and those I thought would remain cool-headed I commissioned. But some of those men might have lost their heads—they might have applied the torch, but it was positively in contradiction to orders. My orders, the chief's orders, Colonel Rooney's orders were to disarm everyone not properly commissioned and absolutely prevent looting and burning.[55]

Adkison's testimony tells us that city officials were responsible for key decisions. First, the highest law enforcement officials distributed commissions. Second, those commissions were distributed without discretion. And finally, the city officials ordered everyone who was not a deputy to be disarmed.

A bricklayer, Laurel Buck, testified in Gustafson's trial about the actions of local officials in the early stages of the riot. After the riot broke out, Buck went to the police station and asked for a commission. He did not receive it, but he was instructed to "get a gun, and get busy and try to get a nigger."[56] Buck went to the Tulsa Hardware Store, where he received a gun. Like many other men, Buck was issued a weapon by Tulsa officials, who were so careless in distributing weapons that they did not even know whom they had issued weapons to. Several weeks after the riot, Gustafson pleaded with Tulsans in the *Tulsa World* to return the weapons:

> Not all persons who borrowed guns from the police station the Tuesday night of the negro uprising have returned them to the station. Chief of Police John A. Gustafson Saturday asked that there be no more delay in returning those firearms. . . . "These guns were only loaned," the chief explained, "and were loaned with the understanding they would be returned as soon as the situation had improved to a point sufficient to justify their return."[57]

Gustafson and the other officials testified—as had Adkison—that their instructions were to "keep a cool head, use common sense, and to do the best to protect property and life."[58] As Adkison recognized, however, the men lost their heads and their hearts as well.

Defending the Temples of Their Gods: Greenwood Bunkers Down

And how can man die better,
Than facing fearful odds,
For the ashes of his fathers
And the temples of his gods?
The Outlook[59]

But our boys who learned the lesson
On the blood-stained soil of France
How to fight on the defensive
Purposed not to take a chance.

Like a flash they came together,
Word was passed along the line:
"No white man must cross the border;
Shoot to kill and shoot in time!"

"Ready, Fire!" And then a volley
From the mob whose skins were white
"Give 'em hell,—boys," cried the leader,
"Soon we'll put them all to flight."

But they got a warm reception
From black men who had no fear,
Who while fighting they were singing:
"Come on Boys, The Gang's all Here."

Rapid firing guns were shooting.
Men were falling by the score.
'Till the white men quite defeated
Sent the word "We want no more."

Nine p.m. the trouble started,
Two a.m. the thing was done.
And the victory for the black men   *deaths?*
Counted almost four to one.

A.J. Smitherman,
The Tulsa Riot and Massacre[60]

As white Tulsa was gearing up, blacks in downtown Tulsa were heading back to Greenwood as quickly as they could. At the Frisco tracks, Greenwood residents made a stand. As some were holding off the whites at the tracks, others back in Greenwood were working to bring calm and make peace. C.F. Gabe and John Smitherman,[61] brother of the editor of the *Tulsa Star,* sought help from J.B. Stradford. They hoped he might help stop the riot. He said, "'Gabe, I ain't going up; if they want me, bring them down to me, I ain't going.'"[62]

Others in Greenwood realized they were already involved in a war. They prepared to ward off the invasion of Greenwood. Veterans, replaying the military techniques they had recently learned, bunkered down. In buildings along the railroad tracks, they found good vantage points from which to defend Greenwood. Some went into the belfry of the new Mount Zion Baptist Church. Later rumors told—

without any basis in fact—that ammunition had been stored there in anticipation of an uprising.[63] Others bunkered down in their homes and businesses. They sought good spots to fire from, like concrete buildings. They put on their uniforms as they prepared to protect their community. As one member of the National Guard recalled years later, "It was surprising to see the number of negroes in army attire . . . found secreted in houses. [They] even wore their war helmets, well supplied with long range Winchesters, often provided with 20 or 30 rounds of ammunition."[64]

Mary Jones Parrish, a teacher in Greenwood before the riot, published a book shortly after the riot entitled *Events of the Tulsa Disaster*. It had her own recollections, as well as those of several prominent Greenwood residents. Parrish described the fighting on the evening of May 31 and early morning of June 1. "[T]hese brave boys of ours fought gamely and held back the enemy for hours. . . . Like Stonewall Jackson of old, our boys stood 'like a stone wall' offsetting each and every attempt to burn Greenwood and the vicinity."[65]

But by about midnight, blacks had been confined to Greenwood. The first edition of the *Tulsa World* reported in a headline that "Negroes Finally Driven into Little Africa." The whites, now heavily armed, were driving around the city. The *World* reported that the men "in motor cars formed a circle of steel about 'Little Africa' and a continuous rattle of rifle and revolver fire could be heard."[66] The circle of cars reminded another paper of the "Indian War Style." The *St. Louis Post-Dispatch* described sixty or seventy cars, "driving slowly round and round after the manner of horsemen in the days of Indian warfare."[67] From that point on, the battle was fought out entirely on the grounds of Greenwood. The resulting destruction occurred when white men—police officers and their deputies, white mobs, and the local units of the National Guard—drove into Little Africa.

The units of the National Guard that were based at Tulsa were the first ones involved in the riot. Their role in the riot is central to understanding it. Yet the Guard's actions are ambiguous and susceptible to several interpretations. The local units struggled to restore order and took some action to protect Greenwood on the evening the riot first began.[68] But their larger effect—as told by their own records—was to facilitate the destruction of Greenwood. They worked in the early morning hours of June 1 in conjunction with local authorities to disarm and arrest the men who were defending it. While ostensibly operating to protect the lives and property of Greenwood residents, the local units of the Guard disarmed and arrested Greenwood residents (and not white rioters), then left their property defenseless, allowing deputies, uniformed police officers, and mobs to loot and burn it.

Shortly after 10:00 P.M., Tulsa officials called the National Guard armory and asked for assistance. Colonel Rooney, the officer in charge, received instructions from Oklahoma Governor J.B.A. Robertson to follow the orders of Tulsa officials. He then sent several dozen soldiers to the courthouse.

Captain Frank Van Voorhis, arrived at the courthouse at 10:30 P.M., with two officers and sixteen men. The Guardsmen went to the police station, across the street from the courthouse, where they apparently began working in conjunction with the police. At 1:15 A.M. they "produced" a machine gun and placed it on a truck, along with three experienced machine gunners and six other enlisted men. They then traveled around the city to spots where "there was firing" until 3:00 A.M., when Lieutenant Colonel L.J.F. Rooney, the officer in charge of the Tulsa Units of National Guard, ordered them to Stand Pipe Hill, just over the western border of Greenwood. At that point, Rooney deployed the men along Detroit Avenue, from Stand Pipe Hill to Archer, where they worked "disarming and arresting negroes and sending them to the Convention Hall by Police cars and trucks."[69] Van Voorhis's report details the "capture" of well more than 200 "prisoners." Van Voorhis's men were able to capture those Greenwood residents without much gunfire. It appears that his men killed no one.

Captain John McCuen's men, however, did kill a number of Greenwood residents in the process of responding to the "negro uprising." McCuen and twenty men guarded the western border between white Tulsa and Greenwood for several hours. They began pushing into Greenwood, using a truck with an old (and probably inoperable machine gun on it), probably around 3:00 A.M. McCuen's men, like Van Voorhis's, were working in close conjunction with the Tulsa police. They arrested a "large number" of Greenwood residents and turned them over to the "Police Department automobiles," which were close by "at all times." These cars "were manned by ex-service men, and in many cases plain-clothes men of the police department."[70] As the night gave way to morning, the riot was about to get worse.

"Running the Negro Out of Tulsa"

Then the white went into council,
Hoping to reprise their loss,
Planned the massacre that followed,
Dared to win at any cost.

June the First at five a.m.
Three long whistle blasts were heard,
Giving sign for concert action
To that cold blood-thirsty herd.

At the signal from the whistle
Aeroplanes were seen to fly,
Dropping bombs and high explosives,
Hell was falling from the sky!

A.J. Smitherman,
The Tulsa Riot and Massacre[71]

[handwritten margin note: where they live separate]

One of the most telling photographs of the riot is a postcard entitled "Running the Negro Out of Tulsa." It shows Greenwood houses
on fire. The fires that destroyed thirty-five blocks of Greenwood were
a central part of the riot. Before the fires were set, the people who
would set them had to get past the well-armed defenders. The local
units of the National Guard were instrumental in the hours before
dawn on June 1 in disarming Greenwood residents; and in disarming
more defenders after dawn. But the Guardsmen are only one part of
the story of the riot. At dawn, white men—members of the police
force, special deputies, and people working in conjunction with
them—were poised on the south end of Greenwood, ready to cross
the railroad tracks.

At the sound of a whistle about 5:00 A.M. on June 1, the invasion
began. Barney Cleaver, a black deputy sheriff, was a witness to the
battle that began with the whistle. Cleaver had stayed at the courthouse until 4:00 in the morning. He finally came back to Greenwood,
with three other black men. At the corner of Greenwood and Archer
he met perhaps twenty armed men and told them to go home. The
city seemed quiet for the time being, but Cleaver feared what might
happen later. When Cleaver got home, he sent his wife and sister-in-
law out to a house they owned about a mile from town and then he

went back to the center of Greenwood. He was in a building near the railroad tracks at five o'clock when "the whistle blew." He recalled he had "never heard such shooting in all my life; well, when they begin shooting, they begin shooting every way." Cleaver saw black men shooting from a hall where the Masons and Odd Fellows met; one man fell out of a window onto the street below. Soon the police were arresting the men who had been shooting from the hall.[72] The policemen took Cleaver out to his house to help rescue his belongings from the fires that were already being set. The heavy shooting lasted for about half an hour.[73]

C.F. Gabe gave dramatic testimony about the destruction that morning. The whistle was central to his account, as it was to Cleaver's account:

> [A]t five o'clock a whistle blowed and when the whistle blowed, maybe a few minutes after five—my mind ain't clear whether it was five or six but it was between there and a whistle blowed and when that whistle blowed you could hear shooting everywhere in town, firing boom, boom, boom, boom. My wife jumped up out of bed and told me there was trouble in town, and when my wife said that, in came some group of men beside my house and says, called me, says "Gabe, get up" and he says, "the white folks is killing all the niggers in town and burning all their houses." And my wife she jumped up and looked out the door and saw fire burning away up high.[74]

It did not take long for the destruction to reach the Gabe home:

> I didn't get up. I thought they was just talking, and after while I heard the shooting up on the hill—I live at the foot of the hill over on Easton and there was somebody up on the hill shooting towards my house, and they shot my piano, and when pieces of the piano began to fall, I stucked my head in the front room and when I stuck my head in the front room I just turned around and said to my wife and the two smaller children, I says "You all get out" and I reached up and got my pistol to fight my way out if I had to do it, and when I found my pistol there wasn't but two bullets in it, I hadn't looked at it for a day or two and I just threw it over on the bed, inside the room, and I went to the door and when I stuck my head out of the door two gentlemen came toward my house.[75]

Those white men told him to "Come out." One said, 'That is Gabe, let him alone' . . . "You go back and get behind the piano and get down in there, we ain't going to bother you, you are all right.'" A few moments later the men, who were continuing up the street, were shot "and both of them fell." Then "came an airplane over, just looked like it was about fifty feet above our heads, and that airplane had some smoke and it seemed like it was all black all around me, I thought it was on the airplane."[76]

Airplanes are an important part of the story of Greenwood's destruction. Mary Jones Parrish also focused on the use of airplanes. "We heard such a buzzing noise that on running to the door to get a better view of what was going on, the sights our eyes beheld made our poor hearts stand still for a moment. There was a great shadow in the sky and upon a second look we discerned that this cloud was caused by fast approaching aeroplanes. It then dawned upon us that the enemy had organized in the night and was invading our district the same as the Germans invaded France and Belgium."[77]

After the riot, black newspapers (and Greenwood residents suing the city) alleged that the police chief, mayor, and other city officials had planned an air attack on Greenwood. The black press presented a stark picture of official involvement in the destruction. Airplanes were central to their stories. One account came from Van B. Hurley, who was identified as a former Tulsa police officer. The papers reported that Hurley, "who was honorably discharged from the force and given splendid recommendations by his captains and lieutenants," named city officials who planned the attack on Greenwood using airplanes. Hurley described "the conference between local aviators and the officials. After this meeting Hurley asserted the airplanes darted out from hangars and hovered over the district dropping nitroglycerin on buildings, setting them afire." Hurley said the officials told their deputies to deal aggressively with Greenwood residents. "They gave instructions for every man to be ready and on the alert and if the niggers wanted to start anything to be ready for them. They never put forth any efforts at all to prevent it whatever, and said if they started anything to kill every b—— son of a b—— they could find."[78]

There remains substantial question whether airplanes bombed Greenwood.[79] At a minimum, it seems airplanes were used to coordinate the attack, according to the *Tulsa Tribune:* "The men in the air were alert for movements of negroes in the sections where shots were being fired from sniping stations at the advancing whites, and they often dipped low in their planes to pick out the exact positions of the barricades. Over outlying portions of the country they watched for groups of negroes reported to be on their way to Tulsa as reinforcements, according to persistent rumors which reached the city all day."[80] In the wake of the riot, airplanes were also used to keep watch over blacks elsewhere in Oklahoma.[81]

The use of airplanes is itself an important signal of the role that technology played in race relations. Airplanes might become an indicator of equality (and vehicles by which salvation is achieved), as Ralph Ellison's essays "Flying Home" and "A Party Down at the Square" suggest.[82] Ellison, writing around the time of World War II, found airplanes symbolic of all that blacks could achieve. At one point he planned to set a novel in a Nazi prisoner of war camp, where the ranking POW was a black aviator.[83] And in Ellison's short story "A Party Down at the Square," a plane, lost in the fog around Birmingham, was drawn to a bonfire where a black man was being burned to death. The plane temporarily interrupted the burning—and held out the hope of salvation. When the plane left, the killing continued. But in Tulsa, the new technology promised not equality but continued—and more effective—destruction.[84]

Gabe's testimony cannot answer the toughest question about the role of airplanes in the riot, for he did not testify whether the plane was dropping bombs. But he did see someone shoot at the plane: "some colored fellows across the street shot at the airplane and hit it, because you could see him, and when he hit the airplane it just went right straight up. I turns around and started back in the house then and there was two fellows came across the street and told me to come on out in the street and make it snappy." Greenwood residents viewed the airplanes as part of the invasion. The image of a plane bombing Greenwood even appeared in a cartoon. Another cartoon depicted the barbaric treatment of Greenwood residents at the hands of Tulsa police and thugs.

Fighting continued in the early hours all over Greenwood. As Mary Parrish looked out a window from her apartment building on the morning of June 1, she saw armed white men gathering near the grainery at the southeastern end of Greenwood, along the railroad tracks. "Then the truth dawned upon us that our men were fighting in vain to hold their dear Greenwood."[85] Soon she left the building, running north on Greenwood Avenue, away from the line of battle, "amidst showers of bullets from the machine gun located in the grainary and from men who were quickly surrounding our district."[86]

Images of airplanes bombing Greenwood appeared in cartoons. Note the plane beneath the flag in "My Country, 'Tis of Thee——," *Chicago Defender* 8 (June 11, 1921).

In War and in Peace

In times of war, when an allied soldier dropped his weapons and raised his hands as a sign of surrender, the "barbarous" Germans spared his life.

In Tulsa, Oklahoma, however, defenseless men, women and children were murdered without a chance for their lives.

"In War and in Peace," *Chicago Defender* 8 (June 18, 1921).

*treated
w/
respect*

Back at Gabe's house, his life was in danger. After he saw the airplane, two more white men came up to his house. One said, "'He is a God damn big nigger,' and says 'kill him' and the other fellow says, 'No, he hasn't got a gun, and you can't hurt him' and says 'Get on up with the crowd.'" Gabe then went up with a group of other black men who were being carried to the Convention Hall for internment. Gabe was driven to the Convention Hall, from there to the Fair Grounds, and from the Fair Grounds finally to Sheriff McCullough's house, where he spent the night.[87]

As Gabe was being arrested by Tulsa deputies, the local units of the National Guard were working elsewhere in Greenwood to disarm and arrest other blacks. Captain McCuen reported that shortly after daylight, he received an urgent request from the Police Department to stop blacks from firing into white homes along Sunset Hill, northwest of Greenwood. "We advanced to the crest of Sunset Hill in skirmish line and then a little further north to the military crest of the hill where our men were ordered to lie down because of the intense fire of the blacks who had formed a good skirmish line at the foot of the hill to the northeast among the outbuildings of the negro settlement which stops at the foot of the hill." The Guardsmen fired at will for nearly half an hour. The Greenwood residents then began falling back, "getting good cover among the frame buildings of the negro settlement." As the Guardsmen advanced, they continued to meet stiff opposition from some "negroes who had barricaded themselves in houses." According to McCuen, the men who were barricaded "refused to stop firing and had to be killed." It is unclear how many were killed. Later, at the northeast corner of the settlement, "10 or more negroes barricaded themselves in a concrete store and a dwelling." The Guardsmen fought alongside civilians, and at this point, some blacks and whites were killed.[88]

A detailed account of one Guardsman based in Tulsa appeared in the *Muskogee Phoenix* a day after the riot. Sergeant T.J. Esley told about his action the morning of the riot. He shot at some black veterans who refused to disarm peacefully:

I could see where the shots were coming from but I couldn't see the niggers. Then I looked under a shack and saw the big feet of one nigger who was doing the shooting. I shot at those feet with my .45 and I could tell I hit them by the way he first picked up one and then the other. He started to run and Bame [another Guardsman] got him. We ran around the corner of the house and I saw a big nigger, one of those who were in the twenty-fourth infantry, good soldiers, stepped in front of us and shot my companion in the stomach. . . . I shot and hit him in the stomach and thigh, tearing half of it away and then he started to run, shooting backward as he did it. Pretty soon he came back from around a nearby house, his hands above his head. I could see he was staggering. He came up to us and said, "Well you boys gave us more than we got overseas. I'm from the twenty-fourth."[89]

The veteran died shortly afterwards.

Why was the Guard disarming Greenwood residents and interning them? Colonel Rooney, who was in charge of the local units of the National Guard, testified during Gustafson's trial that he had initially planned to put a line of troops around Greenwood, but abandoned the plan when he discovered he did not have enough men to protect it. Instead, the Guard began gathering Greenwood residents together and taking them to internment centers around the city. Ostensibly, the Guard did that for the protection of Greenwood residents. The rationale was that if Greenwood residents were collected together, they could be more easily protected against the mob. Some Greenwood residents, however, did not want to give up their guns. "In several cases the negroes made a stand and fought, but with the exception of one case the skirmishes were short. In the one case there were about 50 blacks who scattered in skirmish formation and fought 'like tigers.'"[90]

Some may agree with Colonel Rooney's assessment that the Guard was taking Greenwood residents into protective custody, but the after-action reports suggest that the Guard's work in conjunction with local authorities was designed to put down the supposed "negro uprising," not to protect the Greenwood residents.

As the Guardsmen were advancing, fires appeared all over Greenwood. Apparently, the white mobs trailed closely after the Guardsmen as they swept through Greenwood disarming and arresting the residents. Under the heading, "Mob follows troops," the *Muskogee Phoenix* told of the mob following in the wake of the National Guard. It reported in stark language: "As the troops pressed forward every home was fired." The *Phoenix* pointed out the difficulty the Guard faced. They did not have enough troops in Tulsa to handle the riot. "The spark had been kindled. A hundred militiamen might be able to battle an army of negroes at their front but they could not rout two thousand heavily armed white men."[91] The paper reported on the connections between the actions and the subsequent destruction of Greenwood. "It was after the break of the day that the blackest of the great tragedy was enacted, for it was then that the white mob, their way blazed by the national guardsmen, 'mopped up' the negro section."[92] The fires followed shortly afterwards. In essence, the Guardsmen facilitated the destruction of Greenwood because they removed residents who had no desire to leave and appeared more than capable of defending themselves.

In evaluating the Guard's actions, one should compare the actions of the Guard and the police in protecting white and black Tulsans. They were lined up facing into Greenwood, positioned to protect white property and lives. When the Tulsa police thought that 500 black men were coming from Muskogee, they put a machine gun crew on the road from Muskogee, with orders to "stop these armed men at all hazards."[93] When Colonel Rooney heard a rumor that the 500 black men had commandeered a train in Muskogee, he went off to organize a patrol to meet it at the station.[94] Yet, in contrast, when whites were firing upon blacks who were in the Guard's custody, they responded by hurrying the prisoners along at a faster pace.[95]

The Guard seems to have been too busy working in conjunction with civilian authorities arresting Greenwood residents—or too preoccupied putting down the "negro uprising"—to protect Greenwood property.

Stories of the Riot: Looting and Burning

Strangely minding with their sorrow
As they faced apparent doom,
Came the soft, sweet strains of music,
Pealing forth "One Day in June."

Music has its many virtues,
Plays its part with young and old.
Sometimes soothes the aching heart, but
Not the anguish of the soul.

Bent on murder, out for plunder,
Hoodlums on their mission gay,

Pausing just inside the parlor,
Set the phonograph to play.

Thus they stood there, heartsick, speechless,
Hearing plainly every sound,
Heard the fiends cry out "All ready"
Saw the coal oil trickle down.

A.J. Smitherman,
Tulsa Riot and Massacre[96]

Susan Williams, who was a co-owner of the Dreamland Theater with her husband, testified about the terror in Greenwood. Early on the morning of June 1, sometime around 7:00, Williams saw people shooting and running by her window on North Denver, a few blocks north and west of the Greenwood business district. About 7:30 she saw a black man shot and killed on the street in front of her house. Then some men came, searched their house, and took her husband. Soon, another group of about twenty men came by and again searched the house, and then set it on fire. When Susan Williams tried to put out the fire, she was ordered to "Come out here, we set that house to burn." Then they set the next three houses on fire. Williams stayed by her burning property until about 10:30, when she was taken to the Convention Center.[97]

Similarly, O.W. Gurley, owner of the Gurley Hotel, told how he was ousted from his hotel by men wearing suits:

> Those were white men, they was wearing khaki suits, all of them, and they saw me standing there and they said, "You better get out of that hotel because we are going to burn all of this God damn stuff, better get all your guests out." And they rattled on the lower doors of the pool hall and the restaurant, and the people began on the lower floor to get out, and I told the people in the hotel, I said "I guess you better get out." There was a deal of shooting going on from the [grain] elevator or the mill, somebody was over there with a machine gun and shooting down Greenwood Avenue, and the people got on the stairway going down to the street and they stampeded.[98]

By about 8:30 A.M., neighboring property was starting to catch fire, and Gurley's hopes that the hotel would be spared were vanishing. Gurley, like Gabe and many other Greenwood residents, saw airplanes flying low.[99] Gurley and his wife debated what to do next. They decided they had to leave, and she asked for help with a trunk. Gurley couldn't carry it, so he "desert[ed] the trunk and work[ed] my way down to the head of the people. I told them I was going out and all of them could follow me, I was going to take a chance." As they passed the Dreamland Theater, two men came from behind it and shot. His wife fell and she said "'You get away' and I got away."[100] Gurley began running. There were men shooting from the Oklahoma Iron Works south of Greenwood. A man running alongside him was killed.

Gurley ran up to the schoolhouse and hid in the crawl space. Some men came over and ordered him out. When he did not answer, they shot through a hole in the foundation. He was hiding close to the wall and after those fellows had shot two or three times they concluded that he had already left. Later—perhaps more than an hour later—he realized the school was on fire, so he came out and was immediately arrested. When asked about what he saw when he was arrested, he said, "I was excited, looking to be killed every moment and didn't have time to take observation. When this gentleman told me to put my hands up, I lost sight of everything but the man with the rifle."[101] Then he was marched with about fifteen other men to Convention Hall.

Gurley does not testify to who burned his property, but only that the men who ousted him threatened to burn it.[102] Other Greenwood residents testified about the role of police officers and deputies in the riot.

Green E. Smith, a black man who lived in Muskogee and was in town for a few days to install a cooling system in the Dreamland Theater, testified about the role of the special deputies in Greenwood. He went to the Dreamland around 5:00 in the morning. He planned to install a fan, then catch a train back to Muskogee by 9:00. After the whistle blew at 5:00, Smith heard shooting and watched out of the window. At one point it "looked like the world was coming to an end with bullets."[103] By eight o'clock the shooting had decreased in intensity, but it picked up again. By 9:30, "a gang came down the street knocking on the doors and setting the buildings afire."[104] When asked, "Who were they?" his response was "Policemen, I guess."

Smith did not know the men by face (he knew only the black officers), but they "had on what they call special police and deputy sheriff's badges."[105] How could Smith have seen the badges? "They came and taken fifty dollars of money, and I was looking right at them."

He had been close enough to them to "read the badge[s]." He saw "ten or twelve of them. Some *Special Police*, and others would be *Deputy Sheriff*."

Smith testified that the special deputies knocked on doors, went into buildings, and then set them afire. In simple, direct prose Smith told how the gang worked. He saw the men go in the buildings, then come out and a few minutes afterwards there was smoke. Smith saw the same scenario repeated for many buildings along Greenwood. He stayed at the Dreamland Theater until the men set it on fire as well. Then he left the building and was arrested. He was released at 4:00 that afternoon and returned to Muskogee.

Further evidence comes from a lawsuit filed by J.B. Stradford against the American Central Insurance Company in Chicago in September 1921. Sheriff McCullough testified in Stradford's suit that he drove through Greenwood and tried to stop the burning: "I told everyone I saw not to let them burn those houses, to keep them from it if they possibly could." McCullough could do nothing to stop the burning, for the whites were heavily armed. He concluded that "the Police gave everybody a gun who came in there and everybody had guns the next morning. There were a lot of good white men . . . who were out ready to kill every negro they saw, but that did not set fire to any houses."[106]

McCullough detected the work of the police in the arrests and disarming that morning. When he heard shooting outside the courthouse, he went out to investigate and found some white men. They told him, "We're hunting negroes," then added that they were helping the police.[107] Those men had traveled all over South Tulsa, taking black servants into custody from their white employers.

> When I went down to the police station about nine o'clock the whole place was full; there was a big crowd; that was about the time the soldiers came and they were loading negroes into trucks and everyway and making them come out with their hands up, including some old women who couldn't hurt anyone, and marched them into the police station, all the time with their hands up.

Everyone had guns and the "police seemed to be engineering it."[108]

The picture that emerges is one of coordination in the arrests of Greenwood residents and then burning, perhaps (but perhaps not) under instructions of men who had been deputized. Greenwood residents were awakened, taken into custody, and marched to interment camps around the city—to the police station, the Convention Center, the ball park, and the fairgrounds. Then their property was looted and burned.

Stories of the Riot: Burning and Murder

Then they heard the roaring blazes
When the torch had been applied,
Soon they heard the falling timber,
"Oh—we're lost!" the mother cried.

Through the smoke and almost stifled,
Groping, gasping for their breath.
Mother saved herself and children
From a cruel and fiery death.

Not alone their home was burning,
Not alone they suffered so,
Clouds of smoke ascending skyward
Told the awful tale of woe.

Picture now a quaint old cottage,
Gray with age and weather wear,
Like the aged couple in it—
Man and wife who knelt in prayer.

In they rushed—the mob—the cowards!
"Get out niggers, quick!" they said.
Then a flash from two revolvers
And their victims lay there—dead!

Fifty years they'd lived together,
Loyal, faithful, every day,
As defying death to part them,
Hand in hand the two now lay.

When at last the fight was over,
Might not right had won the day,
Blocks of homes and business places
Now in ruins and ashes lay.

A.J. Smitherman,
The Tulsa Riot and Massacre[109]

The stories of the burning and murder during the riot are difficult to verify with the same level of accuracy as the involvement of the police and their deputies in the systematic disarming and arresting of Greenwood residents, and the subsequent destruction of the community. There seems little question that indiscriminate killing took place. As a *Tulsa World* editorial acknowledged two days after the riot, "Semi-organized bands of white men systematically applied the torch while others shot on sight men of color."[110] There were few limits on the stories of barbarism. For example, one black man had been dragged behind a car in downtown Tulsa.[111]

There is one particularly well-documented cold-blooded killing. Judge Oliphant testified in the trial of Police Chief Gustafson about the behavior of the special deputies. The seventy-one-year-old Oliphant, who lived in the white section just west of Greenwood, went into Greenwood to look after his rental property there. He called the Police Department around eight o'clock and asked for help protecting his homes.[112] No assistance came, but shortly after his call, a gang of men—four uniformed officers and some deputies—came along. Instead of protecting property, "[t]hey were the chief fellows starting fires."[113] Around eight o'clock in the morning he saw Dr. A.J. Jackson emerge from his house, with his hands in the air, saying, "Here I am, I want to go with you." Jackson was surrendering to a group of several dozen armed men. Two shot him and he subsequently bled to death.[114] A few hours after that, Oliphant saw a group of four or five men setting fires to buildings. One was a police officer; the others wore badges or stars. They burned Dr. Jackson's house by throwing "gasoline and coal oil back in the butlery at Dr. Jackson's."[115] The scene of destruction was unreal:

> They were scattered around there, quite a large number of people looting the houses and taking out everything. There wasn't no excitement particularly. Some were singing, some were playing pianos that were taken out of the buildings, some were running victrolas, some were dancing a jig and just having a rolicking easy good time in a business which they thought they were doing that [which] was upright.[116]

Oliphant described the scenes of men, women, and children, going into houses and taking all property—"oceans of it"—from the houses: "pianos, victrolas, clothing, chairs, musical instruments, clothing of all kinds."[117] He was still there a few hours after the blacks had been interned, which he reported had been essentially completed by about 7:00 or 8:00 A.M., trying to dissuade people from burning it. Oliphant feared that fires in Greenwood might set his property on fire, too.[118] Others testified to lesser crimes they saw the police committing. A firefighter, for example, reported seeing a special deputy taking "silk shirts" out of a residence as a gang he was with set the house on fire.[119]

There was other, sketchier evidence of misconduct. Insurance appraiser B.F. Williams went to Greenwood to get a close look at the destruction. On the afternoon of June 1, as he was driving along the border, he saw "a truck load of corpses come out covered with quilts." He estimated there were about six bodies in the truck. "The Militia had charge of the truck." As he drove along a hill, he was stopped by a guard, but he was able to look over and "see people around on top of the hill; at one time we saw people chasing a nigger across the top of that hill at quite a distance, and we couldn't tell whether they were trying to catch him or what, but they were firing at the time."[120]

There are many other stories of people killed. Walter F. White, who came to Tulsa to investigate the riot for the NAACP, reported that four men had been trapped in a house and burned to death. One had escaped, but he was shot and tossed back onto the fire. He may be referring to the same story reported in the *Tulsa World* that about three o'clock in the morning, there were six men shooting from a residence at the border of Greenwood (on Boston Avenue in the block north of the Frisco railroad tracks). It caught fire and the men had to flee. "[F]ive of the six who ran from the house were killed."[121] According to another story, referred to in A.J. Smitherman's poem, an elderly couple was murdered in their home.[122]

As the internments were underway and the lootings and burnings were starting where were the Oklahoma City-based units of the National Guard? Their train arrived in Tulsa about 9:00 A.M. They went first to the police station. Tulsans were surprised by the Guard's actions. When Judge Oliphant saw the National Guard arrive via train around nine o'clock, there was still property that had not burned. But they did not go directly to Greenwood. As he said, "I expected the militia over there but they were just parading around the city having a promenade. I don't know just what they were doing."[123]

By the time the out-of-town units arrived in Greenwood, probably sometime after 10:00 A.M., much of the damage had been done.[124]

Captain McCuen, who was part of the Tulsa-based National Guard, concluded in his report that "all firing" had ceased by 11:00 A.M. The riot wound down not so much because the Guard had succeeded in bringing the white rioters under control, but because the Greenwood residents had been arrested or driven out: "practically all of the negro men had retreated to the northeast or elsewhere or had been disarmed and sent to concentration points."[125]

Even Police Chief Gustafson acknowledged the problems were with whites, not blacks. "In the early hours of Wednesday morning up until the fighting stopped," he testified, "our greatest trouble was to keep the whites back."[126] He estimated that perhaps 200 or 300 people were involved in the looting and burning.[127] Given our hindsight, it is tragic that Gustafson and Adkison, in conjunction with the mayor, deputized men and issued them weapons on the evening of May 31. Those special deputies had become, in the words of Adjutant General Charles F. Barrett, who was in charge of the National Guard, "the most dangerous part of the mob."[128]

Mary Jones Parrish captured the frustration of Greenwood residents with the failure of the police and Tulsa-based units of the Guard to protect them:

> It is the general belief that if [the state troops from Oklahoma City] had reached the scene sooner many lives and valuable property would have been saved. Just as praise for the State troops was on every tongue, so was denunciation of the Home Guards on every lip. Many stated that they [the local guard] fooled [the residents] out of their homes on a promise that if they would give up peacefully they would give them protection, as well as see that their property was saved. . . . When they returned to what were once their places of business or homes, with hopes built upon the promises of the Home Guards, how keen was their disappointment to find all of their earthly possessions in ashes or stolen.[129]

Thus ended the riot. Immediately there were questions about what had happened, why, and what to do next. Many of those questions still confound us. One of the most puzzling questions about the riot is the number of people who lost their lives in it. Even the official estimates of twenty-four blacks and ten whites, which we now realize are implausibly low, make the loss of life high.[130] As contemporaries admitted, the first concern was restoring order and cleaning up after the riot, not counting bodies. There remain tantalizing, unconfirmed stories of bodies stacked like cordwood in Greenwood, of bodies being taken away on flatbed trucks.[131] Some of them come from credible sources, like a white insurance adjustor, who testified shortly after the riot.[132] It is still difficult to obtain a consensus on the deaths. Contemporary estimates often vary between 75 and 150. The most recent study, undertaken for the Tulsa Race Riot Commission, admits we do not have an accurate count.[133]

Perhaps even sadder than the deaths was the destruction of the property of those left alive. Thirty-five blocks burned to the ground— scenes of destruction that rival a modern war zone.[134] More than a thousand families were left homeless. Behind those grim numbers were distinct tragedies. The newspapers reported the utter despair of victims:

> Half lying, half sitting a negro girl with heavy-lidded eyes stared before her with such blank misery in them that more than one person hesitated before her. Someone asked her if she were ill. She raised tear-filled eyes.
>
> "No, I ain't sick." She scarely noticed her questioner. Was there anything could be done for her? "No, I ain't got nothin'." That was all she would say.[135]

There were other stories—sometimes written in dialect—that told of the despair of people who had lost everything. But they had bigger problems than that. They did not know where their families were:

> "Los' somethin'? You ax me has ah los' somethin'? Ah done los' mah home and ah done los' mah close, 'ceptin these heah on mah back, and mah shoes is burned"—she held out a foot in a charred shoe. "An' ah ain't seen mah husband' sence we left this mawnin' with our house a-burnin's. Ah ain't seen mah husban',"—her voice rose to a wail and she wrung her hands. "It seems to me nothin' wouldn't mattah no mo' if I could jes' see mah husban'."[136]

Barney Cleaver, who had spent so much energy trying to prevent the trouble, lost more than $20,000 in real estate. As the fires started, he "entered his home and carried a few of his most valued possessions into the street. Duty called him away and when he returned vandals had stolen everything but a few precious trinkets which he had carried with him in a pasteboard box." Those trinkets were what remained of the Cleaver family possessions. "Yesterday evening at the county jail, when the quieting situation gave him time from his work to think of his own affairs, Cleaver sat down and cried like a child. He has not seen the wife of 30 years, to whom those trinkets belonged, since the night of the outbreak and does not know whether she is alive or dead."[137]

There is other, more credible and less sensational evidence of official culpability from several court cases and from eyewitness accounts of both blacks and whites made at the time of the riot. The best source is William Redfearn's suit against the American Central Insurance Company. The Oklahoma Supreme Court acknowledged that many of the people doing the burning were wearing deputy police badges. It stated simply, "the evidence shows that a great number of men engaged in arresting the negroes found in the negro section wore police badges, or badges indicating they were deputy sheriffs, and in some instances were dressed in soldier's clothes and represented to the negroes that they were soldiers."[138]

The riot was over, but the questions of what to do were just beginning. There were allegations that there was a debt that needed to be paid. The Oklahoma City *Black Dispatch* wrote about that debt:

The white citizens of Tulsa are in debt to the Negroes whose property they burned and the lives they wantonly destroyed, and we believe that there are those who will make some effort to repair the loss which they have caused. They cannot forget it, they admit that it was wrong and they feel deep down in their hearts that they should repay. It will always be a debt until it is paid.

And we are still talking about those questions eighty years later.

Tulsa with her teeming millions
    Paid the toll for racial strife,
    But her black men won a victory
    With their blood they paid the price.

Nobly they had stopped a lynching,
    Taught a lesson for all time,
    Saved a man the Court has since found
    innocent of any crime.

Though they fought the sacrificial
    Fight with banners flying high,

Yet the thing of more importance
Is the way they fought—and why!
A.J. Smitherman,
The Tulsa Riot and Massacre[139]

Editor A.J. Smitherman, who had been so influential in Muskogee and then in Tulsa, whose editorials and activism had saved the lives of others from lynching, whose cool but firm responses had averted race riots in the past, who had been at the center of the discussion on the evening of May 31, was left propertyless. He fled with his wife and their four children to Boston to escape prosecution. There he published an article in the *Boston Herald* about the events and how Tulsa had subsequently failed to repair the damage. He wondered whether America would awaken to the problem of injustice:

> In the wake, above the din of a one-sided battle with machine guns and the roar of flames, above the cannonading sounds of explosives dropped from airplanes, which still lingers in the minds of many of these poor people, comes the heart-rending cries of suffering women and children begging for clothes and food to sustain life through the winter—pleading for justice!
>
> But their cries evidently die in the distance before reaching the lawmaking body of our country, where a few days ago the solons were debating the constitutionality of a bill which, if enacted, would make effective the 14th amendment to the Constitution of the United States. Surely justice sleeps while injustice runs amuck!
>
> In Tulsa, as in many other parts of our country, the calloused spots of indulgence on the souls of black men have been rubbed off by the friction of race hatred, leaving the raw, bleeding sores of injustice and contumely of a half century's accumulation, and they are now smarting under the sting of a growing national indifference to their cause. Will America awake?[140]

Chapter Three

Picturing the Riot

Tulsans took hundreds of photographs of the riot and its aftermath. For us, the photographs preserve in detail the severity and pathos of the riot. But for contemporaries the photographs served other purposes. For whites, the pictures—many of which were made into postcards—served to celebrate the violence. For blacks, who printed and displayed panoramic photographs of the destruction, the photographs served as a reminder of the violence and the courage of the Greenwood community in rebuilding.

Directly after the riot, the black newspapers used the photos to detail the extent and horror of the destruction, printing photos of the devastated central district and the burnt shells of key businesses. Later in the year, photographs showed the resiliency of Greenwood. Around Christmas 1921, the *Black Dispatch* offered its readers a three-foot-long picture as an incentive to subscribe to the paper for the year. Showing the "desolate, smoking ruins of the Tulsa Riot" the paper celebrated the "heroism of the valiant black men and women who have remained in Tulsa and made of that charnel house a fit place for our group to live."[1]

Pictures were also used as dramatic reminders of the violence against blacks in Oklahoma; the paper sent a photograph of a lynching victim to every member of Congress, to garner support for the Dyer Antilynching Bill. Lynching photographs were also private keepsakes.[2] For blacks they were reminders of the lawless lynching spirit pervading America. Lynchers themselves, however, often took pictures in the same spirit as they took body parts of the victims (as souvenirs.[3] A 1911 Kansas photo shows whites posing around their victim.[4]

Today we continue to debate whether these disturbing images should be displayed and the purposes that they serve. Do they remind us of a terrible past and make such scenes less like to occur again, or do they desensitize us to violence and, in some perverse way, perpetuate the subjugation of African Americans?[5] Photographs obviously serve various purposes. The photo essay that follows documents both the stark racial violence and some of the uses to which the images were put.

Greenwood on Fire. White Tulsans went to the rooftops of downtown buildings to watch (and photograph) the progress of the riot.

Greenwood Across the Railroad Tracks. Other white Tulsans went to the railroad tracks, which separated Greenwood on the north from white Tulsa on the south.

"Running the Negro Out of Tulsa." The caption on this postcard tells the story of the riot from the white perspective. As happened in towns throughout the southwest, blacks were "run out of town" through a combination of violence and racially restrictive ordinances.

"Captured Negroes on Way to Convention Hall." This postcard evokes images of war and slavery. It shows Greenwood residents who have been "captured" and rebuts claims made after the riot, that they were being taken into "protective custody."

National Guard marching with Greenwood Residents Under Guard. This photograph suggests that some residents were afforded "protective custody." The men are wearing hats and walk proudly, in stark contrast to "Captured Negroes on Way to Convention Hall" on page 66.

A building's shell after the riot.

The panoramic offered to subscribers of the Oklahoma City *Black Dispatch* in December 1921 portrays the destruction of Greenwood.

Chapter Four

"A White Wash Brush and a Big One in Operation in Tulsa": Tulsa Interprets the Riot

Civilization broke down in Tulsa. I do not attempt to place the blame, the mob spirit broke and hell was let loose. Then things happened that were on a footing with what the Germans did in Belgium, what the Turks did in Armenia, what the Bolshevists did in Russia.

—*Bishop Ed D. Mouzon,* June 1921[1]

The 'race war' was as unjustified as it was unnecessary. Because of it Tulsa is blazoned as a community where tolerance does not exist, where the constitution of the United States can be enforced or suspended at will; where prejudice and race bigotry rules.

—*Tulsa World,* June 2, 1921[2]

As the fires cooled on the evening of June 1, Tulsa and the nation began to question what had happened. By the next Sunday, ministers were telling their congregations of the tragedy of Tulsa. In the newspapers and the pulpits, white Tulsans expressed remorse and promised to help rebuild. Even the *Tulsa Tribune,* which many blamed for sparking the riot with its report of Dick Rowland's assault on Sarah Page, discussed the need to restore law and to rebuild:

Acres of ashes lie smoldering in what but yesterday was "Niggertown." . . . City and county officials are responsible for this distressing story and this appalling loss of property. The insurance companies flatly place the responsibility there. The city and the county are liable . . . because the city of Tulsa and the county of Tulsa stand before the world as unable to protect life and liberty. . . . Let us meet the need and so far as we can redeem the wanton and unnecessary destruction of property. Let us try to be fair to the innocent.[3]

In the days after the riot, Tulsans wondered how this had happened. They frequently laid blame on outside agitators who had stirred Greenwood residents to seek racial equality. Reverend Ed Mouzon, preaching the Sunday after the riot, said that "black agitators" had caused Greenwood residents to become arrogant and aggressive in their haste to protect Rowland. Mouzon singled out W.E.B. DuBois, whom he termed the "most vicious negro in America,"[4] for particular scorn. DuBois had visited Oklahoma in March, and it is likely that he energized sentiments against lynching. Others also pointed to DuBois' visit and the consciences he raised as important precursors to the riot. Oklahoma's governor at the time of the riot, J.B.A. Robertson, told a Dallas insurance agent a few days after the riot that he had instructed the attorney general to investigate DuBois' involvement in the riot:

> "Dr." DuBois . . . is an agitator of the worst type and I have directed the Attorney General who has charge of the investigation now under way at Tulsa, to inquire about his activities and if he is in any way responsible for this outrage, I am going to have him indicted and tried as any other criminal should be.[5]

Oklahoma Attorney General S.P. Freehling saw the riot's origin in the growing idea of "race equality," as promulgated by people like DuBois. Freehling thought the riot "might have happened any-where[,] for the negro is not the same man he was 30 years ago when he was content to plod along his own road accepting the white man as his benefactor."[6] As the black press urged racial equality, it began to tell its readers to arm for protection against lynching. Tulsans thought the black newspapers "are full of just this sort of incendiary stuff. And IT MUST BE STOPPED."[7]

The police suspected that for several months before the riot Greenwood residents had acted on the advice of race agitators to store arms for use against whites.[8] Such lawless behavior as the collection of arms, Tulsans complained, was "allowed to run unarrested in the old 'Niggertown.'"[9] One popular urban myth, retold by both blacks and whites, held that the Tulsa chapter of a black secret society, the African Blood Brotherhood, plotted the insurrection.[10]

Tulsa Mayor T.D. Evans, drawing on such reports, thought the "negro uprising" was inevitable.[11] Evans seemed to take pleasure in the fact that it was Greenwood that was destroyed, rather than white Tulsa. "I say it was good generalship to let the destruction come to the section where the trouble was hatched up, put in motion, and where it had its inception."[12] That destruction would probably ensure that Greenwood residents would not take the law into their hands again.[13]

White Tulsans spread their views widely. Richard Lloyd Jones, the *Tulsa Tribune*'s editor, published an editorial in the *Chicago Tribune* on June 2, laying blame on "bad" "Negroes," who did not respect the law. Jones shifted blame to selected Greenwood residents and a few white Tulsans:

> [T]here is a bad black man who is a beast. The bad black man is a bad man. He drinks the cheapest and vilest whiskey. He breaks every law to get it. He is a dope fiend. He holds life lightly. He is a bully and a brute. A dozen of such collect at the Tulsa county courthouse with firearms when they hear the lynching rumor. . . . As soon as this small band of armed black men came upon this scene the Tulsa police, with or without the aid of county officials, should at once have thrown a line around them and marched them to jail, but they stupidly let the psychological moment pass. Then a white struck a match to the incendiary mob powder by trying to take a gun away from a black man and the fighting began.[14]

Another editorial blamed the riot on a group of "'bad niggers,'" who had used a flimsy excuse that Rowland might be lynched to arm themselves and invade white Tulsa, defiantly taking "the law into their hands."[15] When the papers acknowledged the role of white lawlessness in the riot, they were careful to present it as a response to black provocation.[16]

Sometimes, however, the white papers acknowledged the city's culpability. Two days after the riot, an editorial laid blame on the police and the mob:

> It is a fundamental fact that the existing agencies of government broke down in Tulsa very early in the proceedings Tuesday evening and either stood helpless when needed most or deliberately joined in the mob enterprise. It is an established fact that police officers if they did not openly contribute to the reign of terror failed utterly to adequately oppose their authority against it and did in many instances incite it by spoken words.[17]

Nevertheless, the failure of black men to abide by the law, even in the face of what they believed (with some basis in reality) was a lynch mob, was central to the white interpretations of the riot.

The day after the riot ended, an Oklahoma City paper explained in detail why blacks should have relied upon law rather than acting on their own. It was inappropriate for the veterans to appear at the court-house to protect Dick Rowland, because Rowland was safe. More-over, it was wrong for them to show up with weapons. Only through acceptance of white justice could there be racial harmony:

> Every negro should realize that the American courts are the best friends the negroes have. The negroes can secure complete justice there. Courts do not punish negroes merely because their skins are black. As an instance, a jury in Arkansas recently acquitted a negro accused of attacking a white girl. In a court, there is every opportunity for the negro to present all evidence in his favor, his attorney has the privilege of arguing in his defense, and the judge and jury are bound by certain well-defined rules of law. The negro has an appeal to higher courts, where judges, entirely free from the excitement of a trial court, con-sider the evidence and the rulings cold-bloodedly and render a decision entirely in accord with the facts and the law.[18]

The paper urged further respect for—and faith in—law, even as it pro-claimed that blacks were not equal to whites: "It is true that, strictly speaking, this is a white man's country. But the law guarantees pro-tection to all, and all should have it."[19] The standard white interpre-tation became, then, that it was illegal for the veterans to go to the courthouse. Stirred by misguided agitators, the veterans acted unlaw-fully and that brought destruction on their community.

The arrogance of the Greenwood residents played an important part in whites' interpretation of the riot. The list of offenses to white superiority included the charges that both Democrats and Republi-cans encouraged blacks to take a stand for equality, in order to attract black voters. One person told of the inflammatory imagery of black women being taken "to the polls in automobiles by white men, and in some cases by white women." The black press fostered the new ideas of equality, some thought. They asserted that there was "sys-tematic agitation" in the black newspapers for "equal rights for the negroes." The war had heightened the gap between black and white expectations of the role that blacks should play in Tulsa society. Black men went into the army on an equal footing with white men and they naturally came home feeling they were entitled to the same respect as white veterans. But where the war had increased blacks' aspirations, the war worked little change in whites' attitudes toward blacks. "There was," one St. Louis newspaper article said, "no change in the attitude of the white citizen toward the negro by reason of the war, however, and feeling was increased by the arrogance displayed by many of the returned negro soldiers."[20]

As the status and self-confidence of Greenwood residents rose, they threatened white Tulsa. An important result of the riot was putting Greenwood residents back in their place. A story appearing a few days after the riot in a white paper emphasized Tulsa's seemingly generous treatment of homeless Greenwood residents. Where there had been hatred during the riot, now there was kindness: "The white citizens of Tulsa have forgotten the bitter hatred and their desperation that caused them to meet the negroes in battle to the death Tuesday night and are now thinking of them only as helpless refugees."[21] Once Greenwood residents were reduced to the status of "helpless refugees," they posed no challenge to white authority and could be seen instead as objects of charity and subject to white control.

Blacks were not just helpless, however. In the minds of white Tulsans, they were also criminals, childlike, and arrogant. Greenwood was a place of vice, particularly prostitution, alcohol, and jazz.[22] Like their contemporaries throughout America, white Tulsans saw the cultural openness of Greenwood as dangerous. Jazz and alcohol were part of the vibrant culture of Greenwood, the ways that it operated at the cultural margins. Yet they also symbolized for whites the dangers of Greenwood. Just days before the riot, a Tulsa paper reprinted a story from Chicago called "*Jazz, the Evil Spirit of Music, Incites Hysteria.*" Jazz, following the formula of vodoo chants, "incites to idleness, revelry, dissipation, destruction, discord and chaos."[23] A year after the riot, Tulsans were still concerned that jazz music, "reeking of crime and sexual appeal," was everywhere. "Heaven pity America if her standards of art and morals are to be judged by the weird syncopations of the 'Coontown blues' sample of present popular taste."[24]

Greenwood residents were seen as lazy. A few days after the riot, an editorial demanded that blacks should be compelled to work: "We want no idle, silk-shirted defiant negroes walking the streets of Tulsa, nor will we have them. Let that fact be proclaimed to the world also along side the demonstrated fact that we purpose doing precise justice to all citizens regardless of their color."[25] Sometimes the papers condescended by discussing the Greenwood residents' humor:

The unquenchable humor of the negro race manifested itself even in this dire extremity of the innocent ones who suffered most heavily. "Dem shooters took $40 out 'o my trunk," one negro woman confided to another today. . . . "You'all can't blame dem cause dey wasn't gettin' paid nothin' for their work," the other negro sympathized.[26]

The way that white Tulsans interpreted the riot tells us a great deal about their attitudes. It can also tell us why rebuilding did not happen.

One way that Tulsans coped with the riot was through a grand jury investigation. The grand jury was empaneled to find out what had happened, then issue indictments and a report. The grand jury, which began work on June 7, took testimony from dozens of white and black Tulsans. It operated within the framework established by Tulsa District Judge Biddison. He instructed the jurors to investigate the causes of the riot. Biddison feared that the spirit of lawlessness was growing. The jurors' conclusions would be "marked indelibly upon the public mind" and would be important in deterring future riots.[27] It cast its net widely, looking at the riot as it unfolded, as well as social conditions in Tulsa more generally.

The grand jury report provides a mature statement of the white Tulsa interpretation of the riot. In a now laughable phrase, the *Tulsa Tribune* stated shortly before the grand jury issued its report that "Tulsa, Mr. Mayor, is in no mood to witness another whitewash exhibition."[28] Such a statement is laughable because the grand jury used evidence so selectively and because it articulated a one-sided interpretation of the riot. A whitewash was exactly what was coming.[29] For, as Oklahoma City's *Black Dispatch* wrote, "The truth is, and as usual, we have a white wash brush and a big one in operation in Tulsa."[30]

The bias of the grand jury report appears from the *Tulsa World's* headline the day after it was issued, *"Grand Jury Blames Negroes for Inciting Race Rioting; Whites Clearly Exonerated."*[31] The report, issued June 25, fixed the immediate cause of the riot as "a certain group of colored men who appeared at the courthouse . . . for the purpose of protecting . . . Dick Rowland." From there it laid blame entirely on those people who sought to defend Rowland's life. It denied that there would have been a lynching, or even that there was a threat of lynching: "There was no mob spirit among the whites, no talk of lynching and *no* arms."[32] That denial of the threat was central to exculpating the whites and inculpating the blacks, for it downplayed the threat of lynching and made veterans' actions look less defensible.

Echoing the discussions of the riot in the white Tulsa newspapers, the grand jury identified two remote causes of the riot: the "agitation among the negroes of social equality" and the breakdown of law enforcement. The agitation for social equality was particularly important:

> Certain propaganda and more or less agitation had been going on among the colored population for some time. This agitation resulted in the accumulation of firearms among the people and the storage of quantities of ammunition, all of which was accumulative in the minds of the negro which led them as a people to believe in equal rights, social equality, and their ability to demand the same.[33]

Such was the mind-set of the grand jury that they thought ideas about racial equality were to blame for the riot, instead of explaining why Greenwood residents felt it necessary to visit the courthouse.[34] The second remote cause, the breakdown of law enforcement, also reflects the values of white Tulsa, for the jury focused on the weakness of law enforcement in Greenwood. The report blamed the failure to enforce vice laws in Greenwood. To rectify the problem, the report recommended more strenuous law enforcement throughout Tulsa,[35] that "'colored town' be policed by white officers," and that "every law be positively enforced to the end that a proper relationship may be maintained between the two races."[36] For there had been "indiscriminate mingling of white and colored people in dance halls and other places of amusement."

To make matters worse, while the grand jury spoke about law, the Tulsa legal system did virtually nothing to enforce that law. The grand jury issued several dozen indictments, mostly for blacks.[37] There were no murder indictments and none for arson. So, despite the destruction that left perhaps 150 people dead and thousands homeless, that had humiliated thousands and destroyed their life savings, that had torn up the fabric of the community, the legal system failed to bring justice. While Tulsa prosecutors sought to extradite A.J. Smitherman from Boston and J.B. Stradford from Chicago to try them for inciting riot, notorious offenders like Cowboy Long walked the streets of Tulsa. Police Chief Gustafson was tried in July 1921 for neglect of duty during the riot and removed from office, but there was virtually no effort to prosecute those blacks and whites who were indicted. The law was once again—although not for the last time—victimizing the Greenwood community.[38]

The grand jury report, which is so transparently biased to our eyes, is nevertheless remarkable for the insights it gives us into how Greenwood was viewed by white Tulsans—and, more generally, how blacks were viewed across Oklahoma. In a revealing coda to this picture of the white view of law, the grand jury report was later picked up by the United States Congress in 1922 in a debate over Representative Leonidas Dyer's Antilynching Bill.[39] Many of the same ugly stereotypes of blacks were used in the Dyer debate and many of the same clashes between the goals of white law and notions of equal justice were on display.

The bill provided relatives of a lynching victim with a cause of action against the local officials where the lynching took place. The relatives would be able to recover up to $10,000, on the theory that the local officials failed to prevent the lynching.[40] Supporters hoped that imposing municipal liability would make local officials more vigilant.

The debates over the bill, which passed the House of Representative in January 1922, illustrate the disjunction between those who urged respect for law over lynching and those who viewed lynching as an understandable (and perhaps even appropriate) response to allegations of crime by blacks. The debates demonstrate how white fears impelled lynchings, how the fear of lynchings affected the entire community, and how lynching led to the breakdown of law. In the face of allegations that lynching was the result of the breakdown of law, the Tulsa riot was for many the result of blacks' demands for equality.

Republicans in the House of Representatives, drawing upon images of freedom and law, argued that the bill was essential to the protection of American lives. Supporters drew upon imagery of law against tyranny made popular during the World War: "A nation is not for the benefit of a kaiser or a despot. It is an organized society for the benefit of those who make up its numbers, in which authority must be limited, at least in these modern times of progress, by the rights of the governed, and controlled in accordance with the principles of equality and of the protection of the law."[41]

When President Wilson spoke out against lynching in 1918, he drew upon another powerful image: justice. Every lynching, he said, *not / truful*

was "a blow at the heart of ordered law and humane justice."[42] Wilson harnessed imagery from the World War to ask for action against lynching in the United States. "Let us show our utter contempt for the things that have made this war hideous among the wars of history by showing how those who love liberty and right and justice and are willing to lay down their lives for them upon foreign fields stand ready also to illustrate to all mankind their loyalty to the things at home which they wish to see established everywhere as a blessing."[43] Others echoed President Wilson's sentiments; they feared the breakdown of law that followed lynchings.[44] The bill, quite simply, held out the promise of restoring law.[45]

Opponents saw lynching in terms of social conflict rather than law. They justified lynching as a natural response to crimes, particularly rape, committed by black men. Representative William Chester Lankford of Georgia urged that Congress should not waste time discussing the bill, but should try to understand the relative positions of blacks and whites. Lankford boldly proclaimed the superiority of whites over blacks. "This is a white man's civilization and a white man's Government, and the white man is and will remain supreme. The Negro race can be and should be happy, contented, prosperous, law-abiding, and very helpful to his community and to his Nation." Harmony was best promoted when blacks kept those facts in mind.[46] The opponents had grand theories about black inferiority and violence. The speeches drew upon racist images of violent, impulsive black character. Representative Bill Green Lowry of Mississippi combined those two images:

> But while the Negro is generally unique, docile, and humorous, yet those who have tried hardest to befriend him know best his weaknesses and have often found in him a preponderance of the animal. This is exhibited in his reckless indulgence of physical appetites and passions, and in a trend toward cruelty, which is seen in the merciless and frequent abuse and beating of his children, and in his savage fights with knives and razors. Out of these two traits has come the crime which has been the prolific source of the lynching evil.[47]

Others depicted the horror of rape—and the ways that the community responded. Representative Ward of North Carolina set the stage for his story of how lynchings occurred with reference to an attack in a rural community: "[A]s the day draws near its close and active life is tired—the customary hour for the crime against woman-hood—the horror breaks on this quiet with the stealth of the serpent as he crawled on his belly to carry sin into the Garden of Eden." Then people begin to hear about it. "A farm bell rings. Is it a fire? Is it a sudden death? What is the matter? The phones, if any, are active. As upon the lightning wings of electricity the signal of horror fills the air, and from the four corners excited manhood rushes to the scene."[48] The new technology of phones was important in spreading the word and in preparing for lynching. So vestigial human passions mixed with the most recent developments in technology, as they did during the Tulsa riot, with deadly consequences.

[handwritten margin note: telephone poles]

The debate over the antilynching legislation reflects the passions simmering in Tulsa, between blacks who sought the rule of law against lynching and whites who could not abide blacks taking action to ensure that Dick Rowland survive long enough to receive a trial. Tulsa was a prime example of the trouble that resulted when blacks failed to remember that "this is a white man's government." Representative John Elliott Rankin of Mississippi attributed much of the problem with lynching, even the Tulsa riot, to black propaganda about racial equality: "The relations between the white people and the Negroes in the South are about as pleasant as could be expected under the circumstances, and all we ask is that we be left alone." When "these agitators . . . invade the country and scatter their propaganda," riots like Tulsa were the inevitable result.[49] The struggle between law and lynching that played out with such violent consequences in Tulsa also played out in the halls of Congress. Once again the forces of lynching won, for despite passing in the House, the Dyer Antilynching Bill never passed the Senate.

The white view, as exemplified in the grand jury report, was that the chaos of the riot represented a "breakdown of law." But white Tulsa and black Tulsa could not have been farther apart in their understandings of what exactly had broken down. White Tulsa and the grand jury believed that the social order had collapsed and that the blacks had staged an uprising. The blacks, in their mind, had not abided by the law, but had shown up at the courthouse brandishing weapons. Whites saw the primary duty of law in the riot's wake as the restoration of order. From black Tulsa's point of view, however, the breakdown was not in the "social order" but in the law itself, which had failed to protect Greenwood against violence. Even worse, the government had authorized harm to Greenwood residents and property.

Oklahoma's blacks already had sophisticated terms to use in discussing the failure of law, for they had been talking about the breakdown of the rule of law for many years by the time the violence of the riot shattered their lives. The riot was the worst part of a larger Oklahoma culture that denied blacks equal protection of the law. For, the laws, as interpreted by the courts and on the street by police, subjected blacks to arbitrary rules:

> The most exasperating thing about laws in Oklahoma (when they relate to Negroes) is their adaptability to many and varied interpretations. Whether it was the intent and purpose of the legislature to provide this elasticity or whether by some curious wharp of circumstance this has happened, the fact nevertheless remains that when it comes to the Jim Crow Law, the Election Law or the vital question of Education, we black folk find a tangled web of gibberish, to which can, AND IS GIVEN A THOUSAND DIFFERENT CONSTRUCTIONS.[50]

The grand jury's depiction of Greenwood residents as lawless and violent was at odds with the reality that Oklahoma's blacks, despite their mistreatment by the law, had continued to seek justice through appeals to law. What is perhaps most inspiring about black culture in Oklahoma is that despite statutes that segregated them, and courts and police that gave them unequal treatment, there was still some belief in the principles of law. Blacks saw some hope in the Constitution, for since the 1910s, Oklahoma's blacks had sought to use the courts to obtain equal treatment on railroads, in schools, and—perhaps most important—in voting rights. Blacks had the confidence that someday, perhaps soon, the courts would hold government officials to the requirement that there be equal treatment.[51]

The newspapers were the vanguard of the assault on unequal treatment. They were the places where those who saw the injustice of segregation tried their ideas and mustered their arguments in preparation for the legal challenge to segregation. Railroad segregation received particular attention.[52] Oklahoma's statute on this matter was particularly odious. The legislature was concerned with the economic effect that segregation could have on the bottom line of railroad companies. To reduce the financial burden on railroads caused by requiring separate accommodations, the Oklahoma legislature exempted railroads from hauling luxury cars for blacks, if there was insufficient demand to make the cars economically feasible.[53] In practice, whites could have luxury accommodations, but blacks could not.

That legislation met challenges in both the state and federal courts. J.B. Stradford lost his challenge in the Oklahoma Supreme Court. Ten years before the riot, Stradford had tried to use law as a vehicle for justice. He had sued to challenge Oklahoma's railroad segregation statute. He had purchased luxury accommodations on a trip from Kansas to Tulsa, but was removed from the luxury car when the train crossed into Oklahoma. The Oklahoma Supreme Court denied his claim.[54] Disappointed and defiant, he registered his protest.

The federal courts proved more receptive. Edward McCabe, a Muskogee businessman, also filed suit in federal court to challenge the legislation. McCabe thought that differential treatment—allowing railroads to provide luxury accommodations for whites, but not blacks—violated the principle of equality of treatment required by the United States Supreme Court's 1898 decision in *Plessey v. Ferguson*.[55]

Plessey, which upheld Louisiana's law requiring separate, but equal, accommodations on railroads, is often considered a low point in constitutional law. However, *Plessey*'s requirement that there be equal accommodations provided some hope for Oklahoma blacks, who could use the case to ask for better, even if separate, treatment on railroads and in schools. Such was the state of discrimination in early Oklahoma that truly equal treatment would have been an improvement.

In 1911 the United States Court of Appeals was not quite ready for such an interpretation. It upheld the Oklahoma statute.[56] The court reasoned that there was relatively little demand by blacks for the luxury cars.[57] Judge Hook's opinion took a lenient interpretation of *Plessey*'s requirement of equal accommodations. He concluded that "Equality of service does not . . . mean identity of service; and manifestly this rule does not require permanent provision for equal service, irrespective of the demand for it. . . . [T]he principle of equality of service between the two races in Oklahoma contemplates substantial similarity of service, and this only when conditions and circumstances under which it is required are substantially the same."[58] Such poor reasoning probably cost Hook a seat on the United States Supreme Court in 1912.[59]

McCabe lost at the appellate level, but there was hope that justice might yet be achieved in the United States Supreme Court.[60] On appeal, the Supreme Court affirmed the denial of relief on technical grounds—that McCabe failed to demonstrate that he had actually suffered harm, for he filed the case before any railroad had actually denied him luxury accommodations.[61] The Court, however, indicated that the statute was unconstitutional and thus railroads had to partition their luxury cars. Exemptions based on economic concerns would allow constitutional protections to turn on "the number of persons who may be discriminated against."[62] For the first—although not the last—time an Oklahoma case provided important precedent for the civil rights struggle.[63] By holding courts to the doctrine they had laid down, Oklahoma blacks might remake the world.

Much could be done outside of courts as well. In 1920 William Hutton boarded a train in Tulsa and sat down in the segregated portion of the car. When white men boarded the train, the conductor removed the sign designating the car as reserved for blacks. He tried to get Hutton to move. Hutton stood his ground and the conductor eventually ordered the white men out of the car. The *Tulsa Star* praised Hutton and urged others to follow his lead: "We need more men like Mr. Hutton who know the law, who know their rights under the law and if need be will fight to enjoy them."[64] Such was the attitude of Tulsa's black community. So, in the middle of May 1921, it is not surprising to hear that a black couple, Gilbert Irge and his wife, were arrested for sitting in the white section of a street car. The *Tulsa Tribune* ran a tiny story on it, under the heading *"thought he owned the car."*[65] Through persistent appeals to law, made in the pages of their newspapers, in the courts, and on the street, blacks were shattering the idea that blacks "could obey laws, but not make or interpret them."[66]

Perhaps even more important to Oklahoma's black population than the campaign against lynching—of which the Tulsa riot is an important result—and for equal treatment on railroads, was the campaign for voting rights. Lynching and voting rights were connected in the black mind, for denial of voting rights was a form of lynching. "Practically every Negro in Georgia IS LYNCHED OF HIS RIGHTS AT THE BALLOT BOX," observed the *Black Dispatch*, and "he is lynched in the courts and on the road gang and county farms, every aspiration, inspiration, joy and pleasure is curtailed, destroyed and denied."[67] Voting rights were at the center of the struggle for equality. In September 1920 the *Black Dispatch* editorialized that "The ballot is the only medium with which in a democracy, one may protect his life, his property and his happiness. It is a thing about which men of other races have fought and died. It is a thing which, when fully and completely in our hands, WILL STOP LYNCHING AND EVERY SORT OF DISCRIMI-NATION THAT HAMPERS US."[68]

Black Oklahomans struggling for voting rights took their case to the United States Supreme Court, as they did for equal treatment on railroads. They challenged the Oklahoma Constitution's grandfather clause, which allowed people who were eligible to vote in 1866 (before the Fifteenth Amendment was passed, ensuring all adult male citizens the right to vote)—as well as those descended from men who were eligible to vote before 1866—to register without passing a reading test.[69] In essence, the clause allowed whites to vote regardless of literacy and allowed only blacks who passed the stringent literacy test to vote.

So blacks filed suit, challenging the act directly. In those cases, decided by the Oklahoma Supreme Court as early as 1910, the court upheld the grandfather clause. In fact, the Oklahoma Supreme Court consistently supported the state's restrictions on voting—in addition to the grandfather clause, it upheld the poll tax and capricious reading tests in a series of cases.[70]

Yet Oklahoma's blacks continued to challenge the clause. They found a receptive ear in the federal courts. The United States Supreme Court's 1915 decision in *Guinn v. United States*[71] struck down Oklahoma's grandfather clause as it upheld the conviction of J.J. Beal and Frank Guinn for violating the voting rights of black Oklahomans. They excluded essentially all, if not all, black voters in their district, even those who could pass a literacy test.[72] Chief Justice White's opinion for the Supreme Court upheld the literacy test.[73] The test by itself was not necessarily unconstitutional because it was associated with disfranchisement of blacks. However, in cases where "the plain letter and necessary intendment" of the clause are discriminatory, the Fifteenth Amendment invalidates the otherwise valid literacy test. Such was the case with Oklahoma's grandfather clause.[74] Oklahoma blacks celebrated *Guinn*.[75]

Yet there were continuing attempts to limit blacks' access to the ballot. In 1916, the Oklahoma legislature passed a registration law designed to limit blacks' voting rights and get around the Supreme

Court's *Guinn* decision. The law automatically registered all people who had been eligible to vote in 1914; those who were not eligible had to register during a narrow period—about two weeks.[76] The law basically grandfathered those who had already benefited from the grandfather clause. It, too, was struck down by the United States Supreme Court, but not until 1939![77]

The struggle for voting rights continued. In a front-page article in 1920, the *Black Dispatch* told its readers how to register and where to report voter registration officials who would not follow the law.[78] The paper promised to "put some jail birds where they belong." Blacks needed to tell the registration officials in clear terms that they were determined to register and vote and would use the federal government to back up their right to: "Tell [your register] that this is a federal election and that you appear before him as a citizen of the United States, which by the way, is just a little bigger than a citizen of Oklahoma. Tell him in plain English that you intend to put him in the federal penitentiary."[79] Such language landed the *Black Dispatch* at the center of a political struggle. A prominent white paper labeled the article "An Inflammatory Appeal."[80] Yet the *Black Dispatch* thought it was not their appeal to voters to register, but the law that was "INFLAMMATORY."[81] Oklahoma's blacks would not abide such unequal voting rights; the days of slavery were far behind and it was time for a new order:

> The old order changeth; no longer is the Negro satisfied or clothed with the placidity of spirit of his slave parents. We black men in Oklahoma know that the legislature of this state tried to deprive us of our franchise when it enacted the 1916 Registration act; we know that such a statute is in conflict with the Constitution of the United States and its interpretation by the Supreme Court. NO LONGER WILL WE BE SATISFIED WITH THE PIG TAILS OF CITIZENSHIP; we want to eat farther up on the body of the hog.[82]

The antilynching, voting rights, and railroad segregation trilogy represented perhaps the most prominent causes of civil rights in Progressive-era Oklahoma. But they were not the only ones. The quality of segregated schools and taxation to provide for those schools were central issues for the Oklahoma black community, as were opposition to the exclusion of blacks from juries and ordinances that required racial segregation.

mited Mrs. Bulah Maxwell's home, which she occupied in violation of the ordinance,[94] the city attorney threatened that there would be violence if blacks continued to challenge the ordinance: "One thing is certain," he promised, "if these people don't stop meddling with our ordinances, there is going to be a lot of DEAD NIGGERS around you."[95] And still the *Black Dispatch* appealed to law.

The riot was the worst episode in an ongoing trend of lawlessness in Oklahoma. The headlines of the *Chicago Defender*, perhaps the leading black newspaper at the time, encapsulated the Greenwood perspective: they told of "Armed White Ruffians Who Begged for Guns to Help Murder"[96] and police who killed Greenwood residents.[97] The riot demonstrated the lawless behavior of the Tulsa government and confirmed that Dick Rowland was not safe. The riot itself was the best evidence one could hope for to show that the police would not protect the community. In response to the criticism that blacks should have let the law take its course through "fair courts," the *Black Dispatch* raged:

> Fair Courts! What sort of a court would have done Rowland any good the next morning with his body swinging from a limb? Somebody might say well, the sheriff would not have permitted the mob to take him, but what are the facts on this point. The sheriff of Tulsa county has permitted men to be lynched by the same gang that was at his jail door Tuesday night. But the outstanding fact which proves the contention of the Tulsa Negroes that they were without protection, followed in the absolute rule and authority of the mob during all of Tuesday night and Wednesday.[98]

Once the *Black Dispatch*'s editor Roscoe Dunjee had urged restraint, but now the entire community understood that the veterans' trip to the courthouse was a logical response—and probably the proper one when the community faced a threat of lynching.

Leading black newspapers saw the riot as the result of the failure of the law to protect the black community, for when the community did not receive protection, it had to resort to arms to protect itself. The *Defender* blamed the Jim Crow system "for the whole revolt." Black women and children were treated poorly on the segregated railroad cars and when men protested the mistreatment, they were beaten and thrown off the train. Even worse was law enforcement:

The police department has been flagrant in its attention to law and order. The color of one's skin will determine the manner in which the case is to be handled. Clubs are used instead of justice in the courts. This practice has reached such a state that members of the Race here decided to protect prisoners thrown in jail on "assault charges." It was when the police department failed to grant ample protection to Dick Rowland Tuesday that an armed band of citizens surrounded the jail.[99]

Greenwood residents offered strong responses to whites who thought the black press's demands for equal rights was at the root of the riot.[100] Dr. R. W. Motley, a Greenwood physician, saw the origins of the riot in the breakdown of law in Tulsa. He shifted blame from blacks in general to "a small group of tough white men [who] started out to take the law into their own hands and lynch a negro."
Then a small group of tough Greenwood residents went out to stop them, "intending to kill white men if necessary." Motley explained how the riot unfolded from there:

> Somebody fired a shot and the negroes went crazy and there was shooting. White people then seem to have decided they must exterminate the negroes, fearing there would be a general raid of the white sections by negroes. Negroes, law-abiding and property owning, some of them, fired in protection of their homes.[101]

Dr. Motley spoke about the failure of white Oklahoma to abide the equal protection clause of the Constitution, but he saw the need for peaceful action by Greenwood residents. "At least 90 percent of our people believe in obeying the law, and while we realize we do not have the privileges guaranteed under the Constitution of equal rights to all citizens, those of us who have been educated and who give thought to the problems of our race, know that violence will only delay our advancement, and will not accomplish anything. So we tell our people."[102]

Similarly, the national weekly *The Nation*, frequently a supporter of black causes, broke the code of white Tulsans who charged that the riot was caused by black radicals. Such talk meant that blacks were insufficiently obsequious. They asked for legal rights:

> Negroes were uncompromisingly denouncing of "Jim-Crow" cars, lynching, peonage; in short, were asking that the Federal constitutional guarantees of "life, liberty, and the pursuit of happiness" be given

[handwritten margin note: law unjust, den w/ it to make change]

regardless of color. The Negroes of Tulsa and other Oklahoma cities
are pioneers; men and women who have dared, men and women who
have had the initiative and the courage to pull up stakes in other less-
favored States and face hardship in a newer one for the sake of greater
eventual progress. . . . Those of the whites who seek to maintain the
old white group control naturally do not relish seeing Negroes eman-
cipating themselves from the old system.[103]

The riot was not caused by black radicals; it was caused by lawless
whites who wanted to keep blacks in their subordinate status.

In editorials and news articles black papers told the story of racial
conflict and breakdown of law enforcement. The *Defender* thought
the police were complicit in the violence, for they failed to stop mob
violence: in fact, once a riot starts the officers "join in with the white
mob under the pretext of trying to restore order, and not only kill
every black person they find, but steal their belongings and burn their
homes."[104] The failure of law was complete. White Tulsans who went
to the rooftops of buildings in downtown Tulsa to watch the burning
of Greenwood could not have imagined that the courts might someday enforce notions of equality that had been talked about in Greenwood.[105] Yet, at some point, in what was then far-distant future, that
call for the rule of law triumphed.[106] And so, forces set in motion in
the 1910s and 1920s caused a fundamental reworking of American
law, as white Americans responded to the theme of the rule of law
that featured so prominently in black culture.[107] All of that was in the
distant future, however. Black Oklahomans drew upon their rhetoric
of law to explain what had happened and to make out their case for
the moral and legal duty of Tulsa to help rebuild Greenwood. As
before, they hoped that the courts might provide relief.

Chapter Five

Tulsa Will! Tulsa Will? Tulsa Will Dodge: The Failure of Reconstruction

For those Greenwood residents left homeless by the riot, which had destroyed thirty-five blocks of their community and more than a thousand homes, there were immediate concerns for shelter and long-range concerns for rebuilding. The city had to reestablish order, clean up the damage, reunite families, and provide food, clothing, and shelter to those who had lost their homes, as well as plan for the future. The initial horror led to promises to help rebuild, but those promises were quickly forgotten. Discussion about Tulsa's duty to rebuild Greenwood changed into discussion about relocating Greenwood farther away from white Tulsa—a plan that might have succeed had not Greenwood property owners won a court battle. At the same time, reparations talk turned from the city's moral duty to assist in rebuilding Greenwood to its lack of legal culpability. Then, the Oklahoma courts denied recovery. As had happened before, the legal system left Oklahoma's blacks without redress. The failure of reconstruction related to the city's explanation of what happened, for the minimal efforts actually undertaken correspond with the attitude toward Greenwood residents.

The immediate work of reestablishing order was undertaken by the out-of-town units of the National Guard. The morning after the riot, Adjutant General Charles F. Barrett of the Oklahoma National Guard began to turn the relief work over to local officials. He asked the Tulsa Chamber of Commerce to appoint a Welfare Committee to coordinate relief work.[1]

The head of the Chamber of Commerce, Alva J. Niles, told of plans to make restitution the day after the riot. He referred to the city's admirable record in the war in his appeal to Tulsa's honor. Niles predicted Tulsa would show that same determination in restoring Greenwood:

> Tulsa feels intensely humiliated and standing in the shadow of this great tragedy pledges its every effort to wiping out the stain at the earliest possible moment. . . . A city which put three military units in the field with more than 7,000 men in the service, which contributed in excess of $33,000,000 for war purposes and which established its reputation as a patriotic city during the recent war second to none on the American continent can be depended upon to make proper restitution and to bring some order out of chaos at the earliest possible moment.[2]

The Public Welfare Board announced plans to focus on rebuilding the homes of Greenwood residents. "It is the committee's contention that those who lost their homes lost virtually all they possessed, and as a result were the worst sufferers from the mob's depredations."[3] The board established a hierarchy of reconstruction: those who suffered the most were entitled to the first payments. The whites and blacks who owned businesses and rental property were unlikely to receive assistance in rebuilding.

Promises of aid for rebuilding were common.[4] Both of Tulsa's white newspapers asked Tulsa to rebuild.[5] The *Tribune*, using the popular phrase that "Tulsa Will," assured that there would be rebuilding. The relief would include immediate assistance, as well as help in rebuilding:

> Relief assumes two forms—that which is immediate relief and that which is permanent restitution. The innocent homeless must be sheltered and fed and cared for. That is not merely a today and a tomorrow duty. Most of these people have lost their homes through no fault of their own, and they will not have another home soon unless this city that should protect them now does protect by giving them at least that which they lost. If this cannot be done through public funds it must be done by private contributions of those who love justice and who love the fair name of our fair city and who take pride in our growing prosperity and who are jealous of our growing greatness.
>
> Every city that is worth saving has always built something better out of every shocking disaster. This is not only Tulsa's chance, but Tulsa's duty to itself—and TULSA WILL.[6] Private contributions and private financing would be the primary vehicles for rebuilding.

The *Tulsa World* told its readers that it was their duty to rebuild because whites were the superior race:

> Vandalism has taken the homes and the savings of thousands of people. Tulsa must restore that which has been taken. The sins of a comparative few are thus visited upon the whole community. But it is a cross that must be shouldered willingly and heroically. This restitution, not because of affectionate regard for the colored man, but because of an honorable and intense regard for the white race whose boast of superiority must now be justified by concrete acts.[7]

Tulsans offered other reasons to rebuild. Some made the point from the perspective of simple justice.[8] Tulsans should, quite simply, many believed, give until it hurt.[9]

So the board began collecting money, which came in at a slower rate than was hoped for. The Public Welfare Board decided to apply all the contributions to immediate relief (housing and feeding the homeless and cleaning up Greenwood), before it set any aside for reconstruction.[10] Yet the board passed a resolution to refuse contributions from outside Tulsa.[11] A $1,000 contribution from the *Chicago Tribune* was returned, as was an offer of aid from the Dallas NAACP.[12]

The Public Welfare Board did not govern reconstruction for long, however. In mid-June, Tulsa Mayor T.D. Evans replaced the board, which had been set up by private citizens at the request of the National Guard, with an official city board, the Reconstruction Committee. The motivation behind the replacement is unclear; however, that change shifted control over reconstruction from Judge Martin and Alva Niles, who had made very public promises to rebuild, to Mayor Evans, whose attitude toward Greenwood was more hostile. The day after Evans announced the new Reconstruction Committee, the entire Public Welfare Board resigned.[13] Reconstruction was then in the hands of men hand-picked by Mayor Evans, who was frequently blamed for inept handling of the riot and who had shown little interest in rebuilding Greenwood.[14]

The Reconstruction Committee seems to have focused on minor public works projects for Greenwood, such as encouraging the Sand Springs railroad to extend service to Greenwood and to assist in the conversion of the burned area into a railroad depot.[15] The committee planned such modest relief measures as "old furniture day," to ask Tulsans to donate furniture to riot victims. They also secured washing basins so that Greenwood women could do laundry for white families.[16]

The Reality of Relief

In the hours and days immediately following the riot, as some Tulsans were making optimistic promises of assistance in rebuilding, there were pressing concerns for relief. Five thousand people were interned around Tulsa, at the Convention Center, the ball park, and the fairgrounds. Over the course of the next several days, many were released and given police protection badges, when a white employer vouched for them.[17] Some were out as soon as the afternoon of June 1; many more were released on Thursday, June 2. That evening, only a thousand people were still in the Red Cross's care.[18] Blacks who remained in what the *Tulsa World* referred to as a "concentration" camp—at a time before that phrase acquired the image it now has for us—were put to work, at little or no wages.[19]

The scenes at the camps were chaotic, as white employers looked for their employees. One newspaper story described how the search went: "White people are looking for their maids and porters. Most of them only know these negroes by 'Annie,' or 'Buella,' or 'Aunt Lizzie,' which makes it rather difficult to locate them, especially since there are dozens of Annies and Lizzies in darkeytown."[20]

Greenwood residents were issued demeaning green tags, reading "Police Protection," which were signed by white employers.[21] The tags marked the wearers as acceptable people. Those without tags were similarly marked—and subject to arrest and derision.[22] The *Tribune* celebrated the role of the tags in driving off the "bad negroes": "As always it is the bad who bring misfortune on the good. The bad negro is not helping the cause of his people in any community when he tries mob rule with gun in hand. The city does just what it should do when it gets rid of the negro who cannot give a good account of both his time and conduct."[23]

It is likely that the tags served a function for white society by giving the illusion that it was taking action to classify Greenwood residents, then assist those who were deserving. Yet the tags looked like a hold-over relic of slavery, in which blacks were required to carry passes from their masters. The tags served an important function in white society by subjecting black bodies to further scrutiny and control. But white Tulsa convinced itself that tags helped the "good negroes," by identifying them as respectable:

> The green card does something more than to help the city get rid of the bad negro. It is the certificate of industry and decency to every negro who carries it. It marks him as of the better class, just as the absence of the card brands the other fellow as one to be looked upon with suspicion, if not to be got rid of. In this hour of our reconstruction, let every good negro who is entitled to his green card, get it without delay.[24]

One important factor behind the releases was a shortage of workers. Most restaurants, for example, had lost their staff.[25] Still, despite the shortage of workers, the police prohibited black men from working in hotels, purportedly to limit vice.[26] The mayor ordered those without employers to work for the city[27]—which they did, with little in the way of pay.[28] They were kept busy clearing the debris from Greenwood under the supervision of white veterans:

> Out in the black belt today gangs of negroes are at work clearing away the rubbish and debris from residence lots under the direction of . . . American Legion men. Huge trucks are hauling away the useless rubbish and behind the wreckage gangs, other gangs are following putting up tents as temporary shelters for the homeless negroes. . . . In the residence district the health department has taken the precaution to finish burning the remains of dead animals which perished in the flames.[29]

At the same time the Red Cross began immediate relief. Its first task was housing and feeding the homeless.[30] As it distributed tents and food, it simultaneously compiled lists of survivors to help the homeless locate their families.[31] Many Greenwood residents lived in those tents throughout the summer and some spent the winter in them.[32] Later, the Public Welfare Board turned over all the money it had collected to the Red Cross.[33] The focus later shifted toward more permanent housing (better tents) and assistance with finding jobs. Maurice Willows, the Red Cross director, was central throughout the process. He told Tulsans that Greenwood residents needed to rebuild to have homes for the winter.[34] By the end of the year, the Red Cross had spent nearly $100,000 in relief. Little of that money was spent on rebuilding, however.[35] The Red Cross's lack of funding, which limited its ability to assist in rebuilding, was all the more unfortunate because property losses were great. The initial estimate placed damages between $1.5 and $2 million.[36] The actual damages may have been much higher. There were perhaps $5 million in claims made to the city council for losses sustained during the riot.[37]

The Fire Ordinance and the Reconfiguration of Greenwood

Even as the Welfare Board was undertaking relief and as the white newspapers were interpreting the riot, the Tulsa City Council faced the decision of what to do with the burned district. The day after the riot, some Tulsa businessmen questioned whether the burned houses and businesses should be rebuilt. They had a better idea for Greenwood. The Tulsa Real Estate Exchange, a board established by the Chamber of Commerce, began to consider converting the burned area into an industrial district and expanding the railroad yard. The Real Estate Exchange estimated that the value of the property when used for commercial purposes was more than three times its value when used for residences.[38] They proposed relocating the black section of town farther north, away from white Tulsa.

The Exchange thought the relocation of Greenwood promised another benefit: it would put more distance between blacks and whites.[39] The Exchange promoted the move as something that would reduce racial tensions: "We further believe that the two races being divided by an industrial section will draw more distinctive lines between them and thereby eliminate the intermingling of the lower elements of the two races."[40]

Within a few days the Real Estate Exchange had a proposal that would force the relocation of Greenwood farther north and convert the burned district into an industrial area. It proposed expanding the city's fire regulation, requiring buildings in the burned district to use fireproof material and to be at least two stories high. The city zoning board adopted it on June 7.[41] The ordinance made rebuilding residences in the area prohibitively expensive. The city was moving ahead with plans to convert Greenwood into an industrial district,[42] including beginning work on installing water mains to service the "new" Greenwood.[43]

Greenwood residents were in no mood to accept involuntary relocation and they were prepared to fight in the courts and to hold out against sale of their burned property. "I'll hold what I have until I get what I lost" became their slogan.[44] They began rebuilding in spite of the ordinance, and in August filed suit to enjoin its enforcement.[45] The *Black Dispatch* was so adamant about the use of law to try to attain justice that it printed the petition challenging the ordinance on its front page.[46] The property owners argued that the city was depriving them of their property by such restrictive building regulations.[47] They argued, in addition, that the city could not interfere with property owners in a way that left them homeless, thus endangering their health.[48]

In late August, a three-judge panel of the Tulsa County Court granted a temporary restraining order against the ordinance, which allowed the building of temporary structures.[49] The next day they struck the entire ordinance on the technical grounds that there was insufficient notice when it was passed.[50] The City Commission was not content. It repassed the ordinance, this time giving enough notice.[51]

With the City Commission's action, there was continuing question of when—if ever—the rule of law would prevail in Tulsa. The cold, deliberate restriction on rebuilding was perhaps even worse than the violent destruction of Greenwood, many thought. The worst crime of the Tulsa riot, according to the *Black Dispatch*, was "not the burning of homes, . . . nor the wholesale massacre of black men and women." The worst crime was the city's ordinance, "where white men sat down and deliberately conspired to confiscate the very land and ashes where black men had dwelt."[52] The ordinance illustrated the breakdown of due process; the lawsuits filed to challenge it were testing whether justice could prevail.[53] There was growing sentiment, even in the white community to allow rebuilding of the burned district.[54] The *Tulsa World* editorialized that Greenwood residents should be permitted to rebuild:

> It is reported that a great number of the colored people want to rebuild their property; that many of them have the instant means to do that. In the light of what has been said, what is the community's best interest if not its duty? Is it not to give them permission to proceed and aid them in every way to accomplish their purpose? That is our thought.[55]

Then, in early September, the judges granted a permanent injunction against the ordinance, citing its effect on property rights.[56] At long last, there was an instance in which the courts had functioned properly. The injunction is one of the stories of the triumph of justice in the riot. After it was struck down, a black newspaper proudly proclaimed, "Kill Ordinance!"[57] The sounds of construction were heard around Greenwood, as the residents began rebuilding their world. Within a year, there was a new and better Dreamland Theater at 127 North Greenwood Avenue.[58]

So while some people stayed and rebuilt Greenwood, and in some ways it was grander than it had been before, the vibrant community that had once existed had dispersed. A.J. Smitherman went to Boston with his family, then to Springfield, Massachusetts, where he established the *Springfield New World*. In 1925 he moved again, to Buffalo, where he founded the *Buffalo Star*, later known as the *Empire State Star*. Smitherman continued to edit the paper until his death in 1961. J.B. Stradford moved to Chicago, where he died in 1935.[59]

The Invisibility of Greenwood Residents: The Failure of Reparations Through the Courts

Even though the ordinance was removed, white Tulsa had lost its will to assist in rebuilding Greenwood. As time passed and the grand jury blamed the Greenwood residents, the initial promises to help in rebuilding were forgotten. A.J. Smitherman, the editor of the *Tulsa Star* before the riot, wrote in January 1922 about the shift away from reconstruction toward blame. "Public opinion in Tulsa, which immediately following the riot and massacre seemed to favor the Colored people, was soon crystalizing into a feeling exactly the converse, and instead of expressions of regret and sympathy there was, among some of the whites, open talk of further violence against the Colored people."[60] Black Oklahomans, playing off the popular phrase "Tulsa Will," began to wonder when and whether "Tulsa will" help rebuild. The moral case having failed, Greenwood residents and property owners (many of the people who lost property were white, absentee owners) were left to press their legal cases.

When Greenwood residents spoke of recovery, they questioned where the money would come from. Perhaps through fire insurance polices? On the day after the riot, insurance companies were already telling their customers that they would not pay on the policies containing "riot exclusion" clauses. Most of the policies had such clauses, which absolved the companies of liability for damage caused by riot.[61] Lawsuits against the city did not look any more promising.[62] The city would not pay because, as Tulsa lawyers told the press, Oklahoma law did not hold the city liable.[63]

Nevertheless, black and white Tulsans filed claims with the city amounting to approximately $5 million.[64] Nearly every claim was denied. The only person who received payment was a hardware store owner, Joe Magee, whose store was broken into as the riot began. He received more than two thousand dollars. Tulsa county commissioners set aside $60,000 to pay for relief; the city set aside $40,000.[65] That money was spent on relief, not on reconstruction.

When the city and insurance companies failed to pay, Greenwood residents and some white Tulsans turned to the courts, as the *Black Dispatch* had been urging them to do. Roscoe Dunjee did not want Tulsa's blacks to receive meager handouts; he wanted complete recovery through the courts. In an editorial, "Fight it out in the courts," Dunjee urged lawsuits:

> The Black Dispatch thinks that there ought immediately be started by the Negroes of Tulsa a test case as to the responsibility of the municipality for the destruction of their homes. . . . No attention should be paid to crocodile tears about restitution, based on the theory, "we will GIVE YOU SOMETHING." We have heard the statements which infer that $1000.00 and $500.00 homes will be erected. What can a black man or a white man build for $1000.00? Rather than take such miserable substitute for fairness, we believe that the Negroes should at once institute a test case.[66]

The key for Dunjee was that those who lost property had a legal entitlement to payment. He optimistically told them they were entitled to payment, "NOT AS BEGGARS BUT AS AMERICAN CITIZENS in the courts of the land."[67] Later, Dunjee suggested that suits be brought to federal rather than state court. "We are not strong for the sort of judgment which a Negro petitioner would get in Tulsa county in such a case. The federal proceedings would give the black man his best shot at justice."[68]

By June 1923, more than a hundred suits had been filed.[69] Only two went to trial. The first, filed by Mabel Allen against the city, was tried in March/April 1921. Oklahoma precedent limited the city's liability,[70] so Allen's suit did not even get to the jury. After Allen's attorney finished putting on her case, the judge directed a verdict for the defense. Almost all records in the case have been lost and she seems never to have appealed the case. Thus ended serious attempts to hold the city liable in state court.[71]

The legacy of the United States Supreme Court's decisions in the years after the Civil War,[72] which limited federal criminal liability for violations of civil rights, together with Oklahoma court decisions, immunizing municipalities from liability for injuries to their residents, left Greenwood residents who had lost property during the riot with little recourse against the government. The federal courts were no more helpful than the Oklahoma ones. G.W. Hutchins, a black Tulsa lawyer who had lost his property during the riot, filed a suit in federal court. He alleged that the city was intimately involved in the destruction, but that Oklahoma law limited the city's liability. That limitation, Hutchins thought, was inconsistent with the Fourteenth Amendment's guarantee of equal protection of the law. Hutchins' vague, but suggestive petition, was dismissed before it ever went to trial.[73]

The second suit that went to trial was filed by William Redfearn, a Native American who owned a theater and a hotel in Greenwood. Redfearn initially sued both the city of Tulsa and his insurance company. Yet his insurance company refused payment on the policies covering his Red Wing Hotel and Dixie Theater, citing the riot exclusion clause in the policies. Redfearn filed suit in May 1922, against his insurance company as well as the city. When the case went to trial in April 1924, the suit was limited to claims against the insurance company, probably because Oklahoma law largely immunized cities from liability. After both sides presented their evidence, the judge granted the insurance company's summary judgment motion, which meant that the case never went to the jury. He relied upon the direct testimony that Redfearn's property had been set on fire during the riot.[74] Having lost at the trial level, Redfearn appealed to the Oklahoma Supreme Court.[75] The key question on appeal then became how to interpret the riot exclusion clause.[76]

There was one precedent, the Kentucky Court of Appeal's 1911 decision in *American Central Insurance Company v. Stearns Lumber Company*, which offered some hope to Redfearn. To force rioters out of a building owned by Stearns Lumber, the marshal set the building on fire. The insurance company refused to pay for the damage, claiming that the building burned as a result of the riot. The Kentucky

Court of Appeals interpreted the riot exclusion clause narrowly, and held that the loss was due not to the riot, but to "the wrongful act of the marshal in setting fire to the house without authority."[77] One reasonable reading of *Stearns Lumber*, thus, was that damage caused by state actors during a riot was not subject to a riot exclusion clause.

The *Stearns Lumber* opinion is difficult to interpret, however. At one level there was a link between the riot and the loss of the building. The insurance policy excluded coverage whenever riot was the "direct or indirect" cause of the loss. One might think that the riot was the indirect cause of the loss; the fire was set during the riot, in an attempt to end it. The court assessed the facts differently. Because the loss was due directly to the "unlawful act of the marshal," the court refused to allow the riot exclusion clause to excuse liability. Perhaps the theory was that an indirect cause cannot excuse liability when there is a direct cause that is covered by the contract. The court thought that the "marshal's posse, acting under his orders, were not rioters." One simple conclusion to draw from *Stearns Lumber* is that destruction caused—even during a riot—by police officers is not the result of riot. Redfearn drew the parallels between *Stearns Lumber* and his own situation. In both cases, the loss was caused by police and those acting under police orders.[78] Redfearn cited extensive precedent showing that exclusions from coverage were construed narrowly.[79]

When the case reached the Oklahoma Supreme Court, the issues in the case centered around the cause of the damage and the scope of the riot exclusion clause.[80] Commissioner Ray wrote the opinion for the Court.[81] He described the origin and progress of the riot. It began with rumor that a black man would be lynched that night. Then the "negroes residing in the northeast part of the city of Tulsa, known as the negro section, became excited over the rumored lynching, and a great many of them armed themselves for the declared purpose of preventing the lynching." By 10:00 that evening there were many whites around the courthouse. At that point "armed negroes in automobiles drove around the courthouse two or three times and drove away. They returned, parked their cars, and marched single file down west of the courthouse. As they neared the courthouse a shot was fired, following which there were a great many shots fired and one white man was killed." Commissioner Ray went on to describe the subsequent events: white men broke into downtown Tulsa stores to get guns and

200 or 300 of them gathered at the police station. They "were sent out to different parts of the town ostensibly to guard the town."

From that point until around 10:00 the next morning, there was shooting. Fires broke out beginning around 2:00 A.M. and the Fire Department could not put them out.[82] Ray then described the destruction of Greenwood. At 5:00 A.M., "at the sound of a whistle, shooting became rather general and continued for some time. Armed white men, described as traveling in groups of from a dozen to 20, rounded up the negroes found in the section where the fires were burning, and took or sent them to the convention hall where they appear to have been detained. A number of witnesses testified that these groups of white men, many of them wearing police badges and badges indicating that they were deputy sheriffs, after removing the negroes from buildings, went inside the buildings and, after they left, fires broke out inside the buildings."[83]

Having described the riot, Ray then turned to the legal issues. Where Redfearn argued for coverage because the buildings were burned by police officers, the Oklahoma Supreme Court had a different, narrower interpretation of *Stearns Lumber*. It distinguished *Stearns* from Redfearn's situation in two ways. First, the men wearing police and sheriff's badges who burned down Redfearn's property were not doing so "in order to make an arrest." Ray acknowledged that "the evidence shows that a great number of men engaged in arresting the negroes found in the negro section wore police badges, or badges indicating they were deputy sheriffs, and in some instances were dressed in soldier's clothes and represented to the negroes that they were soldiers." But because there was "no evidence that any negro ever resisted arrest, or that any fire was started in order to make such arrest," he thought the fires were part of the riot. "The only evidence contained in the record tending to show that any person wearing a police or deputy sheriff's badge, or in any way pretending to act in an official capacity, set fire to any building, was after the arrest had been made or where no arrest was being made or attempted."[84]

The Oklahoma Supreme Court drew one other distinction. It questioned whether the men wearing "police badges or sheriff's badges were in fact such officers or acting in an official capacity."[85] If those men were, indeed, not police or deputy sheriffs, then there would be no analogy to *Stearns Lumber*. That statement indicates Commissioner Ray's pro-police bias. The case was appealed from a directed verdict against Redfearn, which meant that the trial judge concluded there was no evidence from which a jury could conclude that the men wearing badges were officers. Yet cases involving resisting arrest routinely conclude that a police badge indicates one's authority to arrest. Simply put, if one of the men involved in the riot resisted one of the men wearing a badge, he could have been prosecuted for resisting arrest. Commissioner Ray could have insulated the insurance company from liability with the statement that, even assuming the men wearing badges were police officers, they were acting beyond their authority and were thus acting as rioters. Ray's inconsistency in applying precedent suggests that his motive was not solely an impartial decision of the case before him, but the insulation of the Police Department and Tulsa from liability. Still, the opinion is striking for its honesty, especially for its acknowledgment of the role of the police deputies in the destruction.

The honesty is remarkable, but *Redfearn* is consistent with the Oklahoma Supreme Court's other opinions at the time, which limited rights of plaintiffs, both black and white. The Court upheld the decision of Guthrie's police chief to prohibit the showing a movie of the prize fight between a black man and a white man in 1910, because of fears of riot.[86] In 1913 it denied recovery to a white woman who was put off a train at the wrong station, then rode in an integrated caboose car to get to her destination. She wanted compensation for having to travel in the same car with black men.[87] When the state hospital placed a white person on a ward reserved for blacks, the Court again denied recovery. The court did not believe there had been sufficient harm to the patient's reputation to warrant a recovery against the hospital.[88]

Even when the plaintiff was a police officer, the Oklahoma Supreme Court limited recovery. In *Kithcart v. Feldman*, the court denied recovery to a Tulsa police officer who had been shot by the hotel's black manager, Walter Rogers. Rogers was described as "vicious in his propensities, quarrelsome in his disposition, criminal in his instincts and tendencies, and possessed of a malevolent disposition toward the police department."[89] In denying liability, the court said the hotel owners were not responsible for their manager's actions, because he was not their slave. It had been sixty-seven years since the Civil War ended, but the slave law continued to be an apt analogy.[90]

Black plaintiffs received no better treatment. Thus, the Oklahoma Supreme Court failed to protect J.B. Stradford's right to ride in the luxury accommodations of a railroad car, even though he had paid for them. Its record of protecting voting rights of blacks was shameful.[91] Courts frequently made reference to the race of plaintiffs, defendants, and witnesses. Sometimes blacks were obstacles,[92] who made a place undesirable to live.[93] A property owner could put up a fence to prevent seeing—or being seen by—blacks.[94] At other times, race was part of portraying plaintiffs as sympathetic. There are references to the "illiterate negro"[95] as well as to "respectable negroes."[96]

On rare occasions, the Oklahoma Supreme Court granted relief to minorities, particularly when railroads violated the state's segregation statutes. A black woman successfully sued a railroad, which failed to have a "step box" to assist passengers in leaving a train. The conductor advised her to detrain through a door reserved for whites, which she refused to do. As she exited from a door for blacks, she fell and injured herself and subsequently had a miscarriage.[97] The case presents a conflict between Oklahoma's segregation statute and the principle of limiting defendants' liability. The segregation law won, although the court apportioned the black woman's damages according to her contributory negligence.[98] When railroads failed to have adequate waiting room facilities equal in comfort to the white facilities, two blacks successfully sued.[99] In another case, a black tenant farmer who was treated grossly unfairly by a bank and its agent recovered $1,500 punitive damages for his mistreatment.[100] In those instances, there was well-established law providing for recovery.

J.B. Stradford tried his luck in Chicago, where he had fled while under indictment for inciting riot. He filed suit against the American Central Insurance Company, claiming that he could not hope to receive a fair hearing in Tulsa. The suit did not go much further than the ones filed in Tulsa. The insurance company took some testimony from whites, portraying the riot as the fault of the blacks—and Stradford in particular. Then it suggested that much of the destruction had come through mobs. Stradford, for obvious reasons, failed to appear in Tulsa, where he had been subpoenaed, to give testimony, and his suit was dismissed in 1925. The other plaintiffs drifted away and dismissed their suits. The final, sad chapter came in 1937, when the remaining suits were dismissed, apparently for failure to pursue them.[101]

Tulsa, which called itself the "magic city"[102] and boasted that it was the wealthiest city per capita in the world, promised to rebuild.[103] Yet those promises were not fulfilled. The city never made reparations to the residents of Greenwood, not even to the whites whose property was burned. The city provided no public funds for rebuilding and relatively little in the way of private funds.[104] Black Oklahomans learned that the phrase "Tulsa Will" really meant "Tulsa Will Dodge."[105] So the question appears: Should some reparations be paid today?

Epilogue

The white citizens of Tulsa are in debt to the Negroes whose property they burned and the lives they wantonly destroyed, and we believe that there are those who will make some effort to repair the loss which they have caused. They cannot forget it, they admit that it was wrong and they feel deep down in their hearts that they should repay. It will always be a debt until it is paid.
—*Black Dispatch*, March 15, 1923

Our age is one of reparations and apologies. There have been reparations from the United States government for the internment of Japanese Americans during World War II, from the United States government to Native Americans for deprivation of property in Alaska, from the United States government to assist with rebuilding Los Angeles after the Rodney King riots in 1992, and from Swiss banks for money deposited before World War II and never returned to the families of holocaust victims. President Clinton apologized for the United States' role in the international slave trade; shortly afterwards the *Hartford Courant*, one of the nation's oldest newspapers, apologized for printing advertisements for runaway slaves.[1] In those instances, the government and corporations making payments and apologies participated in the tragedies—or at least allowed them to happen. Now there is a serious, growing debate, at least at colleges and universities, about reparations for slavery.

The age is also weary of reparations claims, however. There are questions about how to apportion the limited public funds that are available. We cannot possibly compensate for each wrong done in the past.[2] So the question becomes, who has the most compelling claim on the public treasury? American law incorporates the notion of lim-

103

itation for past wrongs with the idea that claims must be filed within a certain period of time (called the statute of limitations) or rights are lost forever.[3] Opponents of reparations think there ought to be a statute of limitations on moral claims as well. They maintain particularly in the case of reparations for slavery that such a long time separates claimants from the oppression that there should be no payments. There is a strong argument that the harm of slavery is continuing— and that the institution of slavery and state-mandated segregation were not effectively dismantled until the late twentieth century. In some ways the legacy of slavery is very much with us today. But arguments over reparations for slavery are beyond the scope of this book.

The vast majority of Greenwood residents who were alive in 1921, those former slaves and former soldiers who lost their homes, their property, their families, are gone. Few traces of the buildings remain. Tulsa has denied the tragedy for so long, that it is easy to forget it ever happened. An interstate highway cuts through Greenwood, exactly where the Dreamland Theater once stood. Yet there are still people today who suffered harm during the riot. There is a direct, human connection between those events in the seemingly distant past and today. And so there is the question, what is to be done about the riot and Tulsa's promises to rebuild, which were never fulfilled? "How can the future deny the past?" we might ask with Ralph Ellison.[4] I hope to use Tulsa as a bridge between supporters and opponents of reparations for slavery, for Tulsa is situated between the Civil War and the present.

Historians rarely discuss the contemporary policy implications of their work. The canons of professional ethics discourage them from making explicit recommendations to policy makers. But historians participate in contemporary debates. Their work sometimes uncovers data that is important in lawsuits and in legislative acts. One of the most prominent cases is Peter Irons' book, *Justice at War.*[5] Irons represented Japanese Americans who had been interned during World War II in their lawsuit against the United States government. More recently, Linda Gordon has explored the abduction of dozens of adopted children from Spanish-American families in a mining town in Arizona in the early part of the twentieth century. Gordon's book, *The Great Arizona Orphan Abduction*, tells the story of community-wide crime, supported by the local mining company and based on religious and ethnic disputes, which has important implications for our understanding of rural communities.[6] Historians stop short, however, of making recommendations regarding reparations.

This epilogue departs in some ways from historians' practice. Given the debate over reparations—and the importance of Tulsa at the crossroads of that debate—it is better to discuss in analytical terms what might constitute a case for reparations to survivors of the Tulsa riot. This is a legal and political case, which is different from the scholarly purpose pursued in the first five chapters. Up until now I have sought to tell the story of the origins and unfolding of the riot. Now I seek to explore the implications of my findings for political action—what a case for reparations might look like and in that way bring some precision to the reparations debate. I aim at issues far beyond Oklahoma: the movement for reparations more generally, from American slavery to Native Americans' land claims, to contemporary civil and voting rights. Tulsa is a merely an example in a larger debate about reparations. Because the facts are particularly compelling and remarkably well-established for a crime that is eighty years old, Tulsa can be the proving ground for legal and, more important, moral claims for reparations. Tulsa can be a turning point in thinking about reparations more generally, which can help us identify factors that are important in deciding when society's scarce resources should be devoted to repair past damages, which are still having important contemporary effects.

The case for reparations in Tulsa rests on establishing a moral claim: that the city and state ought to repair the damage done in this instance. Tulsans once recognized the moral claims. When a delegation of the Tulsa bar announced that the city was not liable legally for their actions in the riot, they were careful to point out Tulsa's moral duty to restore Greenwood.[7] Others articulated the claim as well. As the *Emporia Gazette* said, "Of course, it was not the best of the white race that created the hellish situation in Tulsa. But none the less, the best of the white race is responsible. The leadership of the community is responsible for the deeds of the community."[8]

Identifying the Factors Governing Reparations for Tulsa

The moral case for reparations for Tulsa is particularly strong. There are four key principles that counsel in their favor. First, the city and the state *were* culpable. Quite simply, had it not been for the misconduct of the city police chief and the special deputies, assisted by the local units of the National Guard, we would not now remember the names Dick Rowland and Sarah Page, nor would we be talking about the Tulsa riot—because there probably would not have been much of a riot. At a minimum, the local government forces bear key responsibility for the destruction of Greenwood.

Second, there are still people alive who suffered harm. The riot was a long time ago, certainly; however, there is a direct, living connection between the past and today. That living connection, which has been important in other reparations cases, such as the Japanese Americans interned during World War II, provides a link between the past and the present. Those survivors can understand that now, a lifetime later, the government has recognized that what it did was wrong and is making amends. It promises that justice can—in limited ways—still be done and the survivors can know that the government which wronged them has acknowledged that wrong.

Third, the harm in Tulsa was concentrated in time and place. Reparations for Tulsa is not a claim for general societal discrimination; it is a request to repair very specific damage. There are certainly strong reasons to urge reparations for general societal discrimination, which—particularly in the nineteenth and early twentieth centuries— had enormous consequences that continue to affect people today. Indeed, the movement for reparations for slavery has developed a powerful argument based on its demonstration of the pervasive, systematic, and extraordinary effects of such discrimination.[9] But a case for reparations is much stronger when there is a claim based on concentrated harm. The United States Supreme Court permits affirmative action only by local governments when they show that there has been discrimination by that particular government in the past and that the discrimination was against the particular group now being aided.[10] In keeping with that restrictive standard, reparations are especially warranted when there is a showing of discrimination in that particular location.

Finally, Tulsans at the time understood the moral claim for reparations. They promised to rebuild. This is not a case of reading our twenty-first-century standards of morality back onto events that happened eighty years ago. People at the time understood the moral claim that riot survivors had on public money and—at least until the Tulsa courts immunized the city from liability—some feared the claims. L.J. Martin, chair of the Reconstruction Committee, made a promise to help rebuild:

> Tulsa can only redeem herself from the country-wide shame and humiliation into which she is today plunged by complete restitution and rehabilitation of the black belt. The rest of the United States must know that . . . Tulsa weeps at this unspeakable crime and will make good the damage, so far as it can be done, to the last penny.[11]

These four factors are compelling grounds for awarding reparations; but they are also limiting factors. For those who ask when reparations claims will end, those limiting factors supply a restrictive answer. Reparations payments can be limited to instances where these factors are present: the government that is paying was culpable; there are living survivors; the harm is concentrated in time and place; and contemporaries understood the moral claim.

80+ yr olds, need money?

Critics of reparations often ask, what is the logical stopping point? When will reparations claims cease? Those four limiting principles—governmental culpability, the human connection between the harm and the present, the concentration of the harm in time and place, and the recognition that the victims had been wronged—offer the hope of identifying other cases that particularly cry out for reparations. Those principles may, indeed, be too limiting; there are some cases when reparations are likely owed even though those factors are not met. Reparations for slavery may be one of those cases.[12] There are some cases where reparations have been paid, even though the people who were most directly affected are long-since dead. The payment of $56 million to members of the Seminole tribe, which was relocated from Florida in the 1820s, is one such example.[13] For Tulsa, the case is even stronger. But Tulsa is not alone; there have been reparations claims made—some successfully—for similar crimes. Those precedents can be useful in contemplating the case of Tulsa riot survivors.

Reparations in Other Contexts: Legislative Precedents

Reparations for Riot Victims in Other States

Some states at the time of the Tulsa riot made municipalities liable when they failed to protect—to say nothing of affirmatively destroy—

a community. In the 1920s, a number of states, including Illinois and Kansas, provided a cause of action for damage done by riot when the local government failed to protect against the rioters.[14] If the riot had occurred in Illinois, for example, there would have been a right to recover if the police failed to protect the victims. A 1905 Illinois law provided that the municipality where violence occurred was liable to the families of "lynching" victims. It allowed claims for wrongful death up to $5,000. The Illinois courts construed "lynching" to include deaths during race riots.[15] The families of twenty-two victims of the 1919 Chicago riot sued the city, and the city paid more than $100,000 to the families.[16] Following the 1917 riot in East St. Louis, victims reportedly received more than $400,000 from the city.[17]

The payments made by Chicago and East St. Louis demonstrate that at the time of the Tulsa riot other states and municipalities recognized the moral and legal claims that riot victims had when the police failed to protect them. Tulsans knew about the statutes in Illinois and Kansas and distinguished their own situation from that of Chicago and East St. Louis because there was no similar law in Oklahoma.[18] In Tulsa the culpability of the city and, to a lesser extent, the state counsels even more strongly in favor of reparations than either the Chicago or East St. Louis riots, where the government was less involved in the destruction.[19]

Debate about the propriety of paying reparations to riot victims was common in 1921. Just a few months after the Tulsa riot, Congress debated the Dyer Antilynching Bill. The bill proposed making municipalities liable up to $10,000 whenever a person was lynched within his or her boundaries. Although it did not pass the Senate, its passage by the House of Representatives testifies to the sentiment at the time that municipalities should pay when they failed to protect against violence. Members of Congress told of claims asserted by riot and lynching victims under state law.[20] There was even a small movement within Oklahoma to obtain compensation from the state legislature for the families who had lost property during the August 1918 riot in Dewey.[21] By 1921 Oklahomans would not allow any talk of government-sponsored reparations, even though the culpability of the city, in failing to protect against riot and in affirmatively destroying Greenwood, was acknowledged in the Tulsa county court and in its newspapers.

Other American Reparations

There are ample models of congressional and state reparations for racial legislation and violence.[22] In recent years, Japanese Americans and Native Americans have received reparations. In most, but not all, instances there has been evidence of governmental culpability. There has also been a compelling story, which leads legislators to think that the expenditure of money might repair past injustice, and maybe even lead to reconciliation.

Reparations for Japanese Americans

The most comprehensive model is the compensation to Japanese Americans who were interned during World War II. The Civil Rights Act of 1988, signed by President Reagan, had several components. Its key elements were an acknowledgment of and apology for the fundamental injustice of the internment; a public education fund; and reparations of $20,000 to every then-living survivor who was "confined or relocated."   ~~Why / how calculated ?~~

The Act's goals were to discourage similar events in the future and to make the United States' concerns over human rights more sincere and credible.[23] The primary purpose of the Act was to provide direct compensation to survivors of internment. But it also included a form of community reparations, by establishing a fund to provide education about internment. The Act, which drew wide support, provides important guidance in contemplating whether there should be reparations for Tulsa. There are important parallels. In both cases, the government was instrumental in the deprivation of rights.

In both cases—the internment of Japanese Americans and the Tulsa riot—decades passed before a moral consensus emerged that the deprivations were wrong and that they were based on unfounded fears. For Japanese Americans, the reparations were limited to survivors who were alive in 1985. That reduced the liability of the federal government. Some might think that the limitation of reparations to survivors diminished the federal government's sincerity. However, the limitation also made it possible to contemplate reparations.[24] It is a sad fact that once the group of potential claimants has decreased—due to death—and enough time has passed so that the community can evaluate dispassionately its own culpability and those who had criminal liability have passed from the scene as well, reparations may be more achievable than immediately after an event.

Reparations for Native Americans

Given that this country's history has been one of almost wholesale dispossession of Native American land, it may seem ludicrous to speak about reparations to Native Americans. The United States Congress has, however, provided for reparations to Native Americans on several occasions. The most significant is the Indian Claims Commission of 1946.[25] The Claims Commission was designed to allow tribes to finally settle land claims with the federal government. The United States Supreme Court's decision in 1950 in *Tee-Hit-Ton* limited tribes' claims to cases where the United States had recognized their right to land. The mere fact that a tribe once inhabited land was insufficient, the Supreme Court thought. Tribes needed to have a treaty recognizing their right to the land before they could make a claim for it.[26]

The largest single act of compensation was the 1971 Alaska Native Claims Settlement Act, which set up corporations based around native villages and then gave individuals shares of the corporation. It provided for economic development, as well as reparations.[27] Recently the Native American Graves Repatriation Act required the return of native artifacts for government-supported museums, where specific owners could be identified.[28]

The Future of Reparations for African Americans

For more than two decades, scholars and activists have debated proposals for reparations for slavery.[29] While such claims have been singularly unsuccessful in the courts,[30] some of the most creative work in critical race studies has been on reparations for slavery. The articles and books advocating reparations are brilliant thought experiments, which rethink basic principles in American law.[31] Sometimes they even employ basic legal doctrines to make radical arguments, as happened when Robert Westley excavated unjust enrichment law to suggest a way that descendants of slaves might be able to present a legal argument for recovery.[32] Representative John Conyers of Michigan has introduced legislation to study the effects of slavery and begin looking at reparations.[33] The Chicago City Council is looking at the possibility of reparations for slavery and urging Congress to do the same. Members of Congress are investigating the use of slave labor in building the Capitol building in the eighteenth century.[34] The new research presents provocative images of what law might be. As yet, reparations themselves have been more modest.

One can point to such grand-scale programs as the New Deal and the Great Society, which drew upon a centuries-old tradition in the United States of using government power and spending to improve the lives of citizens. These programs are a form of reparations, although they were not limited to the descendants of slaves. On a more limited scale, there was state legislation that provided causes of action against municipalities that permitted lynching and, more recently, government-sponsored programs for rebuilding after the riots of the 1960s.[35] There are other examples of money set aside in the aftermath of riots. As part of a $1 billion urban development program, Congress provided funding for development after the 1992 Los Angeles riot, for example.[36]

In 1994, the Florida legislature provided a $2 million fund to compensate survivors of the 1923 Rosewood Massacre. It allowed individual property claims of up to $150,000, as well as a modest education fund for descendants of the residents of the town.[37] The case for compensation of victims of the Tulsa riot is substantially stronger than Rosewood, because in Tulsa the police took an affirmative hand in the riot. In Rosewood the government failed to protect the residents, but did not take a direct role in the massacre.

Exercising the Restorative Power
for Other Oklahoma Tragedies

Just after the riot, Mayor Evans claimed that white Tulsans were as blameless as if the destruction had been caused by a cyclone.[38] While the evidence belies Evans' statement, even if the riot was merely an act of nature, there is still precedent in Oklahoma for government action to help rebuild. Following the May 3, 1999 tornado—the worst tornado anywhere in recorded human history—which swept through Oklahoma, leaving more than $1.1 billion in damages, the federal government and the state of Oklahoma spent more than $280 million to help clean up and restore damaged property.[39]

Is Justice Possible?: Contemplating the Utility of Reparations, Limiting Factors, and Building a Theme of Justice

> How can the future deny the past? . . . [T]he answer lies in remembering that, given the nature of our vision, of our covenants, to remember is to forget and to forget is to remember selectively, creatively! Yes, and let us remember that in this land to create is to destroy, and to destroy—if we will it so and *make* it so, if we pay our proper respect to remembered but rejected things—is to make manifest our lovely dream of progressive idealism.
>
> —Ralph Ellison, *Juneteenth*[40]

> It is not fair that a city like Tulsa, especially the part belonging to the weaker part of the citizenship, should be so wrecked. The city of Tulsa should be loyal enough to rebuild that part of the city that was destroyed by fire and otherwise pay other damages done.
>
> —*Oklahoma Guide*, June 9, 1921[41]

Are truth, justice, and forgiveness possible? To answer this question, we can now join the case for the culpability of the city and state in the Tulsa riot with reparations given in analogous contexts to make the case for reparations in Tulsa. Yet even with the precedents of reparations in analogous contexts, there is the nagging question: what good will reparations do? One danger of reparations is that they anger members of the community. For, as one Oklahoma politician opposing reparations says, "you have to wonder if this doesn't just make blacks hate whites."[42]

A primary goal of reparations is to do justice, to the extent that can be done. Reparations offer the hope of several benefits. First, they make good on a promise and represent some effort to repair decades-old damage. Second, they suggest that justice is possible. Third, in holding out the promise of moving in the direction of justice, they can build trust in the community. Moreover, they make similar events—in which the community collectively fails to enforce the law—less likely to happen again.

Reparations payments obviously cannot restore the community, which is gone. They can, however, symbolically demonstrate that Tulsa and Oklahoma more generally have accepted responsibility for their role in the riot. That acceptance is an important part of healing, since there is no longer a denial of the crime. That acceptance of responsibility may be one of the few, meaningful actions that can still be taken. One benefit, as we have learned from the Truth and Reconciliation Commission in South Africa, is that forgiveness follows confessions of wrongdoing.[43]

Even if the Oklahoma legislature were never to pay reparations—which apparently it never will—we at least have a history that presents a balanced interpretation, which demonstrates that the destruction was caused by the deliberate actions of the city and was the fault of the city and state. At least there is no longer "a white wash brush and a big one in operation in Tulsa."[44] For decades, adding up to nearly a century, there have been black and white histories of the riot. And for too long the white history, which has denied the culpability of the city, has been dominant. That white history, which owes much to the obviously biased grand jury, found Greenwood residents to blame for the riot. Once that biased interpretation had been accepted and disseminated, it became easy to avoid reconstructing "Little Africa." Even further violence against Greenwood was contemplated.[45] What is needed at a minimum is a history that fair-minded interpreters can agree upon.

Greenwood residents were doubly victimized by the law. They were not protected. Indeed, their property was actually destroyed by the government. Then came the zoning ordinance, which made rebuilding impossible (at least until the ordinance was overturned). "The greatest crime committed," editorialized the *Black Dispatch*, "was in a certain meeting of the city commissioners, where white men sat down and deliberately conspired to confiscate the very land and ashes where black men had dwelt. Men can be excused for some of the things they do when they are lashed in the throes of anger, but when sober men sit down to rob dead men of their property, they are ghouls, grave robbers, below the level of a common thief."[46] Even after the zoning ordinance was struck down by the Tulsa district court, the Oklahoma courts prevented recovery against the city or local units of the National Guard. Oklahoma law occupied an important place in the prohibition of justice.

Contemplating Types of Reparations

What types of remedies are most appropriate? How can we begin to repair the damage—or should we even try? There are several basic models for reparations. The simplest are apologies and truth commissions. Then there are remedies that involve expenditure of money to help the victims, their survivors, and the victimized community. The Oklahoma legislature and city of Tulsa might consider a combination of these models, such as a fund for community development for Greenwood, as well as direct payments to survivors of the riot, in addition to acknowledging the government's role in the destruction of Greenwood.[47]

Apologies and Truth Commissions

Apologies are inexpensive in terms of money, but they are not necessarily easy to obtain. The difficulty in obtaining them suggests how meaningful they can be—to both the people who make them and those who receive them. Apologies are part of a struggle for interpretation of past events. They offer hope to victims and descendants of victims that pride can be restored. They become a part of contemporary debate and can be the basis for interpretation of events that are currently happening. Apologies for slavery, for instance, are part of the reconstruction of black and white interpretations of the past. They can affect how we currently see the world.

Truth commissions are another form of interpretation. They offer the opportunity to collect testimony and evidence about the causes and consequences of tragedies. Then they may provide an official story about the events. Thus, they can re-create our view of the past. Truth commissions hold out the promise of vindication for victims and blame for offenders. The official stories they tell can remake our understanding of why people were victims and can lay blame on offenders. That in itself—while seemingly so small to many—tells the world a different story from the one they have been told. It is part of the reordering of the stories. If we measure who has won a struggle using the adage "winners write history," then a truth commission signals to the world that the victims have won. For it is the victims whose history is recorded and retold to future generations. Truth commissions, when looked at from that perspective, provide powerful, lasting forms of reparations. For those interested in long-term struggles, the way that past actions are viewed can have important consequences for current debates. Those interpretations channel how the struggle for power is discussed.[48]

Community and Individual Reparations

In other instances, reparations move beyond apologies and new official histories to payments to victims. Ideally, the payments go to the
specific individuals harmed, or their immediate heirs. The payments
come, in many instances, from the government or corporation that
caused the harm. At other times, however, it is impossible to pay reparations to the people most directly harmed. In the wake of the Los
Angeles riots in 1992, Congress provided for more than $1 billion in
funding for urban renewal. Los Angeles residents were eligible for
assistance, even if they had not been victims of the riot. The idea moti-
vating the assistance was that the federal government—which no one
thought was directly responsible—might make the community where
the riot occurred better. In other instances, the individuals harmed
may not be alive or they may not be identifiable.

Community-based remedies are frequently employed in cases
involving racial discrimination, from school desegregation to voting
rights to race-based set-asides for affirmative action.[49] There, remedies reach people who may not have been the specific victims of discrimination; they reach the community harmed. For race-based
remedies, the United States Supreme Court requires evidence of specific past discrimination by the actor now making amends. In *Richmond v. J.A. Croson*,[50] the leading case governing a city's right to
award race-based set-asides, the Supreme Court required a narrow
tailoring of affirmative action programs to remedy past discrimination in that specific location and against the specific racial
groups being benefited.[51] The destruction of Geenwood provides the
basis for race-based affirmative action, should Tulsa ever decide to
pursue it.

A Blueprint for Justice: In Tulsa and Elsewhere

The city and state law enforcement officials were largely to blame for
the destruction of the Greenwood community. The community rebuilt
itself and, a little more than a year after the riot, Oklahoma City's
Black Dispatch printed a picture of the new Dreamland Theater,
which the Williams family had rebuilt using their own resources. Neither the city nor their insurance company had assisted them.[52]

There remains the question of how the Oklahoma legislature and the city of Tulsa might fulfill the promises made decades ago. In considering reparations, it is important to consider what is politically realistic, as well as what is morally justified. One modest plan could compensate survivors who are still alive at a set rate, perhaps $20,000, as the Civil Rights Act of 1988 did for Japanese Americans interned during World War II. Such a plan has several distinct advantages. Some people may consider a proposal to compensate only those who are still alive, along with a modest fund for community development, as laughably small. But this is a political argument, looking to what is realistic, not an academic one that looks to abstract justice.

Such a reparations plan is both realistic in terms of cost and effective in terms of achieving the goal of justice at least partly. First, it incorporates a limiting factor. To receive compensation, one must be currently alive, so there is an upper limit on the liability. There are currently approximately a hundred survivors, meaning $2 million would provide a token payment of $20,000 per survivor. Second, there is a direct connection between present payments and past wrongs. While 1921 is more than a lifetime ago for the vast majority of Americans, it is within the lifetime of some people who suffered at the hands of their government. Thus, there is a direct, living connection between past harms and the present. That human connection provides both a limitation on the number of people who can recover (and thus may satisfy those who are concerned that Tulsa reparations would set a dangerous precedent) and assures that the money is targeted at those who suffered the harm most directly. It also holds out the promise that those who suffered *finally* receive assistance, which might be of some benefit to them. Many of the survivors do not have much—and one of the reasons they don't is that they lost what they had in the riot.

Most important, however, reparations to now-living riot survivors would make good on promises made a lifetime ago. Those promises acknowledged a moral debt, which many people in Tulsa and around the United States understood was owed to the victims. Those promises were made by many people. The *Tulsa World* thought "There is but one way in which Tulsa can rehabilitate itself in either its own eyes or the eyes of the outside world. That is by rebuilding that which has been destroyed."[53] Tulsans understood that Greenwood residents had been mistreated and they promised to make good the damage. They still have that opportunity, even if payments are terribly small in comparison to the harm that has been suffered.

Those opposing reparations say the current generation should not have to pay for a previous generation's sins. They see a moral as well as a legal statute of limitations. Certainly, a great deal of time separates the riot from the present. Indeed, at the time of the riot, Tulsa residents were closer to the era of slavery than we are to the riot. Nevertheless, there are living connections between the riot and the present. Limiting payments to surviving victims provides an important, direct connection between those who have been harmed and relief. That limiting principle connects the harm caused by the riot and the present in important ways. Quite simply, it closes the gap between an event eighty years ago and today. The present generation may still be asked to pay for the sins of the past, but it is asked to pay only for those sins when there is a direct, living connection to the past.

The lingering effects of the riot, which was exacerbated by the state, however, counsels in favor of some sort of reparations. The city benefited because it never paid damages to the riot victims it was responsible for harming. To ask the city now to return that benefit it has retained, which it rightfully should have paid to many more victims, is consistent with well-established equitable principles.

The riot represented the complete breakdown of the rule of law. It was the product of a failure of white Tulsans to uphold the law against lynching. The destruction was itself further evidence of the lack of the rule of law in Tulsa. The payment of reparations holds out the promise of allowing the rule of law to reign in the Tulsa riot, even if eighty years later. Unfortunately, as of the spring of 2001, the Oklahoma legislature seems to have decided against direct payments to Tulsa riot survivors. After limited debate, the legislature passed the "1921 Tulsa Race Riot Reconciliation Act," which gave official recognition to the "staggering cost" of the riot. It also created (but did not fund) committees to design a memorial and assist in economic development. It also established a mechanism for distributing scholarships to descendants of riot victims and other deserving students, but did not fund the scholarships.[54] The legislature also passed a joint resolution authorizing the award of medals to the 118 known, now-living survivors of the riot.[55]

Looking Beyond Tulsa

The case for reparations in Tulsa, many people believe, is compelling. Even staunch opponents of reparations for slavery support reparations in Tulsa.[56] The question remains, however, what the case in Tulsa tells us about other reparations movements. Can Tulsa form the basis for larger reparations, even for slavery? Or does Tulsa tell us that reparations will never be available for the great societal tragedies—the wholesale inequalities that are legacies of slavery, colonialism, and centuries of neglect of Native Americans? That at best there will be reparations when harm is concentrated and when the number of recipients of reparations is relatively limited?[57]

The factors that counsel so strongly in favor of reparations for Tulsa—the harm was caused by the government, there are still living survivors, the harm was concentrated, and the government's actions were recognized as wrong at the time—provide a strict limit on the number of other reparations claims that might be successful. One supporting reparations for slavery might argue for them using a slightly expanded version of the Tulsa factors. The United States government was intimately involved in the maintenance of the institution of slavery; there are certainly living victims of the legacy of slavery, people whose educational, employment, housing, and voting opportunities were limited because the system of slavery had not been effectively dismantled during their lifetimes. The harm being remedied was concentrated on people based on race, and many people argued at the time that slavery was wrong—and that there should be action to elevate the former slaves after slavery ended. One of the many tragedies of slavery is that so little was done to remove its effects after the United States government formally ended it. The former slaves, instead of being ensured education, opportunity for credit to build businesses, and voting rights, were provided with black codes, aimed at reestablishing white control.

Before the Civil War, one of the most powerful arguments against abolition of slavery was made by Thomas Roderick Dew, a professor of history at William and Mary College in Virginia. Dew wrote a pamphlet opposing the abolition of slavery, which the Virginia legislature was considering in the early 1830s. Slavery, the legacy of the millennia, might "require *ages* to remove," he told the legislature.[58] Dew understood, as did many others, that the legacy of slavery would require generations to eradicate—and he used that argument effectively to *prevent* abolition of slavery. And yet so little was done, once slavery ended as a formal system, to repair the damage. The only serious consideration given to reparations after the Civil War ended was to whether former slaveholders should receive compensation. And in Washington, D.C. they did.[59]

Perhaps we can begin to reconsider the legacy of slavery and other tragedies like the dispossession of Native American lands, understand how those tragedies have a dramatic effect on the lives of people today, and then work toward repairing the harm they caused. In that way, the future might deny the past. For too long, the losers in the Tulsa riot have been left alone "to grapple with the issues that are left unresolved."[60]

Notes

Prologue

1. W.E.B. DuBois, BLACK FOLK THEN AND NOW vii (1975 ed., Kraus-Thomson Organization) (originally published 1939), quoted in George Hutchinson, THE HARLEM RENAISSANCE IN BLACK AND WHITE 63 (1995).

2. *See Redfearn v. American Central Ins. Co.*, 243 P 929 (Okla. 1926).

3. *J.B. Stradford v. American Central Ins. Co.*, Cook County Superior Court, Case No. 370,274 (1921).

4. Ralph Ellison, *Going to the Territory,* in THE COLLECTED ESSAYS OF RALPH ELLISON 591, 594 (John F. Callahan, ed., 1995).

5. *Grand Jury Blames Negroes for Inciting Race Rioting; Whites Clearly Exonerated,* TULSA TRIBUNE 1 (June 26, 1921).

6. Brent Staples, Unearthing a Riot, NEW YORK TIMES MAGAZINE 64–70 (December 19, 1989).

7. *See* THE TULSA RACE RIOT: A SCIENTIFIC, HISTORICAL AND LEGAL ANALYSIS (John Hope Franklin and Scott Ellsworth, 2000). The report is incorporated into the Riot Commission's Final Report, and is available at the Oklahoma Historical Society's website: *http://www.ok-history.mus.ok.us/trrc/freport.htm.*

8. Ralph Ellison, INVISIBLE MAN xvii (1952).

Chapter 1

1. *Going to the Territory,* in THE COLLECTED WORKS OF RALPH ELLISON 600 (John F. Callahan, ed., 1995). *See also id.* at 602–3 ("Geography is fate, and in moving west they were repeating a pattern begun by runaway slaves and by the Negroes who accompanied the Indian tribes along the death march which took so many lives that it became known as the 'Trail of Tears,' a march initiated by Andrew Jackson in fulfillment of the treaty of Dancing Rabbit").

2. *Id.* at 601. *See also* Ralph Ellison, *Remembering Richard Wright*, in THE COLLECTED WORKS OF RALPH ELLISON 659 (John F. Callahan, ed.,

1995) ("I grew up in a state which possessed no indigenous tradition of chattel slavery.").

3. *Id.*

4. *See McCabe v. Atchison, Topeka, and Santa Fe Ry.*, 235 U.S. 151, 163 (1914); *Guinn v. United States*, 238 U.S. 347 (1915).

5. Brief for Defendant in Error, *Redfearn v. Am. Cent. Ins. Co.*, 243 P. 929 (Okla. 1926) at 60.

6. The World War was central to that elevation of spirit. *See The Negro After the War*, MUSKOGEE CIMETER 2 (March 30, 1918); *The Negro and the War*, MUSKOGEE CIMETER 1 (May 18, 1918).

7. *The Source From Which the Mob Spirit Springs*, BLACK DISPATCH 4 (August 2, 1918) ("Freedom of movement and safety in law are two of the cornerstones of American institutions, and because we, as a race group, has felt that America was striving for higher ground in the realm of justice and equity we have given freely our boys to go to the death line to champion, with their blood, the cause of freedom").

8. *Bristow Celebrates*, BLACK DISPATCH 1 (January 4, 1918). *See also Jim Crow Must Go: Florida Negroes Define Democracy*, BLACK DISPATCH (March 21, 1919); *What Black Men are Thinking Today*, BLACK DISPATCH 1 (January 10, 1919).

9. *See Buchanan v. Warley* 245 U.S. 60 (1917); *McCabe v. Atkison, Topeka, and Kansas Rwy.* 235 U.S. 151 (1915).

10. *See The Maul of Patriotism*, BLACK DISPATCH 1 (May 10, 1918). The cartoon was accompanied by an editorial of the same title. *See The Maul of Patriotism*, BLACK DISPATCH 4 (May 10, 1918). *See also Service Rendered*, BLACK DISPATCH 4 (May 10, 1918).

Peonage referred to a once-common practice of imprisoning blacks for debt and then releasing them to whoever would pay their debt. Alexander M. Bickel and Benno C. Schmidt, THE JUDICIARY AND RESPONSIBLE GOVERNMENT, 1910–21, at 775–84 (1984). The United States Supreme Court outlawed peonage in 1911, although there continued to be allegations that workers in debt to farmers were threatened with jail on vagrancy charges if they failed to work.

11. *See What Santa Claus Brings*, BLACK DISPATCH 1 (December 21, 1917).

12. *A New Reconstruction*, BLACK DISPATCH 1 (July 18, 1919). *See also The True Basis of Democracy Defined*, BLACK DISPATCH 4 (May 9, 1919).

13. *DuBois Says North Blacks Right: On the Great Deep*, BLACK DISPATCH 1 (September 5, 1919).

14. *See, e.g., Jewish Army Stops Pogroms*, BLACK DISPATCH 2 (February 22, 1923).

15. *Upright Men Shall be Astonished*, BLACK DISPATCH 4 (August 15, 1919) (quoting article from THE OUTLOOK, August 1919).

16. *Nero Fiddled While Rome Burned*, BLACK DISPATCH 4 (February 16, 1922).

17. *See* Ralph Ellison, *Roscoe Dunjee and the American Language*, in THE COLLECTED ESSAYS OF RALPH ELLISON, *supra* note 1, at 451, 458–59 ("The whole concept of changing segregation through appeals to the Supreme Court was present in Oklahoma City when I was a boy, and was propagated through the columns of a weekly newspaper").

18. *See, e.g., Jim Crow Democracy: Black Troops Suffer in Filth at Chickasha*, BLACK DISPATCH 1 (February 22, 1918); *Grady County Jails Black Lieutenant*, BLACK DISPATCH 1 (March 8, 1918).

19. *Are we entitled to the moral leadership of the world?* BLACK DISPATCH 4 (August 15, 1919).

20. *Id.*

21. *See The Future: Shall These Horrors Await Our Future Generations?* TULSA STAR (February 21, 1920).

22. *See Untitled Cartoon*, TULSA STAR 1 (May 1, 1920).

23. 60 P. at 110.

24. *See Norman Mob after Singie Smith Jazz*, BLACK DISPATCH 1 (February 9, 1922) ("Negroes are occasionally seen on the streets of Norman in the daytime, but the 'rule' that they leave at night is strictly enforced. Several other Oklahoma towns have similar customs"); *Stealing Our Money*, BLACK DISPATCH 4 (October 20, 1921).

25. *Wants Negroes Driven Out*, NORMAN TRANSCRIPT (September 2, 1898). Thanks to Les Sparks for calling this article to my attention and for sharing his paper on the *Wallace* case.

26. There are elliptical references to it in the STAR and BLACK DISPATCH. *See, e.g., A Near Lynching at Bristow, Okla.*, TULSA STAR 1 (August 24, 1918) (referring to plea to editor A.J. Smitherman to assist in preventing "a repetition of the Dewey outrage"); *What Black Men are Thinking Today*, BLACK DISPATCH 1 (January 10, 1919) ("Since the last convention of this legislature several men of color have lost their lives at the hands of the mob. Recently in the town of Dewey, the whole colored section of the city was reduced to ashes and their owners driven from the city. Several of these people had sons fighting in France, and they were attempting to keep the Home Fires burning until their brave loved ones returned. Instead, fires were made of their homes").

27. *See* BLACK DISPATCH (March 19, 1919) (discussing bill in Oklahoma legislature to provide aid to victims of attack). Other racial attacks occasionally led to attempts at reparations. *See Sisters of Slain Man File Suits*,

BLACK DISPATCH 1 (November 1, 1923) (reporting suit by relatives of lynching victim).

28. *See Blacks are Chased from Town*, DAILY OKLAHOMAN 1 (February 16, 1908); *Bartlesville Officers Drive Out Undesirable Negroes*, TULSA STAR (October 18, 1913); *Frank Greer Would Run Negro Porters Out of Town*, TULSA STAR 1 (March 28, 1914). For other examples, close in time to the Tulsa riot, of fear that someone (not always blacks) would be run out of town, *see Negro Whipped and branded by Ku Klux Klan*, TULSA TRIBUNE 1 (April 2, 1921) (Klan terrorizes black man in Dallas, Texas); *Residence Dynamited, None Hurt*, TULSA TRIBUNE 1 (March 30, 1921) (tenants' house blown up as a way of driving them off; four men arrested); *Oilton Riot Anti-Cleanup Move, Claim*, TULSA TRIBUNE 1 (March 30, 1921) ("best citizens" warned to leave town, which they refused to do).

29. When the LITERARY DIGEST ran a story on "*Mob Rule a National Menace*," the MUSKOGEE CIMETER reprinted it. MUSKOGEE CIMETER 2 (November 8, 1919) (reprinted from the *Literary Digest*). *See also 63 Lynched in U.S. in 10 Months; 11 Burned, 20 Shot; 19 Hanged*, MUSKOGEE CIMETER 1 (November 8, 1919); *Federal Government and Lynching*, TULSA STAR 1 (May 23, 1919); *The Lynching Season*, BLACK DISPATCH 4 (June 1, 1922) ("Lynching is a race crime; it is the ritual by which the white race signifies its intention to deprive the black man of the rights and privileges which under the federal constitution are guaranteed to every American citizen").

30. 62 CONGRESSIONAL RECORD (67th Cong. 2nd Sess.) 1371 (January 18, 1922).

31. *Id.* at 1426 (January 19, 1922) (referring to Memphis, where "Every newspaper, every minister of the gospel, and practically every other citizen has discouraged lynching in every possible way." Then, "[t]hings went from bad to worse, until one morning the whole community was shocked by one of the most horrible crimes ever committed by a human being").

32. CONGRESSIONAL RECORD 1375 (January 18, 1922). *See also id.* ("Upon the passage of the bill it would be found that it would be understood by some—from the very name of it—to be a law enacted to protect the guilty from the extreme penalty, and it would encourage the would-be rapist to more boldly attempt to do his fiendish work").

33. *Id.* at 1721 (Representative Sisson). Representative Sisson continued: "It is horrible to think of taking a little child into a court room and making her describe, as one must in a court room, the horrible details of the crime of rape." It is also difficult to contemplate a dead child giving any testimony in a courtroom on this earth. But that internal inconsistency in Representative Sisson's account seems not to have bothered him or his audience.

34. *Id.* at 1299 (Representative Ward of North Carolina).

35. *Id.* at 1785.

36. *Id.* at 1427.

37. *Id.* at 1724 (referring to attempts to use Fourteenth Amendment to "promote domination of Anglo-Saxons of the reconstructed States by the African black man").

38. *Another Lynching in Oklahoma: Colored Man swung up and dedicated to Gov. Cruce*, Tulsa Star (November 8, 1913).

39. *One Hundred Men Lynch Negro Woman Near Waggoner*, Tulsa Star 1 (April 4, 1914) ("These conditions are becoming very alarming and a serious calamity is sure to follow if something is not done to force all citizens to respect the law").

40. *Claude Chandler Hung by Mob, Posse Follows Too Late: Body Found West of City*, Black Dispatch 1 (September 3, 1920).

41. *And this is the White Man's Law?* Black Dispatch 4 (September 3, 1920).

42. *Id.*

43. *Id.*

44. *Id.*

45. *Terrible Lessons*, Black Dispatch 4 (August 22, 1919) ("The officers sometimes come and disarm Negroes, ONLY Negroes, and then they withdraw and on comes the mob. If this happens too often, the Negro will naturally conclude that there is a connection between the disarming officer and the mob. And then the black man will naturally prefer to die with his gun in his hands rather than without it").

46. Ralph Ellison, *The Perspective of Literature*, in The Collected Essays of Ralph Ellison 768 (John F. Callahan, ed., 1995). Similarly, as an Oklahoma City police officer roughly handled a woman suspected of stealing from her employer, she told him to "mind what you are doing. There is a law against such treatment." "By God, I am the law," was the reply. *See Story Like Unto Dark Ages*, Black Dispatch 1 (June 21, 1918).

47. Ralph Ellison, *The Perspective of Literature*, in The Collected Essays of Ralph Ellison, *supra* note 1, at 768.

48. That law was struck down too: in 1934! *See Lane v. Wilson*, 307 U.S. 268 (1934).

49. *Not a Child Race*, Muskogee Cimeter (June 17, 1916).

50. *See Terrible Lessons*, Black Dispatch 4 (August 22, 1919).

51. *See Guinn v. United States*, 238 U.S. 347 (1915).

52. J.B.A. Robertson to S.P. Freehling, August 30, 1920, in Attorney General's Case File 1018, Oklahoma State Archives ("[T]he excuse as given in the Daily Oklahoman this morning by the jailer is altogether too flimsy to be believed, and is the stock excuse of all other officers on such occasions. To me it simply proves that the officers were in collusion with the leaders of

the mob, or else wholly unfit by lack of physical courage and otherwise, to discharge the duties of the officer which they held").

When he promised to punish the lynchers, the TULSA STAR headline read, "Governor Invokes Law Versus Mobbists." *Gov. Invokes Law vs. Mobbists,* TULSA STAR 1 (September 4, 1920).

53. *The Mountain that he must climb,* BLACK DISPATCH 4 (September 10, 1920).

54. *See Oklahoma v. G.L. Johnson,* Oklahoma County District Court 20,092. The sheriff was not, however, convicted.

55. *Let Judgement Run Down as Waters,* BLACK DISPATCH 4 (September 17, 1920).

56. *Upright Men Shall be Astonished?* BLACK DISPATCH 4 (September 10, 1920).

57. *Id.*

58. *Respect for the Law Must Go, Lynching Must be Supreme,* BLACK DISPATCH 1 (August 6, 1920) ("The most powerful instrumentality in the world is public sentiment"). *See also* David Margolick, STRANGE FRUIT: BILLIE HOLIDAY, CAFE SOCIETY, AND AN EARLY CRY FOR CIVIL RIGHTS (2000).

There was also discussion of potential legal responses to lynching and of the rule of law. *See, e.g.,* James Harmon Chadbourn, LYNCHING AND THE LAW (1933): Walter Francis White, ROPE AND FAGGOTT: A BIOGRAPHY OF JUDGE LYNCH (1922); J.N. Flowers, MISSISSIPPI AND THE MOB (1926); Albert E. Pillsbury, *A Brief Inquiry into a Federal Remedy for Lynching,* 15 HARVARD L. REV. 707 (1902).

59. *Misguided Oklahoma Patriots,* TULSA STAR 4 (September 4, 1920).

60. *The Outrages at Durant,* MUSKOGEE CIMETER 1 (September 2, 1911). *See also Vision of a Lyncher,* 3 CRISIS 122 (January 1912) (reprinting what appears to be a painting of Durant lynchers and their victim tied to a board).

61. *Bryan County Negroes Organized,* MUSKOGEE CIMETER 1 (September 2, 1911) ("The word has been 'sent down the line' and the Negroes all over the county are preparing for the worst. They are no longer depending on the law to protect them but will protect themselves").

62. *D——— Cowards,* MUSKOGEE CIMETER 1 (June 2, 1917) (responding to a report in MUSKOGEE PHOENIX that there were fifty men contemplating lynching two black men held in jail in Muskogee).

63. *Adding Insult to Injury,* BLACK DISPATCH 4 (September 10, 1920) ("[T]o the credit of the Oklahoma City Negroes, th[ey] were present on that disgraceful night, some of the Negroes were known to the authorities and, when they had made their presence known, the guns were returned to their owners and the disarmed Negroes permitted to proceed with their fellows in pursuit of the mob").

64. Testimony of J.B. Saunders, at 8, Attorney General Case No. 1018, Oklahoma State Archives.

65. *And this is the White Man's Law?* BLACK DISPATCH 4 (September 2, 1920).

66. *The Facts Remain the Same,* TULSA STAR 8 (September 18, 1920).

67. *Id.; cf.* Ralph Ellison, INVISIBLE MAN 454 (1952) (asking, about the police following a riot in Harlem, "Why hadn't they come when they could have stopped it all?").

68. *The Facts Remain the Same,* TULSA STAR 8 (September 18, 1920) ("No man or set of men have any right to conspire and arm themselves to desecrate the law, but any man or set of men may rightfully and legally take up arms to defend and uphold the law").

69. *Id.*

70. *Grand Jurors Probe Takes a New Angle,* TULSA TRIBUNE 1 (June 13, 1921).

71. *Mob Foiled in Attempt to Lynch Man!* TULSA STAR 1 (March 6, 1920). *See also Republicans and Jim Crow Car Disgrace,* TULSA STAR 1 (January 31, 1920); *America's Pastime—Lynching!* TULSA STAR 1 (July 31, 1921). There was also frequent talk about legal rights and the use of courts to enforce them. *See e.g., Colored Woman Shamefully Mistreated,* TULSA STAR (May 15, 1920) (reporting suit by I.H. Spears against Midland Valley Railroad for mistreatment of black woman by baggage agent); *Colorado Court Upholds Civil Rights Law,* TULSA STAR (June 19, 1920).

72. *Mob Rule and the Law,* TULSA STAR 8 (March 6, 1920). *See also id.* ("But if our laws were properly enforced the action of the Colored men would have been unnecessary because the mob would have been arrested, even if it had been necessary to order out the militia. Our laws must be ample to protect prisoners as well as punish them. Otherwise either our laws or our officers are inadequate"). It turned out that law enforcement officers had already spirited Chap Davis away before the mob reached Shawnee, where he had been convicted of attempted assault, so there was no confrontation.

73. *Mobs Lynch White Boy at Tulsa and a Colored at Oklahoma City,* TULSA STAR 1 (September 4, 1920) ("Sad to relate, Oklahoma shook hands with the American lynching state of Georgia last Saturday night at Tulsa and Sunday night at Oklahoma City by lynching of a white boy and a colored boy by mob violence").

74. *See* Attorney General's Investigation of Lynching of Roy Belton, Oklahoma Attorney General, Case File 1017, Oklahoma State Archives. The sheriff phoned the jail when he heard that a mob was about to take Belton. He instructed the jailer, A.F. Basham, to "do all we could to save the prisoner, but be careful not to hurt anybody." *Id.* at 25 (August 28, 1920). A few minutes later, when the mob appeared outside the jail (which was on the

top floor of the Tulsa courthouse), the sheriff ordered his deputies to open
the door. When they did, they found about two dozen men. Some were pointing guns at the sheriff and he instructed the deputies to let the men in. The
deputies complied and then Sheriff James Woolley told them, "I guess you
just as well turn him over to them." *Id.* at 30. The deputies then went and
got Belton out of the "colored dungeon" where he was being kept and turned
him over. *Id.* at 33.

After Belton was taken from the jail, the police made no effort to catch
the people who took him out. *Id.* at 66–67 (testimony of Wilburn Woolley,
deputy sheriff and son of Sheriff James Woolley). In fact, they went to the
place where Belton was to be lynched and then stood by while he was exe-
cuted.

According to the attorney general's witness notes, George Donahue saw
Chief Gustafson, Officer Nick Remickel, and other officers at the lynching
scene. *See* Witness Notes, Oklahoma Attorney General, Case File 1017, at 4.

A reported for the TULSA TRIBUNE recalled that he saw Belton carried out
of the jail by a group of masked men. The reporter jumped on the running
board of the car carrying Belton out to Red Fork, where he would be lynched.
When the car arrived at Red Fork, the reporter saw about a thousand people and several police officers:

> [When] we got out there, everybody got out of the cars, . . . then a
> bunch of police held us back with guns and while we were standing
> there, there was a big crowd that gathered that filled that whole street.
> There must have been over a thousand people. . . . I thought I saw two
> or three men in uniform. I am almost sure one [was a] Negro and I
> thought I saw one white man.

Testimony of William N. Randolph, in Attorney General's Investigation of
Lynching of Roy Belton, Oklahoma Attorney General, Case File 1017, at
117.

75. *Near Race Riot is Staged at Okmulgee,* BLACK DISPATCH 1 (October
15, 1920). A headline in the TULSA STAR proclaimed "Colored Men Armed
for Self-Defense, Waited for Attack that Did Not Come." *Riot Averted by
Race Men in Okmulgee,* TULSA STAR 1 (October 16, 1920).

76. *Near Race Riot Is Staged at Okmulgee: One Thousand Negroes Arm
to Defend Homes; Cowardly Mob Burns Isolated Black Man's Hut; Woman
Say They Got Wrong Man,* BLACK DISPATCH 1 (October 15, 1920). The STAR
told how blacks foiled the lynching of Adkinson. The sheriff moved him from
Okmulgee to Muskogee and from there to the state penitentiary at McAlister. *Lynching Averted by Race Men,* TULSA STAR 1 (October 16, 1920).

77. *See also Near Lynch Victim Proved to be an Innocent Man*, TULSA STAR 3 (October 23, 1920).

78. *See Just a Little Less Talk of White and a Little Less Talk of Black*, BLACK DISPATCH 4 (April 22, 1921).

79. *See White Man Shot in Race Trouble*, TULSA WORLD 1 (April 17, 1921).

80. *Id.*

81. Other events, like the April 29, 1921, lynching of a man in Missouri, was probably on the minds of Greenwood residents. *See On Way to Prison, Negro is Lynched*, MUSKOGEE PHOENIX 3 (April 20, 1921). There were also fears of riots reported in Tulsa shortly before the riot. *See Two Slain, Riot Feared in Springfield*, TULSA TRIBUNE 1 (April 16, 1921).

82. *A Near Lynching at Bristow, Okla.: Cowards Failed to Lynch a Colored Man*, TULSA STAR 1 (August 24, 1918); *Smitherman is Dead*, BUFFALO CRITERION 1 (June 24, 1961). I would like to thank John Schlegel for sending me Smitherman's obituary and for sharing his knowledge of Buffalo, where Smitherman worked from 1926 until his death in 1961. While in Buffalo, Smitherman founded and edited the *Buffalo Star*, later known as the *Empire Star*.

83. We know about the conversation between Smitherman and Stradford because Henry Sowders, a white man who worked as a motion picture operator in the theater, was eavesdropping on it. Sowders listened though a hole in the floor. He testified in a suit brought to recover insurance payments after the riot about attitudes and events in Greenwood as the riot was beginning. Sowders heard Stradford and Smitherman talking about the event in Muskogee, along with E.E. Cotton, the manager of the Dreamland. Sowders became interested in their ideas, and every chance he got, he looked in the black newspapers. Then he came across the article they were discussing that night he overhead them in the Dreamland. *See* Sowders Deposition in *Stradford v. American Central Ins. Co.*, Superior Court of Cook County, No. 370,274 at 126 (1921).

84. *Id.* Other evidence of the increasing militancy of Greenwood residents comes in elliptical fashion. In the middle of May 1921, for example, a couple were arrested for refusing to sit in the segregated portion of a street car. A brief story about it appeared in a white newspaper. *See Thought he owned the car*, TULSA TRIBUNE (May 16, 1921).

85. *The Place Where Lynchers are Born*, BLACK DISPATCH 4 (July 16, 1920); *Likened Unto White Sepulchers*, BLACK DISPATCH 4 (June 10, 1920); *Just Before the Dawn*, Black Dispatch 4 (June 10, 1921).

86. *The Place Where Lynchers are Born*, BLACK DISPATCH 4 (July 16, 1920).

87. *Upright Men Shall Be Astonished*, BLACK DISPATCH 4 (August 15, 1919).

88. *Cf. We Must Reach the Cause of the Trouble*, BLACK DISPATCH 4 (October 3, 1919) ("If there must be a separate law on public carriers a program ought to be arranged by which the plain operation of that law could be lifted out of the hands of those who many times to the positive knowledge of the writer, act unfair and court just such trouble in this city as has been this week the concern of all of the citizens black and white"). *See also Reconstruction: Prominent Men of both Races Discuss A Program for the Improvement of Race Relations*, BLACK DISPATCH 1 (October 10, 1919) (proposing self-enforcing segregation law for street cars).

89. *White Conscience*, BLACK DISPATCH 4 (May 15, 1924).

90. *Reconstruction*, BLACK DISPATCH 1 (October 10, 1919).

91. *Grand Jury Blames Negroes for Race Rioting: Whites Clearly Exonerated*, TULSA WORLD 1, 8 (June 26, 1921). For a sampling of complaints about vice in Tulsa generally before the riot, *see Twenty Joints Running Here, Shot Claims*, TULSA TRIBUNE 1 (April 14, 1921); *Chief to Ask Movie Censor in Clean-Up*, TULSA TRIBUNE 1 (March 15, 1921); *Gustafson to talk on Enforcing Laws*, TULSA TRIBUNE 9 (March 11, 1921).

92. Defendant's Brief *Redfearn v. Am. Cent. Ins. Co.*, 243 P. 929 (Okla. 1926), at 48.

Chapter 2

1. *See, e.g., Raped White Girl a Myth—Negro Business Section and Better Home Section Laid Waste by Torch*, WILMINGTON ADVOCATE (June 11, 1921) ("The attempted rape incident has turned out to be nothing more than a discovery of the fact that a giddy white girl has become infatuated with a comely young Negro lad of scarcely more than twenty years of age").

2. O.W. Gurley reported that the TRIBUNE stated "there was going to be a lynching." Whether he was referring to the front-page article or the editorial is not clear. Gurley Deposition, at 83, in *J.B. Stradford v. American Central Ins. Co.*, Cook County Superior Court, Case No. 370,274 (1921).

3. *The False Story which set Tulsa on Fire*, BLACK DISPATCH 1 (July 1, 1921).

4. *Misuse of Word "Assault" Led to Tulsa Charge*, CHICAGO TRIBUNE 14A (June 5, 1921) ("An afternoon newspaper in reporting the incident that caused the excitement used the word 'assault,' but gave insufficient information to confine the term to a mere agitation. The public got the meaning that rape had been attempted, which was untrue"); *Mob Fury and Race Hate as a National Danger*, LITERARY DIGEST 9 (June 18, 1921); *cf.* Walter White, *What a lyncher looks like*, BLACK DISPATCH 7 (April 20, 1922).

5. Walter J. White, *The Eruption of Tulsa*, THE NATION 909 (June 29, 1921).

6. B.C. Franklin, MY LIFE AND AN ERA 196 (John Hope Franklin, ed., 1993).

7. *Barney Cleaver Dismissed from Tulsa Police Force*, BLACK DISPATCH 1 (April 1, 1921).

8. Gurley Affidavit, Attorney General Files 1062, Oklahoma State Archives.

9. McCullough Deposition, Stradford Suit, *supra* note 2, at 15.

10. *First Detailed Story of How Riot Started*, ST. LOUIS POST-DISPATCH 21 (June 3, 1921).

11. McCullough Deposition, in Stradford Smith, *supra* note 2, at 16–17.

12. *Id.*

13. Brief for Plaintiff in Error, *Redfearn v. Am. Cent. Ins. Co.*, No. 15,851, 243 P. 929 (Okla. 1926) at 48.

14. Brief for Defendant in Error, *Redfearn v. Am. Cent. Ins. Co.*, 243 P. 929 (Okla. 1926) at 101–2. *See also* Gurley Deposition, in Stradford Suit, *supra* note 2, at 83 ("You ought to go home. . . . All you fellows ought to be put in jail").

15. Gurley Deposition, in Stradford Suit, *supra* note 2, at 87.

16. A.J. Smitherman, THE TULSA RIOT AND MASSACRE (circa January 1922), available in NAACP Papers, Library of Congress, A.J. Smitherman File.

17. *The Facts Remain the Same*, TULSA STAR 8 (September 18, 1920); *cf.* Ralph Ellison, INVISIBLE MAN 454 (1952) (asking, about the police following a riot in Harlem, "Why hadn't they come when they could have stopped it all?").

18. *When Riot Stalked in Tulsa*, TULSA WORLD 7 (June 2, 1921) (quoting Cleaver). *See also* Defendant's Brief, *supra* note 14, at 92–93 (Cleaver's testimony) ("I went out there and said, 'Boys, where are you going?' They said they come over to see about the lynching. I says, 'Now this boy is upstairs and the cage is locked upstairs and there is no way anyone can get to him go back.' And they turned around and went back on Boulder. I came back in the Court House and we was all in there talking and so on, and pretty soon some lawyer came, . . . and says, 'Here are a whole lot of niggers up here with guns.' Well, I come out on Boulder then again, me and the Sheriff, and there was a quite a few out there").

19. Defendant's Brief, *supra* note 14, at 76. *See also When Riot Stalked in Tulsa*, TULSA WORLD 7 (June 2, 1921) (discussing McCullough).

20. Bell to Rooney, *Report on Activities of the National Guard on the Night of May 31st and June 1st, 1921* (July 2, 1921).

21. Attorney General Files, Oklahoma State Archives. McCullough later

told a reporter that the trouble began when someone called a movie theater in Greenwood and alerted people there that Rowland might be lynched. *See Sheriff Says Telephone Call Started Riot*, TULSA TRIBUNE 1 (June 3, 1921).

22. Stradford memoirs, quoted in Jonathan Z. Larsen, *Tulsa Burning*, CIVILIZATION (February 1, 1997), available at www.britannica.com/bcom/magazine/article/0,5744,4702,00.html.

23. *Id.*

24. Defendant's Brief, *supra* note 14, at 76.

25. *See* Gurley Affidavit, Attorney General Files, Oklahoma State Archives.

26. Smitherman, *supra* note 16.

27. *Negro Tells How Others Mobilized*, TULSA TRIBUNE 1 (June 4, 1921).

28. *Id.* After the riot Mann formed a corporation to sue the insurance companies for fire insurance coverage. *See Negro Adjustment Firm: Gets Chance to Aid Riot Victims Collect Insurance*, TULSA TRIBUNE 3 (August 5, 1921).

29. *See* Scott Ellsworth, DEATH IN A PROMISED LAND: THE TULSA RACE RIOT OF 1921 52 (1982); Plaintiff's Brief, *supra* note 13, at 47. *See also Guardsmen With Machine Guns Ready for Any Emergency*, ST. LOUIS POST-DISPATCH 2 (June 1, 1921) ("One version of the beginning of the trouble says the first firing came shortly after dark, when a negro was stopped by an officer and his gun taken away. He attempted to resist, according to the officer, and was shot dead. Three hours later his body was picked up from the street and taken to Police Headquarters, which was used as a temporary morgue"). Another account reported that one man said, "Disarm? You can bet we won't disarm." *Race War Rages for Hours*, TULSA WORLD 3 (June 1, 1921).

30. McCullough Deposition, Stradford Suit, *supra* note 2, at 19.

31. *Id.* at 19–20. Lawyer Luther Jones gave a similar account of the start:
And there were several cars and truck loads of negroes that drove around the court house two or three times, as I remember it, and the white, people were making—they were yelling and had their guns in the cars and the trucks and some of the white people were making a good deal of complaint about it, you could hear it at different places here, I circulated around through the crowd in this street (indicating) and on Boulder. And some of the officers came out and requested the negroes, to leave, Bill McCullough for one, and they drove off down east on Sixth Street that was the next to the last time I saw them. Then they came back in a few minutes, and I was down here south of the Court House door; they drove down there and parked their cars some place, I didn't see where, and they marched single file down west of the Court house, and they got along over there and I heard a pistol shot or a gun shot in this direction (indicating). They was, I guess there must have been fifteen hundred people around the Court House here, women and children and men,

and when that shot was fired, then there must have been fifty other shots. I, like a lot of other people, run into a house on the corner here. I stayed there until the firing ceased and I came out and went over to the Elks Club. It must have been about nine thirty or ten o'clock at that time, and I heard shooting scattered at different places after I went over there.

Defendant's Brief, *supra* note 14, at 152–53.

32. *See* F.W. Prentice, *Oklahoma Race Riot*, 90 Scribner's 151, 152 (August 1931). Cleo Shumate, a white man who died about 10 p.m., may have been the first victim. *See* The Known Dead, TULSA WORLD 1 (June 2, 1921). Or it may have been Walter Daggs, another white man who also died about 10 p.m. *See Riot Death Toll Reduced to 20 by Rechecking*, TULSA WORLD 1 (June 3, 1921).

33. Defendant's Brief, *supra* note 14, at 103.

34. Tulsa City Commission Minutes, August 13, 1921.

35. *Two Whites Dead in Race Riot*, TULSA WORLD, 1 (June 1, 1921) (1st edition).

36. *Id.*

37. Smitherman, *supra* note 16.

38. Defendant's Brief, *supra* note 14, at 78.

39. *Id.* at 79.

40. *Id.* at 79–80. Gabe's reference to "ting" meant "shooting."

41. *Id.* at 80–81.

42. J.L. Dailey Deposition, Stradford Suit, *supra* note 2, at 78.

43. *Id. See also* Plaintiff's Brief, *supra* note 13, at 71–72 (testimony of fire-fighter B.J. Johnson regarding fires on the morning of June 1).

44. Plaintiff's Brief, *supra* note 13, at 48.

45. TULSA WORLD 8 (June 1, 1921) (1st edition).

46. Defendant's Brief, *supra* note 14, at 42.

47. Pack also testified in the Redfearn trial. Pack's testimony offers the possibility of reconstructing the interlocking experiences of the characters of the riot. *See* Plaintiff's Brief, *supra* note 13, at 52.

48. *See* Plaintiff's Brief, *supra* note 13, at 43. *See also* Defendant's Brief, *supra* note 14, at 90.

49. Smitherman, *supra* note 16.

50. *Id. See also White Dead are Forgotten, Rev. Cooke Charges*, TULSA TRIBUNE 11 (June 9, 1921); *Warning Against Further Trouble*, TULSA WORLD 1 (June 4, 1921) ("Negroes held in detention camps have been turned loose indiscriminately. There is a general feeling in the city that Tulsa is no safer tonight than it was Tuesday night. Without proper police protection, with the Negroes resentful over the loss of their property, there is an increasingly apprehensive feeling that something else is going to happen").

51. *See, e.g., Race War Rages for Hours After Outbreak at Courthouse;*

Troops and Armed Men Patrolling Streets, TULSA WORLD 1 (June 1, 1921) ("In response to a call from Muskogee, indicating several hundred Negroes were on their way to the city to assist Tulsa negroes should fighting continue, a machine gun squad loaded on a truck, went east of the city with orders to stop at all hazards these armed men").

52. *Id.* ("The arrival of Major Rooney and a bunch of national guard men on an army truck was a signal for shooters. 'Now let the niggers come if they dare,' the crowds shouted").

53. *See Weapons Must be Returned,* TULSA WORLD 3 (June 4, 1921) (asking for return of weapons and threatening prosecution if they are not).

54. Plaintiff's Brief, *supra* note 13, at 68.

55. *Curiosity Drew Mob, No Violence from Whites Until Armed Negroes Went Past Courthouse,* TULSA WORLD 1, 7 (July 19, 1921). I am indebted to Robert Norris for this citation. *See also* Testimony of Laurel Buck, 30, Attorney General's Civil Case Files, RG 1–2, A-G Case no. 1062, Box 25 (Oklahoma State Archives) (discussing instructions given to Laurel Buck, a white man, to "get a gun, and get busy and try to get a n———-er"). According to pleadings in a suit filed by a black riot victim, one deputy officer gave instructions to "Go out and kill you a d——- nigger." Petition in *Robinson v. Evans, et al.,* Tulsa County District Court, No. 23, 399, May 31, 1923.

56. Testimony of Laurel Buck, *supra* note 55, at 30.

57. *See Guns Taken During Riot, Still Sought by Tulsa Policemen,* TULSA WORLD 2A (June 19, 1921); *Weapons Must be Returned,* TULSA WORLD 3 (June 4, 1921) (asking for return of weapons and threatening prosecution if they are not). Once again I am indebted to Robert Norris for alerting me to this evidence.

58. TULSA WORLD 3 (July 21, 1921). As Adkison recognized, however, the men lost their heads and their hearts as well. *Id. See Chief and Officers Take Witness Stand,* TULSA WORLD 1 (July 20, 1921) (reporting testimony of Police Captain Blaine).

59. *DuBois Says North Blacks Right: On the Great Deep,* BLACK DISPATCH 1 (September 5, 1919) (quoting THE OUTLOOK).

60. Smitherman, *supra* note 16.

61. Defendant's Brief, *supra* note 17, at 79–80. John Smitherman was arrested for inciting riot. *See Smitherman, Held for Inciting Riot, Released on Bond,* TULSA TRIBUNE 2 (July 11, 1921). The indictments returned against Greenwood residents—many of whom fled Tulsa after the riot—is an example of the ways that legal mechanisms were used to drive out even more Tulsa blacks. *See 38 Indicted in Race Riot Probe,* TULSA WORLD 2 (June 19, 1921) (reporting that first indictments returned by the grand jury were against blacks and that most had fled the city). *See also Bye, Bye Tulsa Is Song of Many Blacks Without Jobs Here,* TULSA TRIBUNE 2 (June 11, 1921).

62. Defendant's Brief, *supra* note 14, at 80.

63. *See, e.g.,* Muskogee Phoenix (June 2, 1921) (discussing rumor of ammunition).

64. Interview with Major Frank Van Voorhis, by Effie S. Jackson (October 25, 1937), available at Oklahoma Historical Society. Major Van Voorhis concluded that "There is no doubt but what some factions had been preparing for a revolt of some kind, but the mass of negroes were innocent victims."

65. Mary Jones Parrish, Events of the Tulsa Disaster 19 (circa 1921) (reprinted 1998).

66. *New Battle Now in Progress,* Tulsa World 1 (June 1, 1921) (2nd edition). *See Whites Advancing into 'Little Africa'; Negro Death List is About 15,* Tulsa World 1 (June 1, 1921); *Race War Rages for Hours After Outbreak at Courthouse: Troops and Armed Men Patroling Streets,* Tulsa World 1 (June 1, 1921) (subheading: "Negroes Finally Driven into 'Little Africa'").

67. *Autos Circle Slowly About Negro Section in Indian War Style,* St. Louis Post-Dispatch 1 (June 1, 1921).

68. *See, e.g., Mob Held Back by Major Daley for Two Hours,* Tulsa Tribune 7 (June 5, 1921). Major Daley also told how the volunteer guard were almost converted into members of the mob at the train tracks that evening. Indeed, had he not been there, it is likely that the group would have started shooting into Greenwood.

On the evening the riot started, a few more police officers might have been able to keep whites away from Greenwood. But as Major Daley of the National Guard told the Tulsa Tribune, when he called for reinforcements from the Police Department, he found that "everyone was out in the hills or in the other parts of town protecting people or conveying the negroes into camp." *Mob Held Back by Major Daley for Two Hours,* Tulsa Tribune 7 (June 5, 1921).

69. Frank Van Voorhis, *Detailed Report of Negro Uprising for Service Company, 3d Inf. Okla. Nat'l Guard* (July 30, 1921).

70. John W. McCuen, *Duty Performed by Company 3d Inf. Okla. National Guard at Negro Uprising May 31st 1921* (undated), Oklahoma State Archives. *See also Rooney Explains Guard Operation,* Tulsa World 18 (June 4, 1921).

71. Smitherman, *supra* note 16.

72. Defendant's Brief, *supra* note 14, at 95.

73. *Cf. 5000 Negroes Held in Fairgrounds Camp,* Tulsa World 2 (June 2, 1921) ("The heaviest fighting took place between midnight and 6 o'clock Wednesday morning. Mobs of white men invaded Little Africa, intent upon killing every Negro in sight. Several pitched battles ensued in which casualties occurred on both sides").

74. Defendant's Brief, *supra* note 14, at 83.

75. *Id.*

76. *Id.* at 84.

77. *See* Parrish, *supra* note 65.

78. *Ex-Police Bears Plots of Tulsans: Officer of Law Tells Who Ordered Airplanes to Destroy Homes,* CHICAGO DEFENDER 1 (October 25, 1921). *See also Attorney Scott Digs Up Inside Information on Tulsa Riot,* BLACK DISPATCH 1 (October 20, 1921).

79. *See Red Cross to Spend Months Aiding Blacks,* TULSA TRIBUNE 6 (June 4, 1921) ("We wuz all asleep when they beginst to shootin' an' de airplanes to swoop down an' den Sam went out to get de calf," one Negro woman was explaining to a group of interested listeners. "I yells to Sam, sez I 'Sam yo all let that calf alone and come on heah wide me.' 'Sam come an' we run fo' ouah lives'"); *Ex-Police Bears Plots of Tulsans: Officer of Law Tells Who Ordered Airplanes to Destroy Homes,* CHICAGO DEFENDER 1 (October 25, 1921) (reporting allegations of former Tulsa police officer that city officials plotted attacks on Greenwood using airplanes, and then "the airplanes darted out from hangars and hovered over the district dropping nitroglycerin on buildings, setting them afire"); *From Midnight to Dawn: The Story of What Can Happen under the Stars and Stripes,* BLACK DISPATCH 8 (June 10, 1921) (reporting accounts of airplanes shooting at Greenwood residents). The BLACK DISPATCH printed one report from W.I. Brown, a porter on a train that carried the National Guard troops from Oklahoma City to Tulsa on the morning of the riot:

> Airplanes were circling all over Greenwood. We stopped our cars north of the Katy depot, going towards Sand Springs. The heavens were lighten up as plain as day from the many fires over the Negro section. I could see from my car window that two air planes were doing most of the work. They would every few seconds drop something and every time they did there was a loud explosion and the sky would be filled with flying debris.

Loot, Arson, Murder: Four Million Dollar Lost, BLACK DISPATCH 1 (June 10, 1921). *See also False Rumor Starts Second Exodus,* BLACK DISPATCH 1 (July 8, 1921) ("The body of Ed Lockhart, a well known Negro, was quite recently found about nine miles from the city. The Negroes allege that he was shot from one of the airplanes, which they charge chased innocent Negroes many miles into the countryside"); *Ask Federal Investigation of Use of Air Planes and Machine Guns in Tulsa Riot,* BLACK DISPATCH 1 (August 26, 1921) ("I am also informed that no attempt has been made to apprehend the persons using aeroplanes, from which the defenseless citizens allege high power rifles were fired and turpentine bombs exploded"). At other times, machine guns might protect black communities. *See Machine Gun Protects N.C. Prisoners,* TULSA STAR 1 (July 25, 1920).

80. *See Air Observers Watched Blacks for the Police,* TULSA TRIBUNE 3 (June 2, 1921). *See also* B.F. Ingraham, *In Defense of Officers,* TULSA WORLD 4 (June 9, 1921) ("But when the airships began to hum, I again went to the main part of the city and saw police out bending every effort to take care of our city").

81. *See Trip by Airplane Disproves Rumor,* TULSA WORLD 7 (June 7, 1921) ("Innumerable and persistent rumors of further threatened uprisings by negroes were set at rest Monday morning when Police Captain George H. Blaine made a scouting trip by airplane to virtually all of the negro settlements in this section of the state, and to all white towns where the negro population is heavy"); *The Disinterested Spectator,* TULSA TRIBUNE 16 (June 7, 1921). The most authoritative investigation of airplanes concludes that it is impossible to tell what role airplanes served. *See* Richard S. Warner, Airplanes and the Riot, in *The Tulsa Race Riot: A Scientific, Historical and Legal Analysis* 144–54 (John Hope Franklin and Scott Ellsworth, eds. 2000).

82. *See A Party Down at the Square,* in Ralph Ellison, FLYING HOME 3 (John F. Callahan, ed., 1996); *id.* at 147.

83. *See On Initiation Rites and Power,* in Ralph Ellison, THE COLLECTED ESSAYS OF RALPH ELLISON 520, 522 (John Callahan, ed., 1995).

84. The machine entered the garden to destroy it. *Cf.* Leo Marx, THE MACHINE IN THE GARDEN: TECHNOLOGY AND THE PASTORAL IDEAL IN AMERICA (1964).

85. Parrish, *supra* note 65, at 19–20.

86. *Id.* at 20–21.

87. The next morning he "went back down home" and saw that Greenwood was burned down. *See* Defendant's Brief, *supra* note 14, at 83–84. The sisters who lived through the riot, Julia and Alverta Duff, present a similarly harrowing account of the terror. See Paul Lee, *The Day Greenwood Burned,* ESSENCE 106 (May 2001) (reprinting and interpreting a Letter written by the sisters shortly after the riot).

88. McCuen, *supra* note 70, at 2.

89. *Boy Started Fire to Avenge Mother Shot by Negroes,* MUSKOGEE PHOENIX 1, 5 (June 2, 1921).

90. *Citizens Uphold Officers' Story,* TULSA WORLD 1, 3 (July 21, 1921).

91. *See* Van Voorhis Report, *supra* note 69, at 3 (reporting the "capture" of "negro prisoners"). *Cf.* Defendant's Brief. *supra* note 14, at 160 (reporting "soldiers' involvement in arresting Greenwood residents"). *Boy Started Fire to Avenge Mother Shot by Negroes,* MUSKOGEE PHOENIX 1, 5 (June 2, 1921). *See also id.* at 1 ("As the white men who searched the houses for arms

and warned the people left[,] the others, the riff-raff, came along and set them afire") (quoting white woman, Mrs. A. Germine, who witnessed the riot).

92. *Id.* See also *Desolate Scene in Wake of Riot,* MUSKOGEE PHOENIX 2 (June 2, 1921) ("The police, too, after they got on the job, had no trouble with the white men and they too went from one negro house to another ahead of the flames, demanding the surrender of the negro men. Several were shot down by the officers when they refused to surrender but opened fire from windows and behind barricades upon the officers").

93. There were fears, for example, that blacks were coming from Muskogee to reinforce the Greenwood residents: "In response to a call from Muskogee, indicating several hundred negroes were on their way to the city to assist Tulsa Negroes should fighting continue, a machine gun squad loaded on a truck, went east of the city with orders to stop at all hazards these armed men." *Race War Rages for Hours After Outbreak at Courthouse; Troops and Armed Men Patrolling Streets,* TULSA WORLD 1 (June 1, 1921).

94. *Id. See also* C.W. Daley Information on Activities During Negro Uprising. May 31, 1921 (July 6, 1921), Oklahoma State Archives ("Upon receiving information that large bodies of negroes were coming from Sand Springs, Muskogee and Mohawk, both by train and automobile. [sic] This information was imparted to the auto patrols with instructions to cover the roads which the negroes might come in on. At this point we received information that a train load was coming from Muskogee, so Col. Rooney and myself jumped into a car, assembled a company of Legion men of about 100 from among the patrols who were operating over the city, and placed them in charge of Mr. Kinney, a member of the American Legion, and directed him to bring men to the depot, which was done in a very soldierly and orderly manner. Instructions were given that the men form a line on both sides of the track with instructions to allow no negroes to unload but to hold them in the train by keeping them covered. The train proved to be a freight train and no one was on it but regular train crew").

95. *See* Van Voorhis Report, *supra* note 69. The white men were firing from a distance and it is not certain that the Guard could have arrested the white shooters. But the contrast illustrates the difference in approach toward whites and blacks.

96. Smitherman, *supra* note 16.

97. Defendant's Brief, *supra* note 14, at 118–19.

98. *Id.* at 50.

99. Gurley Deposition, Stradford Suit, *supra* note 2, at 90.

100. Defendant's Brief, *supra* note 14, at 107.

101. Gurley Deposition, Stradford Suit, *supra* note 2, at 105–6.

102. Similarly, Susie Williams, who lived in Greenwood at the time of the

riot, saw two groups of men set fire to her house. *See id.* at 65–66. Williams did not mention whether the men were wearing badges or not. Her testimony shows the organized nature of the burning, not who did the burning.

103. Defendant's Brief, *supra* note 14, at 114.

104. Plaintiff's Brief, *supra* note 13, at 55.

105. *Id.* at 61.

106. McCullough Deposition, Stradford Suit, *supra* note 2, at 24.

107. McCullough Deposition, Stradford Suit, *supra* note 2, at 25.

108. *Id.* at 26.

109. Smitherman, *supra* note 16.

110. *See The Disgrace of Tulsa*, TULSA WORLD 4 (June 2, 1921).

111. *Whites Advancing into "Little Africa"; Negro Death List is About 15*, TULSA WORLD 1 (June 1, 1921) (2nd edition) ("One negro was dragged behind an automobile with a rope about his neck, through the business district").

112. Testimony of John A. Oliphant, at 2, Attorney General's Civil Case Files, RG 1–2, A-G Case No. 1062, Box 25 (Oklahoma State Archives).

113. *Id.* at 6. Oliphant tried to dissuade them from burning. "This last crowd made an agreement that they would not burn that property [across the street from my property] because I thought it would burn mine too and I promised that if they wouldn't, . . . I would see that no negroes ever lived in that row of houses any more." *Verdict Returned After Six Hours of Deliberation*, TULSA WORLD 1 (July 23, 1921). I would like to thank Eli Hellman for sharing his research on Gusfason's trial. *Instruction is Denied by Court*, TULSA WORLD 1, 2 (July 16, 1921).

114. *See* Oliphant Testimony, Attorney General Files, at 4–5 A-G Case No. 1062, Oklahoma State Archives.

115. *Id.* at 7.

116. *Id.*

117. *Id.* at 8–9.

118. *Id.* at 6–7.

119. *Witness Says Cop Urges Him to Kill Black*, TULSA TRIBUNE 1 (July 15, 1921) ("C.O. McEnturff, a Frisco fireman, formerly on the police force, told the jury he saw a man with a special officer's badge taking silk shirts out a negro residence his companions were setting on fire.").

120. B. F. Williams Deposition, Stradford Suit, *supra* note 2, at 10–11.

121. *Whites Advancing into "Little Africa;" Negro Death List is About 15*, TULSA WORLD 1 (June 1, 1921) (probably 3rd edition).

122. *See* Walter F. White, *The Eruption of Tulsa*, THE NATION 909, 910 (June 29, 1921); *Boy Started Fire to Avenge Mother Shot by Negroes*, MUSKOGEE PHOENIX 1 (June 2, 1921).

123. Oliphant Testimony, *supra* note 114, at 6. *See also* Prentice, *supra*

note 32, at 155 (portraying the Guard as eating a leisurely breakfast before entering Greenwood). Prentice appears to be a somewhat fictional account of the riot, so the "breakfast story" is subject to some question.

124. The records for the out-of-town units of the Guard are, unfortunately, missing. Robert Norris, an expert on the National Guard, speculates that the Guard went directly to the police station to assess the riot. He believes it would not make sense to go immediately to Greenwood.

125. McCuen, *supra* note 70, at 2. *See also First Detailed Story of How Riot Started*, St. Louis Post-Dispatch 21 (June 3, 1921) ("Last night 1000 or more negroes were being cared for in concentration camps").

126. Gustafson Deposition, Stradford Suit, *supra* note 2, at 29.

127. *Id.* at 33.

128. 1 Charles F. Barrett, *Oklahoma After Fifty Years: A History of the Sooner State and It's People, 1889–1941* 209 (1941).

129. Parrish, *supra* note 65, at 31.

130. "Two More Negroes Dead, Boosts Total Death Toll to 34," Tulsa Tribune 5 (June 7, 1921).

131. *See* Sapulpa Herald 1 (June 2, 1921). *See* Clyde Snow, *Confirmed Deaths in the Tulsa Race Riot of 1921: A Preliminary Report*, in The Tulsa Race Riot, *supra* note 81, at 155–96.

132. *See* B.F. Williams Deposition, Stradford Suit, *supra* note 2, at 10 ("We drove down the west side of the street along with western border of the burned district and saw a truck load of corpses come out covered with quilts; I should say about six. The Militia had charge of the truck and it appeared to be about six people covered with quilts or some kind of covering like that"). Williams testified that he also saw "some people chasing a nigger across the top of that hill at quite a distance, and we couldn't tell whether they were trying to catch him or what, but they were firing at the time." *Id.*

133. *See, e.g., Police Turn Criminals, Small Tulsa Death List*, Chicago Defender 3 (June 11, 1921) (estimating 150 deaths); '*A Bunch of Burglars*': *Soldier's Subdue Big Race Riot*, Chicago Defender 1 (June 2, 1921) (estimating seventy-seven deaths); Snow, *supra* note 130, at 158.

134. Maurice Willows, Report in Bob Hower, Angels of Mercy; 1921 Tulsa Race Riot and The American Red Cross 161, 164 (1993).

135. *Negroes Gladly Accept Guards*, Tulsa World 3 (June 2, 1921).

136. *Id.* The dialect stories, which were run more frequently in the Tribune than the World, are suspect. They often accompany stories with thinly veiled racist messages. *See, e.g., Negro Finds $600 in Melted Gold in Ruins of His Home*, Tulsa Tribune 3 (June 2, 1921); *Red Cross to Spend Months Aiding Blacks*, Tulsa Tribune 6 (June 4, 1921) (reporting alleged statements of Greenwood resident) ("De good Lawd sho' has sent terrible punishment

on us niggahs! I sho hopes dey kills dem bad niggahs dat is responsible fo' dis misery").

137. *Negro Office is Heavy Loser in Race Riots*, TULSA TRIBUNE 3 (June 2, 1921).

138. 231 P. at 930. *See also id.* at 928–29. ("A number of witnesses testified that these groups of white men, many of them wearing police badges and badges indicating that they were deputy sheriffs, after removing the negroes from buildings, went inside the buildings and, after they left, fires broke out inside the buildings.")

139. Smitherman, *supra* note 16.

140. A.J. Smitherman, *How Tulsa Has Treated the Negroes Since the Riot*, BOSTON HERALD 6D (January 15, 1922).

Chapter 3

1. BLACK DISPATCH 5 (December 8, 1921).

2. *Civilization in Oklahoma: Jake Brooks*, BLACK DISPATCH (January 26, 1921) (reprinting picture of lynching victim).

3. *America's Pastime—Lynching!*, TULSA STAR 1 (July 31, 1920). Members of the mob who witnessed a white man's lynching near Tulsa in 1920 claimed pieces of rope and coat buttons as souvenirs. Then someone took a shoelace and another witness, finding "there wasn't anything left," took a shoe. He brought the shoe back to town and showed it to guests at the rooming house where he was staying, then he left it in lobby. He testified, "I didn't get it as a keepsake. I just got it because everybody else was getting them." Testimony of Gordon Bowman, in Attorney General's Investigation of Roy Belton Lynching, *supra* note 24, at 98. See also Testimony of John Woolley, in *id.* at 146 (testifying about men collecting souvenirs).

4. TOPEKA PLAINDEALER, quoted in 3 The Crisis 60 (December 1911), quoted in turn in Leon F. Litwack, TROUBLE IN MIND: BLACK SOUTHERNERS IN THE AGE OF JIM CROW 287 (1998).

5. See Brent Staples, *On the Perils of Growing Comfortable with Evil*, NEW YORK TIMES (March 16, 2000) (discussing problems of a recent exhibit of lynching photographs at the New York Historical Society); Litwack, *supra* note 6, at 290–92.

Chapter 4

1. *Black Agitators Blamed for Riot*, TULSA WORLD 1 (June 6, 1921). *See also Agitators were cause of riots: Propaganda Responsible for Ill Feeling Among Races Mouzon Says*, TULSA WORLD 2 (June 3, 1921).

2. *The Disgrace of Tulsa*, TULSA WORLD 2 (June 2, 1921).

3. *The State in Action*, TULSA TRIBUNE 1 (June 2, 1921).

4. *Black Agitators Blamed for Riot*, TULSA WORLD 1 (June 6, 1921)

5. J.B.A. Robertson to D.P. Bailey, June 7, 1921, Governor's Papers, Oklahoma State Archives.

6. *Propaganda of Negroes is Blamed*, TULSA TRIBUNE 1 (June 18, 1921). Freehling continued:

So, with the continued tirade against the white race launched by negro publications throughout this nation the negro has come to look upon the white man as his oppressor. And, so, they have in a large way become organized since the war, and in this organization there lies a force that is liable to start trouble any time.

7. *It Must be Stopped*, TULSA TRIBUNE 4 (June 11, 1921). The incendiary stuff the TRIBUNE referred to was a report from the NEW YORK TIMES that the president of the Liberal League of Negro Americans told a rally in Harlem that blacks should arm themselves and that no one "should be surprised if we see three splendid race riots by next September." *Id.*

8. *Police Say They Knew of 'War' Plans*, TULSA TRIBUNE 1 (June 3, 1921); *Mayor Warned of Uprising Negro Avers*, TULSA TRIBUNE 1 (June 6, 1921). *See also Warning Against Further Trouble*, TULSA WORLD 1, 11 (June 4, 1921) ("Chief Gustafson and I have made several trips into 'Little Africa' and on those occasions told the negroes that if there ever was a uprising we would hold them responsible. We told them to talk down the possibility of a race riot") (Mayor T.D. Evans). *See also White Dead are Forgotten, Rev. Cooke Charges*, TULSA TRIBUNE 11 (June 9, 1921) (alleging that whites killed in the riot were instrumental in putting down a negro uprising). Even after the riot, Greenwood residents were viewed with suspicion, as people ready to revolt. *See Warning Against Further Trouble*, TULSA WORLD 1 (June 4, 1921) ("Negroes held in detention camps have been turned loose indiscriminately. There is a general feeling in the city that Tulsa is no safer tonight than it was Tuesday night. Without proper police protection, with the negroes resentful over the loss of their property, there is an increasingly apprehensive feeling that something else is going to happen").

9. *It Must be Stopped*, TULSA TRIBUNE 4 (June 11, 1921).

10. *Military Control is Ended at Tulsa*, NEW YORK TIMES 1 (June 4, 1921) (referring to African Blood Brotherhood); *Denies Negroes Started Tulsa Riot; Head of Brotherhood Defends the Purpose of the Organization*, NEW YORK TIMES 21 (June 5, 1921). *See also Tulsa and the African Blood Brotherhood*, THE CRUSADER (July 1921) (discussing involvement of the African Blood Brotherhood in the Tulsa riot); *Negroes Blamed for Race Riots*, TULSA WORLD 2 (June 14, 1921). At least it appears to urban mythology!

11. *Public Welfare Board Vacated by Commission*, TULSA TRIBUNE 2 (June 14, 1921) ("Let the blame for this negro uprising lie right where it

belongs—on those armed negroes and their followers who started this trouble and who instigated it and any who seek to put half the blame on the white people are wrong and should be told so in no uncertain terms"). Evans mentioned that armed Greenwood residents had twice before come to the white section of Tulsa "and made certain demands under threat of force." He proudly proclaimed that "we wager that trip number two will not take place soon." *Id.*

12. *Id.*

13. But just for good measure, Evans proposed a law prohibiting blacks from owning guns. *Id. See also Negroes Denied Arms*, TULSA WORLD 5 (June 2, 1921) ("More than a hundred negroes visited various hardware stores here today in an effect to purchase firearms and ammunition. . . . Many of the negroes were questioned as to what they wanted to do with the ammunition and some said they wanted to go to Tulsa to take part in the race riot there"); *Weapons are being seized by officials; all sales of guns stopped at Beggs following Negro Gathering*, TULSA TRIBUNE 7 (June 21, 1921) (reporting that blacks were not permitted to purchase guns at Beggs, Oklahoma); *Armed Negro Band Routed Near Beggs*, TULSA TRIBUNE 5 (June 20, 1920).

14. *See* Richard Lloyd Jones, *Powder of Race Hate Lighted by Spark of Crime*, CHICAGO TRIBUNE 2 (June 2, 1921).

15. *Bad Niggers!* TULSA WORLD 4 (June 4, 1921).

16. *Niles Blames Lawlessness for Race War*, TULSA TRIBUNE 4 (June 2, 1921) ("A bad psychological condition occasioned by a spirit of unrest and some unemployment dovetailed into the lawlessness which grew like a snowball and rapidly got beyond control of officials. The situation was quickly taken advantage of by some of the lawless element among the whites").

17. *Martial Law*, TULSA WORLD 4 (June 3, 1921).

18. *The Tulsa Race War*, DAILY OKLAHOMAN 4 (June 2, 1921). Thanks to Lee Rezabek for showing me this editorial.

19. *Id.*

20. *Citizens of Tulsa Tell of Conditions There Preceding the Race Riot*, ST. LOUIS POST-DISPATCH part II, 1 (June 5, 1921).

21. *To Rebuild Homes for Negro Owners and Probe Blame*, MUSKOGEE PHOENIX (June 3, 1921). The TULSA WORLD drew upon similar sentiments to urge kindness to Greenwood. Some wanted to "drive them out forever." But the WORLD asked:

To where? In calm reason let that question be answered. Helpless women and babes were roaming the woodlands round about Tulsa for thirty-six hours. Surrounding towns had reared a barrier of armed guards to keep them out. They were pariahs upon the face of the earth. They had been driven out, and they had nowhere to go.

See An Appeal to Reason, TULSA WORLD 4 (June 3, 1921).

22. *Raid "Choc" Joints*, TULSA TRIBUNE 1 (June 8, 1921).

23. *Jazz, the Evil Spirit of Music, Incites Hysteria*, TULSA WORLD (May 22, 1921). I would like to thank Randy Krehbiel for providing me with this reference.

24. *Jazz Becoming Anthem of U.S., Musician Says*, TULSA WORLD (May 28, 1922). *See also Jazz Burglars Get Busy*, TULSA WORLD 9 (June 7, 1921) ("[B]urglars turned on the lights, started jazz music on the phonograph to cover their activities and ransacked the place"). The WORLD sometimes admitted that jazz had some positive potential. Shortly after the riot, an article asked, *Have You Any Jazz in Your Make Up?* TULSA WORLD 6 (July 10, 1921). Along with music, movies also threatened disorder. *See Mayor Warned of Uprising Negro Avers*, TULSA WORLD 1 (June 6, 1921) ("The wide-open Sunday is then condemned as a commercial movement which should be counteracted by the churches. The crime films and lurid sex stories of the motion picture houses are denounced and the tendency of motion pictures to corrupt the morals of the younger generation is openly charged"). *See also Movies Rapped as Breeders of Immorality*, TULSA TRIBUNE 2 (July 2, 1921) ("The movie picture show is the greatest feeder of wickedness that exists in the United States today. . . . The only thing worse than the modern picture show is the dance. It is the hotbed of lust, and the majority of fallen girls of this country fell as the direct result of the dance. . . . [T]here is no use to try to correct these things with a white-washed set of officials who will put things over in spite of evidence") (statements of evangelist preaching in Tulsa). *See also Dreary Days! Dances Dull but Decent*, TULSA TRIBUNE 4 (April 26, 1921).

Greenwood residents thought differently, of course. In the last surviving issue of the TULSA STAR was an article entitled *"Everybody Loves Jazz." See*, TULSA STAR (January 21, 1921) ("It is a well recognized fact that everybody is delighted with the new syncopated melodies which are now so popular throughout the country and called 'jazz'"). *See also Jazz Blues and Fickle Women*, BLACK DISPATCH 1 (April 6, 1922) (reporting popularity of jazz).

Ralph Ellison recalled in the early 1960s the importance of the Blue Devils. *See* Interview with Richard G. Stern, *That Same Pain, That Same Pleasure*, in THE COLLECTED ESSAYS OF RALPH ELLISON 63, 67 (John F. Callahan, ed., 1995). For a sampling of the music of the Oklahoma City Blue Devils, which was heard in Tulsa about the time of the riot, visit: *http://www.redhotjazz.com/bluedevils.html*. For some jazz inspired by Tulsa, listen to "Tulsa Blues," available at: http://www.redhotjazz.com/bmkc.html.

25. *In Work There is Salvation*, TULSA WORLD 4 (June 5, 1921).

26. *Red Cross to Spend Months Aiding Blacks*, TULSA TRIBUNE 6 (June 4, 1921). There were also occasional references to superstition. *See Still is*

Located through a Guard, TULSA WORLD 8 (June 3, 1921) ("The cemetery nearby evidently had been used to frighten curious negroes away").

27. *Judge Biddison's Instructions to Grand Jury*, TULSA TRIBUNE 1 (June 9, 1921).

28. *It Must be Stopped*, TULSA TRIBUNE 4 (June 11, 1921). What was the whitewash the TRIBUNE feared? That the Tulsa police had been negligent in policing Greenwood: "It appears to be reasonably well established that certain lawless negroes had for some time been collecting arms and ammunition. It is also well established that lawlessness was allowed to run unarrested in the old 'Niggertown.'" *Id. See also Prison for Riot Chiefs, Jury Order*, TULSA TRIBUNE (June 5, 1921) (reporting that Judge Biddison did not expect the grand jury to be a whitewash).

29. *Cf.* Ralph Ellison, INVISIBLE MAN 202 (1952) ("White! It's the purest white that can be found. Nobody makes a paint any whiter. That batch right here is heading for a national monument"); *White Justice Likened Unto White Sepulchers*, BLACK DISPATCH 4 (June 4, 1920) ("[H]e does not deny, in fact he admits that he stood out with his fellow citizens and helped protect his humble cottage when that second murderous crowd of 5000 snarling hounds of perdition swooped down upon the Negro District. He did what any negro with a spark of manhood in his body would try to do and any Judge in America who would permit such a verdict in his court, against a citizen is making a shambles of justice. . . . Truly as saith the Book of Books, such a court and such a Judge is 'Likened unto white sepulchers, which while beautiful on the outside are full of dead men's bones and all uncleanness'"); *Annanias Uses his Whitewash*, BLACK DISPATCH 4 (September 24, 1920) ("It is impossible, at this date, to determine just what the outcome will be in this now, notorious lynch case, but if whitewash counts for ought, there is going to be a clean bill of health given to the rankest criminals who ever dodged a jail door"). Or, as an editorial in the last surviving issue of the TULSA STAR noted: "We have become slaves to the white color as applied to human beings. All kinds of powders, paints and false skins are made to create white impressions. We have discarded all other colors for the human family. Everybody must be white to be popular. And why?" *Colored Dolls, Why Not?*, TULSA STAR (January 21, 1921) (reprinting editorial from PITTSBURGH COURIER).

30. *In Name Only*, BLACK DISPATCH 4 (July 8, 1921) ("We observe that the only really definite statement made in the whole [grand jury] report is that the NEGRO IS TO BLAME, a conclusion they seemed to have arrived at through evidence unsupported by any facts which they present").

31. *Grand Jury Blames Negroes for Inciting Race Rioting; Whites Clearly Exonerated*, TULSA WORLD 1, 8 (June 26, 1921).

32. *Id.*

33. *Id.*

34. Similar statements appeared elsewhere. In debate over antilynching legislation in Congress in January 1922, one representative blamed lynchings on blacks who crossed "the social dead line":

> Some gentlemen present may feel that they are doing a wonderful thing for the entire colored race, but believe me when I tell you that you are only playing to some of the so-called "big Negroes" of the North, who are, in my opinion, the worst enemies that the mass of the colored people have. The Negro of the South, and that is where the Negroes live, knows that the southern white man understands him and wants to treat him right if he himself will keep his place and behave. But while the southern white man will treat the colored people right, he will never change the social dead line, well established and well understood, and whenever the Negro oversteps the white man's dead line he knows, and he is so informed by the right-thinking members of his own race, that he thereby takes his life in his own hands.

62 Congressional Record 1375 (January 18, 1922) (Representative Jeffers).

35. *See Lawlessness Is Rapped in Final Report*, Tulsa Tribune 1 (June 26, 1921) ("The props were knocked from under the recent municipal white-wash court of inquiry into the conduct of the police department in the final report of the race riot grand jury. . . . Booze joints and houses of prostitution have operated in complete and open defiance of the police, while lawless whites have been allowed to roam the city unmolested by city officers, the report shows"). In reviewing a claim that children were white and could attend a white school, the Oklahoma Supreme Court emphasized the importance of the issue by observing that it is "a well-known fact that white persons and negroes do not associate with each other on terms of social equality." *Cole v. District Board of School District No. 29*, McIntosh County, 123 P. 426 (1912).

Reports of the sale of alcohol and drug dealing in Greenwood were frequent. *See, e.g., Choc Joint First to Open in Burned District, He Says*, Tulsa World 5 (June 3, 1921) ("The first negro establishment to open yesterday was a 'choc' joint and notorious place where liquor was sold and where men and women of questionable character congregated"); *"Dope" Center Gone: Riot Fire Destroyed Rendevous for Drug Peddlers that was Raided a Few Weeks Ago*, Tulsa World 21A (June 5, 1921); *Drug War Goes on as Addicts Get Long Terms*, Tulsa Tribune 2 (June 19, 1921) ("Joe Fornan, confessed addict, who said he was a Cherokee Indian, declared he bought his morphine for a dollar from a negro at the corner of Boston and Archer street").

36. *Grand Jury Blames Negroes for Inciting Race Rioting, supra* note 31, at 8. In reviewing a claim that children were white and could attend a white school, the Oklahoma Supreme Court emphasized the importance of the issue by observing that it is "a well-known fact that white persons and negroes do not associate with each other on terms of social equality." *Cole v. District Board of School District No. 29*, McIntosh County, 123 P. 426 (1912).

37. *See* S.P. Freehling to James E. Markham (November 2, 1921) (discussing indictments and mentioning that nearly 100 were returned); *Grand Jury Gives Report to Courts*, TULSA WORLD 2 (June 16, 1921) (reporting return of more than fifty indictments against blacks and whites).

38. *See Bring Stradford Back for Trial*, TULSA WORLD 3 (June 7, 1921); A.J. Smitherman file, Series A, reel 3, "Discrimination in the Criminal Justice System," NAACP Papers, Library of Congress (discussing Oklahoma's attempt to extradite Smitherman). Smitherman's concern for his safety increased after the BOSTON HERALD published his home address with an article he wrote about the riot (*How Tulsa Has Treated the Negroes Since the Riot*, BOSTON HERALD D6 [January 15, 1922]). *See also* Charles T. Smith file, Series A, reel 3, NAACP Papers, Library of Congress (discussing attempt to extradite Smithie from Minnesota). The Minnesota governor deferred Oklahoma's extradition request pending the outcome of the trials of other black men accused of inciting rioting. *See* James Markham to William F. Seaver (December 20, 1921), in *id.* The other trials never took place and the matter ended with no extradition. *See In re Robinson et al.*, case 2227, Tulsa County Court (1921) (criminal cases against William Robinson and other black men not prosecuted).

On Gustafson's trial, see *Verdict Returned After Six Hours of Deliberation*, TRIBUNE WORLD 1 (July 23, 1921). I would like to thank Eli Hellman for sharing his research on Gustafson's trial with me.

39. *See Grand Jury Blames Negroes for Race Rioting; Whites Clearly Exonerated*, TULSA WORLD 1, 8 (June 26, 1921).

40. 62 CONGRESSIONAL RECORD 1429 (January 19, 1922) (describing provisions of Dyer's bill); *id.* at 1292–93 (analyzing each section of bill); *id.* at 1744–45 (amended bill). *See also* Claudine Ferrell, NIGHTMARE AND DREAM: ANTILYNCHING LEGISLATION IN CONGRESS, 1917–1922 (1986); Amii Larkin Barnard, *The Application of Critical Race Feminism to the Antilynching Movement: Black Women's Fight Against Race and Gender Ideology, 1892–1920*, UCLA WOMEN'S LAW JOURNAL 1 (1993); Emma Coleman Jordan, *Crossing the River of Blood Between Us: Lynching, Violence, Beauty, and The Paradox of Feminist History*, 3 JOURNAL OF GENDER, RACE AND JUSTICE 545 (2000); Barbara Holden-Smith, *Lynching, Federalism, and the Intersection of Race and Gender in The Progressive Era*, 8 YALE

As early as 1890, Oklahoma law mandated separate schools for black and white students. Initially, the legislature provided that the race of the majority of the voters in each county would define the race of the majority school.[83] Then, in 1913, as it became apparent that there might be a few counties in which blacks were the majority race—and hence would be entitled to attend the majority school—the law was changed to provide that the superintendent of schools in each county could define which race would go to the majority school and which to the separate school.[84] That had important implications, because, despite the legislature's statement that the majority and separate schools should be equal, the majority school had superior facilities.

When local authorities denied sufficient funding to maintain equal facilities in the black and white schools, the Oklahoma Supreme Court refused to compel taxation to provide for equal facilities.[85] The *Black Dispatch* saw through the schemes of the legislature to shift funding away from black schools, and it spoke of the "rotten education law" in January 1921.[86]

Then there was housing. In 1916, the Tulsa City Council passed an ordinance that prohibited anyone from purchasing a house on a block if 75 percent of the residents on the block were of a different race. Blacks could live on a majority white block, however, if they were employed at least five days a week as domestic servants at property on that block.[87]

The Tulsa ordinance was based on a Louisville one, which had been upheld by the Kentucky Supreme Court.[88] The court there spoke of the "gravity of the race problem as it exists in our country today," and the government's right, as a consequence of that problem, to regulate property.[89] Expediency, as determined by judges and city councils, was at the center of the movement for housing segregation. But constitutional rights are not always judged by expediency. The act aroused "indignation" in the Greenwood community and some vowed to challenge the act in court.[90] The year after Tulsa passed its ordinance, the United States Supreme Court struck down zoning ordinances that segregated on the basis of race.[91]

Oklahoma City passed a segregation ordinance in the fall of 1918, *after* the Supreme Court's decision.[92] The city commissioners, who knowingly violated the law, modeled illegal behavior.[93] The city attorney then seemed to encourage further violence. When someone dyna-

JOURNAL OF LAW AND FEMINISM 31 (1996); George C. Rable, *The South and the Politics of Antilynching Legislation, 1920–1940*, 51 J. SOUTH. HIST. 201–20 (1985); Beth Crabb, *May 1930: White Man's Justice for a Black Man's Crime*, 75 J. NEGRO HIST. 29–40 (1990).

41. 62 CONGRESSIONAL RECORD (67th Congress, 1st Sess.) at 1277 (January 17, 1922) (Representative Burton). *See also id.* at 1278–81 (reprinting editorials from newspapers, including southern newspapers, about the importance of upholding the law).

42. *Id.* at 1302.

43. *Id.* at 1303 (quoted by Representative Yates).

44. The community in which a lynching occurs is more deeply injured than the individual who is its victim, even though he be burned by the torch. After all, his tortures are necessarily brief, soon ending in death. . . . But the men who perpetrated the lynching can never again be the same law-abiding loyal citizens they were before taking a human life by such barbarous methods. Nor can the community which permits it ever pass from out the dark shadow of it. Never again can it be felt sure that there the law will be under restraint. When the castle walls that surround the citadel of the law are broken down in one direction by armed bands to avenge in lawless fashion one offender against the law, the breach remains after the vengeance has been effected.

Id. at 1710 (Representative Cockran).

45. *Id.* at 1311 ("It will set up the standard of the law to be revered and worshiped by all who live under its folds"). *See also id.* at 1296 ("It is generally conceded that our lack of respect for law and order constitutes the greatest danger existing in our community today").

46. 62 CONGRESSIONAL RECORD 1371 (January 18, 1922).

47. *Id.* at 1713 (Representative Lowery).

48. *Id.* at 1299.

49. 62 CONGRESSIONAL RECORD 1428 (Representative Rankin of Mississippi) (January 19, 1922). Similarly, Representative Hatton Sumners of Texas cited the grand jury report laying blame for riots on race agitators and contact between blacks and whites. *See* CONGRESSIONAL RECORD 1783, 1786 (January 26, 1922).

50. *Oklahoma's Rotten Educational Law*, BLACK DISPATCH 4 (January 21, 1921). *See also The Negro Before the Law*, BLACK DISPATCH (January 28, 1921) (reprinting editorial from SAVANNAH TRIBUNE, which began, "There can be little inducement nowadays for Negro people to have confidence in the laws by which we are governed, in view of the brand of justice which is being meted out to Negroes in our courts").

51. *The Jim Crow Evils*, Tulsa Star (April 24, 1920).

52. *See, e.g., Outrages at Jim Crow Depot*, Muskogee Star 1 (February 12, 1909) ("Colored women have to suffer all kinds of discomfort and the toilet is a disgrace even to savages. The R.R. police are as discourteous as it is possible to be and on many occasions they arrest strangers who come to town and charge them with loafing").

53. Revised Law of Oklahoma, 1910 sec. 860 (1910) ("Separate Coach Law," passed December 18, 1907). The legislation was, on its face, racially neutral. The law required separate accommodations, but then added that nothing contained in the act should be construed to prevent railway companies "from hauling sleeping cars, dining or chair cars attached to their trains to be used exclusively by either white or negro passengers, separately but not jointly." *Id.* The statute was interpreted as exempting railroads from providing separate luxury accommodations whenever there was insufficient demand for the accommodations to make them financially viable.

54. *Stradford v. Midland Valley R.R. Co.*, 128 P. 98 (Okla. 1912).

55. 163 U.S. 537 (1896).

56. 186 F. 966, 970 (8th Cir. 1911).

57. *Id.*

58. *Id.* at 971.

59. *Judge Hook*, Muskogee Cimeter 1 (February 10, 1912).

60. *See McCabe v. Atchison, Topeka, and Santa Fe Ry.*, 235 U.S. 151, 163 (1914). *See also* Alexander M. Bickel and Benno C. Schmidt, The Judiciary and Responsible Government, 1910–21 775–84 (1984).

61. *See McCabe v. Atchison, Topeka, and Santa Fe Ry.*, 235 U.S. 151, 163 (1914).

62. *Id.* at 161. *McCabe* served as precedent for later civil rights cases. *See, e.g., Barrows v. Jackson*, 346 U.S. 249 (1953); *Missouri ex rel. Gaines v. Canada*, 305 U.S. 337, 351 (1938). *See* Randall Kennedy, *Race Relations Law and the Tradition of Celebration: The Case of Professor Schmidt*, 86 Colum. L. Rev. 1622, 1644–45 (1986) (questioning the importance of *McCabe*).

63. *See, e.g., Guinn v. United States*, 238 U.S. 347 (1915); *Hollins v. Oklahoma*, 295 U.S. 394 (1935); *Lane v. Wilson*, 307 U.S. 268 (1939); *Sipuel v. Board of Regents of Univ. of Okla.*, 332 U.S. 631 (1948); *Skinner v. Oklahoma ex rel. Williamson*, 316 U.S. 535 (1942).

64. *The "Jim Crow" Evils*, Tulsa Star 4 (April 24, 1920).

65. *Thought He Owned Car*, Tulsa World (May 13, 1921).

66. Ralph Ellison, *The Perspective of Literature*, in The Collected Essays of Ralph Ellison 766,766 (John Callahan ed. 1995). Ellison mentioned two of his Oklahoma City mentors, Roscoe Dunjee, editor of the Black Dispatch, and J.D. Randolph, custodian of the state law library,

as people who shattered the white myth that blacks could not interpret the law.

Kenneth Mack has explored the ways that social norms reinforced the movement toward segregation statutes in the early twentieth century. *See* Kenneth W. Mack, *Law, Society, Identity, and the Making of the Jim Crow South: Travel and Segregation on Tennessee Railroads, 1875–1905*, 24 LAW AND SOCIAL INQUIRY 377–409 (1999). Formal law existed independently of blacks' interpretations of "law" in Mack's world, as well as in Tulsa. By the 1920s, however, the worlds of law in the minds of black and white Tulsans were so distinct that they rarely intersected.

Even though the courts might enforce the requirement of equal accommodations, the railroads did not always provide them. In January 1914, Tulsa's black residents had had enough. The TULSA STAR ran a front-page story on Mrs. Lee Terrell, who alleged that she paid for a first-class ticket from Tulsa to Pawhuska. When thirty or more drunken white men entered it, the conductor moved her to a baggage car for the remainder of the trip. "The law specifically provides that equal accommodations be given the two races in Oklahoma, but there is not a railroad in the state today complying with the law," the STAR's editor, A.J. Smitherman, reported. *Colored Woman Forced to Ride in Baggage Car*, TULSA STAR 1 (January 17, 1914). I could locate no record of her suit.

A few days later, Smitherman had a similar experience. He claimed that in the early evening of January 20, 1914, he boarded a train bound for Tulsa, at Sapulpa, about 14 miles away. He sat in the portion of the car designated for blacks. Afterwards, more than a dozen whites entered the car and the conductor told him to move to another car, which Smitherman refused to do. The conductor then returned with a porter and the two together forcibly removed Smitherman from the car and put him in another one, which had neither heat nor light, for the rest of the trip to Tulsa. Unfortunately, the court records do not record the outcome of the suit; however, the mere fact that it was filed testifies to Smitherman's determination to employ the courts to fight discrimination. *See Andrew J. Smitherman v. James W. Lusk, et al.*, Tulsa County Superior Court (January 30, 1914).

67. *Lynching in Georgia*, BLACK DISPATCH 4 (July 9, 1920).

68. *Senseless Negroes*, BLACK DISPATCH 4 (July 9, 1920).

69. See Oklahoma Constitution, quoted in *Guinn v. United States*, 238 U.S. 347, 357 (1915) ("No person shall be registered as an elector of this state, or be allowed to vote in any election held herein, unless he be able to read and write any section of the Constitution of the state of Oklahoma; but no person who was, on January 1st, 1866, or at any time prior thereto entitled to vote under any form of government, or who, at that time, resided in some foreign nation, and no lineal descendant of such person, shall be denied

the right to register and vote because of his inability to so read and write"). 129 P. 34, 37 (1912).

70. *See Atwater v. Hassett*, 111 P. 802 (1910) (upholding constitutionality of grandfather clause); *Cofield v. Fannelly*, 134 P. 407 (1913) (upholding Oklahoma's grandfather clause in denying the right to vote to Theodore Cofield). *See also The Grand Father's Clause Upheld*, TULSA STAR (August 1, 1913).

71. 238 U.S. 347 (1915).

72. *See Guinn v. United States*, 228 F. 103, 109 (8th Cir. 1915) (describing voting qualifications of blacks who were prevented from voting).

73. 238 U.S. at 366.

74. *Id.* at 366–67.

75. *Registration Law Unconstitutional: Oklahoma City Judge so Holds in Granting Injunction Against State*, MUSKOGEE CIMETER 1 (June 3, 1916). Periodically the black newspapers talked about their efforts to enforce *Guinn*. In 1918, for instance, amid allegations that blacks were being denied the right to vote, the *Muskogee Cimeter* promised a "*Big Fight: Negroes Will go in the Federal Courts No Begging for assistance of any political party.*" MUSKOGEE CIMETER 1 (October 21, 1918).

76. *See* "Registration Law," 1916 Session Laws, chap. 24, at 33. *Cf. Black v. Geissler*, 159 P. 1124 (Okla. 1916) (unsuccessfully challenging registration law).

77. *Lane v. Wilson*, 307 U.S. 268 (1939).

78. The issue of the BLACK DISPATCH containing the article has been lost. Fortunately, the article was reprinted two weeks later. *See The Nigger Peril*, BLACK DISPATCH 6 (October 29, 1920).

79. *Id.*

80. *An Inflammatory Appeal*, BLACK DISPATCH 4 (October 15, 1920) ("This law operated, as it was intended by its sponsors, to place the Negroes at a disadvantage although it did not bar them from the right of registration. It was the nearest approach to a grandfather clause that could be enacted at that time in face of the stringent attitude of the federal government against franchise discrimination because of race"). *See also The Black Dispatch Wants Negro Equality*, BLACK DISPATCH 6 (October 29, 1920) (reprinting story from McALESTER NEWS-CAPITAL).

81. *An Inflammatory Appeal*, BLACK DISPATCH 4 (October 15, 1920).

82. *Id.*

83. *See* Oklahoma Compiled Laws 1909, sec. 8193. The first segregation act was passed in 1890. *See* Sec. 1, art. 9, c. 28, Sess. Laws 1901, at 205; Comp. Laws Okla. 1909, sec. 8200, *Jones v. Carnes*, 87 P. 652 (1906). The laws permitting the superintendent of schools to designate the majority school was upheld against a challenge that it violated the due process rights

of blacks. The Oklahoma Supreme Court rejected the argument that such redesignation violated the Fourteenth Amendment's requirement of equal treatment. When counties began to face the issue of whether schools should be consolidated, blacks were not allowed to vote in elections to decide that issue; the justification was that "the election pertained only to schools of the white race."

84. *See* 1913 Okla. Session Laws, chap. 219, art 15, sec. 3 ("The county separate school in each district is hereby declared to be that school in said school district of the race having the fewest number of children in said school district; provided, that the school superintendent of public instruction of each county shall have authority to designate what school or schools in each school district shall be the separate school and which class of children, either white or colored, shall have the privilege of attending such separate school or schools in said school district"). *See also Jumper v. Lyles*, 184 P. 1084 (Okla. 1919) (interpreting act as providing that "the separate school in each district is that school of the race having the fewest number of children in said school district, unless the county superintendent designates the other school"); *School District No. 71, Oklahoma County v. Overholser*, 87 P. 665 (Okla. 1905).

State ex rel. Gumm v. Albritton, 224 P. 511 (1924). *Gumm* explained how the separate school system worked. The school districts hired and paid the teachers of the majority school; the counties hired and paid the teachers of the separate schools. Each county's school superintendent chose which race would attend the majority school and which the separate school. *Id.* at 513. Thus, whites might constitute a minority of voters in a particular district, but they could still be designated to attend the majority school. The court refused any relief from the decision of the school superintendent on the grounds of denial of equal protection. In a nonsensical interpretation of the equal protection clause, it said that "while a state may not deny to persons of different races equal accommodations in schools, it may deny them identical accommodations." *Id.* The court concluded: "however arbitrary the action of such superintendent may seem it cannot be said that the equal protection clause of the Fourteenth Amendment is violated, because it is not shown that accommodations or facilities equal [*sic*], though not identical with those of white children, are afforded to the colored children." *Id.*

In other cases, the courts allowed the superintendent of education to designate the majority school. *See Jumper v. Lyles*, 185 P. 1084 (Okla. 1919); *Jelsma County Treasurer v. Butler*, 194 P. 436 (Okla. 1920). In 1931 a federal court similarly refused relief on equal protection grounds. *See School Dist. No. 7, Muskogee County v. Hunnicutt*, 51 F.2d 528 (E.D. Okla. 1931). It ruled that there is no equal protection violation if "equal advantages are granted." *Id.* at 529. *See also Ervin v. Seikel*, 119 P. 2d 563 (Okla. 1941); *Musick v. School Dist. No. 41*, 98 P. 2d 590 (Okla. 1940).

See Ratliff v. State ex rel. Woods, 191 P. 1038, 1040 (1920). *Ratliff* addressed the adequacy of notice for a special election to abrogate the consolidation of the Cole school district. The county election officials failed to give any notice to black voters and the Oklahoma Supreme Court, citing a 1910 law that provided "one race shall not participate in any election pertaining to the schools of the other race," refused relief. "This being a school election which pertained simply to the schools of the white race, the negro race were not interested therein, nor were they qualified voters, or entitled to notice." *Id.* at 1040.

85. In *Board of Education of Guthrie v. Excise Board of Logan County*, the Oklahoma Supreme Court faced a board of education seeking sufficient funding to have equal facilities. The court refused to require the excise board (the taxing authority, which had the duty of taxing to support the Guthrie schools) to increase taxes to provide for equal facilities. 206 P. 517 (1922). *See also Thompson v. Rhyner*, 206 P. 609 (1920) (denying writ of mandamus to compel building of separate school). The denial of mandamus, which is a writ compelling action, in *Thompson* is, perhaps, not surprising. The standard for mandamus—that there be an unambiguous duty—is difficult to meet.

The Oklahoma Supreme Court granted the taxing authorities wide power over assessing taxes. It rejected, for instance, a claim by a railroad that it had overpaid school taxes used to support separate schools. *See Chicago R.I. & P. Ry. v. Lane*, 170 P. 502 (Okla. 1917). It remains unclear what the result would have been if the railroad had prevailed. It might—but probably would not—have signaled the end of separate public schools. *Cf. Lusk v. White*, 173 P. 1128 (Okla. 1916) (upholding taxation imposed by county excise board at equal level for both majority and separate schools); *Olson v. Logan County Bank*, 118 P. 572 (Okla. 1912); *Atchison, Topeka, and San Fransisco Ry. v. State*, 113 P. 921 (Okla. 1911).

The problems involved with determining whether a person was black or white—and hence entitled to attend the better schools—demonstrate the complex involvement of the state in the defining race and maintaining segregation. *See, e.g., Cole v. District Board*, 123 P. 426 (Okla. 1912) (interpreting race of children, to determine which school they could attend); *Blake v. Sessions*, 220 P. 876 (Okla. 1923). *See also Jones v. Board of Education of Muskogee*, 217 P. 400 (Okla. 1923); *Court Dodges Constitutionality*, BLACK DISPATCH 1 (July 26, 1923).

86. *See Oklahoma's Rotten Educational Law*, BLACK DISPATCH 4 (January 21, 1921).

87. *See Segregation Passes City Council*, TULSA STAR 1 (August 5, 1916).

88. *See id.* (referring to *Harris v. City of Louisville*, 177 S.W. 472 (1915)).

89. *Id.* at 475 ("The advance of civilization and the consequent extension

of governmental activities along lines having their objective in better living conditions, saner social conditions, and a higher standard of human character has resulted in a gradual lessening of the dominion of the individual over private property . . . so that today all private property is held subject to the unchallenged rights and power of the State to impose . . . reasonable regulations as are deemed expedient for public welfare"). *See also Carey v. City of Atlanta*, 84 S.E. 456 (Ga. 1915); *Harden v. City of Atlanta*, 93 S.E. 401 (Ga. 1917).

90. *See Negroes Wage Bitter Fight Against Act*, TULSA STAR (August 9, 1916).

91. *See Buchanan v. Warley*, 245 U.S. 60 (1917); *Segregation Invaded Due Process Clause*, BLACK DISPATCH 1 (November 9, 1917). In celebration, the BLACK DISPATCH printed key excerpts from the opinion on the front page. *Our Rights*, BLACK DISPATCH 1 (November 23, 1917).

92. *See Officials Deny the Supreme Court*, BLACK DISPATCH 1 (August 2, 1918). Those actions made the Oklahoma city commissioners breakers, rather than upholders, of the law. *See The Source From Which the Mob Spirit Springs*, BLACK DISPATCH 4 (August 2, 1918) ("The day when men of the standing and intelligence of the City Commissioners learn to regard and respect the supreme law of the land, that day the common people will also reverence it").

93. A black man, William Floyd, challenged the ordinance. He purchased property on a majority white block, entered the house, and was arrested. Floyd sought an injunction in federal court, while a state court in Oklahoma City began to hear his case. *See Bumps Segregation*, BLACK DISPATCH 1 (May 30, 1919); *Negroes Fight Unfair Ordinance*, BLACK DISPATCH 1 (May 23, 1919).

The state court eventually dismissed the indictment. *See Dodge Federal Issue: Judge Says Floyd Has Not Violated City's Segregation Ordinance*, BLACK DISPATCH 1 (June 20, 1919). *See also No State Court! Cottrell Says City's Only Relief, By Amendment of U.S. Constitution*, BLACK DISPATCH 1 (June 6, 1919); *Immeasurable Damage*, BLACK DISPATCH 4 (June 6, 1919).

94. *Cowards Dynamite Woman*, BLACK DISPATCH 1 (September 1, 1919); *Where the Blame Lies*, BLACK DISPATCH 1 (September 19, 1919).

95. *See Defies Justice*, BLACK DISPATCH 1 (June 13, 1919). *See also Whatsoever is the Law, Should be Obeyed*, BLACK DISPATCH 4 (June 13, 1919) ("IF BLACK MEN START OUT TO GET AN INTERPRETATION OF THE LAW THEY ARE ENTITLED TO THAT INTERPRETATION, AND WHAT SO EVER IS THE LAW SHOULD BE OBEYED BY BLACK AND WHITE CITIZENS ALIKE"); *The Reason Why*, Black Dispatch 4 (June 20, 1919) ("[T]he black man will continue to insist upon the right to add to his property interests as the population increases, the HUNS OF AMERICA TO THE CONTRARY NOTWITHSTANDING").

96. *Armed White Ruffians Who Begged for Guns to Help Murder*, CHICAGO DEFENDER 1 (June 11, 1921) (discussing contributory causes of riot). Randy Krehbiel has called into question the accuracy of the DEFENDER account. *See* Randy Krehbiel, *Post-Riot Lawsuits Reveal Clues, Mysteries*, TULSA WORLD (February 6, 2000).

97. *Police Turn Criminals, Swell Tulsa Death List*, CHICAGO DEFENDER 1 (June 4, 1921).

98. *A White Man's Country*, BLACK DISPATCH 4 (June 3, 1921).

99. *Bombs Hurled from Aeroplanes in Order to Stop Attacks on the Whites*, CHICAGO DEFENDER 1 (June 4, 1921).

100. *Citizens of Tulsa Tell of Conditions There Preceding the Race Riot*, ST. LOUIS POST-DISPATCH, sec. 2, at 1 (June 5, 1921).

101. *Id.* at 11.

102. *Id.*

103. Walter F. White, *The Eruption of Tulsa*, THE NATION 909 (June 29, 1921). A more extended account of White's testimony appeared in *What a Lyncher Looks Like; Hair Raising Exploits of NAACP Investigator Down in America's Congo; Out-Bluffing the Bluffers*, BLACK DISPATCH 7 (April 13, 1922).

One justice on the Georgia Supreme Court explained the origins of an Atlanta riot in this way: "this one thing of the street car employees being required by their position to endure in patience the insults of negro passengers was, more largely than any other one thing, responsible for the engendering of the spirit which manifested itself in the riot." *Georgia Railway & Elec. Co. v. Rich*, 71 S.E. 759, 760 (Ga, 1911).

104. *Id.*

105. Ellison, *Going to the Territory*, in RALPH ELLISON, GOING TO THE TERRITORY at 135 (1986).

106. *See generally Climbing the Ladder of the Law*, in B.C. Franklin, MY LIFE AND AN ERA 238–47 (John Hope Franklin and John Whittington Franklin, eds., 1997). *See also* J. Clay Smith, EMANCIPATION: THE MAKING OF THE BLACK LAWYER, 1844–1944, 504–11 (1993) (discussing black lawyers in Oklahoma and their role in opposing segregation); *Evil Blossometh*, BLACK DISPATCH 4 (February 9, 1922) ("In respect for law lies the safety of any nation; contempt for law has brought us to the abyss of chaos where we stand today").

107. *See, e.g.,* A.J. Smitherman, *Aftermath of the Tulsa Race Riot*, BLACK DISPATCH 2 (January 26, 1922) (quoting editorial "An Appeal to Reason," from the June 3, 1921, *Tulsa World*, which warned that "The wretched mob spirit still smolders. . . . Standing high above every recognizable fact is this tremendous unsurmountable truth: these people have a right to life, to the pursuit of happiness and to their earthly possession. To deny them those

rights is to set aside the basic law of the land and deliberately take a keystone from the arch of the government in this country"); *cf.* Ralph Ellison, *Homage to Duke Ellington on His Birthday*, in ELLISON, GOING TO THE TERRITORY, *supra* note 68, at 217, 223–24 (referring to slaves' remaking of American dance and music traditions). One wonders if Ralph Ellison should not have begun his essay, "What would America be like without blacks" with a reference to the contribution of the black press to the rule of law. *See* Ralph Ellison, *What Would America Be Like Without Blacks*, in ELLISON, GOING TO THE TERRITORY, *supra* note 68, at 104–12.

Chapter 5

1. *See Officials Under Fire at Meeting*, TULSA WORLD 1 (June 3, 1921); *Citizens to Help Rebuild "Little Africa,"* TULSA WORLD 8 (June 3, 1921) (estimating that $500,000 would be needed for reconstruction). For a detailed description of the Reconstruction Committee, see *Local Situation is Well in Hand*, TULSA WORLD 2 (June 7, 1921).

2. *Niles Blames Lawlessness for Race War*, TULSA TRIBUNE 4 (June 2, 1921).

3. *Citizens to Help Rebuild "Little Africa,"* TULSA WORLD 8 (June 3, 1921). *See also A Grand Jury Riot Probe: And Tulsa Business Men Will Rebuild Negroes' Homes*, KANSAS CITY STAR 1 (June 3, 1921) ("A subscription of one-half million dollars will be asked . . . and the homes actually owned by the negroes will be reconstructed. No attempt will be made by the Committee to rebuild the business buildings in the district, many of which were owned by white persons, or homes which were rented, members said").

4. *Tulsa is Repentant Now*, KANSAS CITY STAR 6 (June 3, 1921). As one would expect, black papers were firm in urging assistance in rebuilding. *See, e.g.*, OKLAHOMA GUIDE 4 (June 9, 1921) ("It is not fair that a city like Tulsa, especially the part belonging to the weaker part of the citizenship, should be so wrecked. The city of Tulsa should be loyal enough to rebuild that part of the city that was destroyed by fire and otherwise pay other damages done").

5. *See, e.g., Tulsa Will*, TULSA TRIBUNE 5 (June 3, 1921). As Tulsa's resolve lessened, Greenwood resident S.D. Hooker, the chair of Tulsa's Relief Committee, asked about Tulsa's will. "Can Tulsa afford to sustain a law that keeps hundreds of its taxpayers in tents to be exposed to the cold winters that are common in Oklahoma?" *Tulsa Will?* BLACK DISPATCH 1 (August 28, 1921). "Immediately following the great disaster, Tulsa published to the world that she would restore every dollar's worth of property destroyed. The world thinks Tulsa is keeping her promise. Can Tulsa afford to deceive the public? Will Tulsa dodge her moral responsibility behind the technicalities of the law?" *Id.*

6. *Tulsa Will,* TULSA TRIBUNE, June 3, 1921.

7. *The Disgrace of Tulsa,* TULSA WORLD 4 (June 2, 1921). *See also Give Until It Hurts,* TULSA WORLD 4 (June 5, 1921) ("All of this should not be construed as sympathy for the colored people so much as penance on the part of the superior race").

8. *See, e.g., Give Until It Hurts,* TULSA WORLD 4 (June 5, 1921) ("The fact remains—stands out like a lighthouse in a fog—that Tulsa must exert itself to the upmost to retrieve the ground lost"); *An Appeal to Reason,* TULSA WORLD 4 (June 5, 1921) ("The wretched mob spirit still smolders. . . . Standing head-high above every other recognizable fact is this tremendous insurmountable truth: These people have a right to life, to the pursuit of happiness and to their earthly possession. To deny them those rights is to set aside the basic law of the land and deliberately take a key-stone from the arch of the government in this country").

One editorial appealed to base economic motives. The riot disabled the city's economic life, because businesses and white households lost their workers. Unless something was done to restore Greenwood, Tulsa would stop growing, for no city ever "prospered under the domination of such prejudiced provincialism." The editorial continued:

> Only negro property in the northeast section of the city was destroyed, it is true. But every foot of real estate in Tulsa was depreciated thereby and it will continue to depreciate until the real Tulsa exerts itself over ruffianism and restores that which has been destroyed. It may not at this moment be popular to say this much, but it is the truth around which must crystalize the sentiment of the community eventually. The better nature of Tulsa citizenship must dominate the situation that exists. In that alone is there hope.

An Appeal to Reason, TULSA WORLD 4 (June 3, 1921).

9. *See Give Till It Hurts,* TULSA WORLD 4 (June 5, 1921).

10. *Need Relief Funds: Sixty-Five Thousand More Needed for Temporary Work,* TULSA TRIBUNE 1 (June 6, 1921). *See also 'Give at Once' Avery's Plea to Save City,* TULSA TRIBUNE 1 (June 5, 1921).

11. *City to Meet Demands Out of Own Purse,* TULSA TRIBUNE 1 (June 3, 1921). *See also City Awakens to Fact That It Must Give,* TULSA TRIBUNE 2 (June 7, 1921).

12. *See Dallas Offers Assistance,* TULSA WORLD 3 (June 4, 1921) ("Thank you for your wire of June 2 stating negroes of Dallas desire to raise funds for food and clothing for Tulsa negroes. Tulsans can handle situation, however, but deeply appreciate your kind interest").

13. *Public Welfare Board Quits Job,* TULSA WORLD 1 (June 16, 1921).

14. *See Riot Statement Made by Mayor*, TULSA WORLD 1 (June 15, 1921). *See also Tulsa Will*, TULSA TRIBUNE 5 (June 3, 1921) (calling Evans' statements blaming Greenwood residents part of a whitewash of "obvious inefficiency").

15. *Invite Negroes to Meet Board*, TULSA WORLD 14 (June 18, 1921). *See also Reconstruction Plans Approved*, TULSA WORLD 2A (June 19, 1921); *New Board on Tour of Burned Area*, TULSA TRIBUNE 1, 11 (June 15, 1921).

16. *See Wash Tubs Given to Negro Women: Problem of Having the Washing Done Is Made Easier*, TULSA WORLD 10 (June 22, 1921).

17. *See Order Replaces Chaos in Camp*, TULSA WORLD 8 (June 3, 1921).

18. *Id.*

19. *War Vets Relived Soldiers as Guards*, TULSA WORLD 1 (June 4, 1921); *Work Negroes on City Street Job*, TULSA WORLD 16 (June 14, 1921) (reporting that men worked for the city in exchange for three meals and housing and concluding that "Several armed guards have been placed near the workers to keep them company"). *See also Civic Workers Care for Negroes Held in Concentration Camps*, TULSA TRIBUNE 4 (June 1, 1921); *Sunday Services at Concentration Camp*, TULSA WORLD 6 (June 6, 1921).

20. *Red Cross to Spend Months Aiding Blacks*, TULSA TRIBUNE 6 (June 4, 1921) ("The registration and employment bureau at the YMCA is attempting to straighten out all of these tangles. All negroes are requested to register and white people who have employment for the negroes can get them through this employment bureau").

21. *Dick Rowland in South Omaha, No Trace of Girl*, BLACK DISPATCH 1 (June 17, 1921) ("'It is humiliating to the greatest degree to the Negroes of the city to have to go around labeled with green cards as though they are dogs or some other kind of animals,' said this doctor, and as soon as they are able, they all evince a spirit to shake the dust of Tulsa from their feet"); *Negro Insurance Company Has Half Million for Tulsa*, BLACK DISPATCH 1 (June 24, 1921) ("These identification cards are issued on the presumption that every Negro works for some white man. At any rate, you are not free to pass on the streets of the Oil City unless you have one of these cards signed by some white man designated as 'employer'").

22. *All Blacks Must Wear Green Tags*, TULSA WORLD 9 (June 7, 1921) ("Police Commissioner J.M. Adkison Monday afternoon issued an order to the police force to arrest all negroes seen on the streets after Wednesday morning unless they were wearing green identification tags which will be issued by the police department"); *Thousands of Green Tags are Issued to Negro With Jobs*, TULSA TRIBUNE 1 (June 8, 1921); *Blacks Given Green Cards*, TULSA WORLD (June 8, 1921). Some thought the tags such a good idea that they should not be limited to blacks. *See All Go to Work*, TULSA

WORLD 4 (June 10, 1921) ("I say tag everybody, white and black. See to it that everybody works, white and black alike").

23. *Get a Green Card*, TULSA TRIBUNE 10 (June 8, 1921).

24. *Id.*

25. *Improvement in Labor Condition*, TULSA WORLD 2 (June 3, 1921).

26. *See Police Order Negro Porters Out of Hotels*, TULSA TRIBUNE 1 (June 14, 1921); *Police Launch New Drive to Cleanse Hotels*, TULSA TRIBUNE 3 (June 17, 1921) (announcing modification of original order barring all blacks from working in "second-rate" hotels; the new order "declared they must not act as clerks nor at any time be left in charge of the place").

27. *Must Work or Go to Jail is Edict of Mayor Evans*, TULSA WORLD 1 (June 4, 1921); *Police Order Idle Blacks to Fair Camp*, TULSA TRIBUNE 4 (June 7, 1921); *Arrest Negro Idlers*, TULSA WORLD 2 (June 11, 1921). Men remaining in the camps were quickly put to work, although few stayed at the fairgrounds for more than a week; most were released by that time. *Want $100,000 for Relief Work*, TULSA WORLD 8 (June 11, 1921) (reporting that fewer than thirty men were still at the fairgrounds).

28. *Blacks Must be Self-Sustaining*, TULSA WORLD 15 (June 8, 1921); *Dick Rowland in South Omaha, No Trace of Girl*, BLACK DISPATCH 1 (June 17, 1921) ("O.A. Steiner, street commissioner, made a bunch of refugees in the Fair Grounds unload several loads of crushed rock, last Monday, receiving in return 'THREE SQUARE MEALS AND A BED'").

29. *Red Cross in Field Until All are Well*, TULSA TRIBUNE 1, 6 (June 4, 1921).

30. *Id.*

31. *Local Red Cross is Reorganized*, TULSA WORLD 1 (June 3, 1921); *Reorganize for Work of Relief*, TULSA WORLD 1 (June 4, 1921); *Red Cross has Two Busy Weeks*, TULSA WORLD 3 (June 13, 1921).

32. Maurice Willows, Report, in Bob Hower, ANGELS OF MERCY: 1921 TULSA RACE RIOT AND THE AMERICAN RED CROSS 161–225 (1993).

33. *Welfare Board Drops Control of Relief Fund*, TULSA TRIBUNE 1 (June 9, 1921). The Red Cross also received the right to collect money from the city for temporary police work paid for by the Public Welfare Board.

34. *See Action Urged on Union Station Project*, TULSA WORLD 14 (June 24, 1921) (urging the construction of housing for Greenwood residents). *See also Negroes Fear Winter, Build in Riot Zone*, TULSA TRIBUNE 8 (August 8, 1921).

35. Other groups assisted with rebuilding, as well. *See, e.g, Tulsa Churches in Mercy Work*, TULSA WORLD 9 (June 3, 1921).

36. *Total Loss in Fire is Fixed at $1,500,000*, TULSA TRIBUNE 1 (June 5, 1921). *See also 'A Bunch of Burglars': Soldiers Subdue Big Race Riot; 77*

Known Dead, CHICAGO TRIBUNE 1 (June 2, 1921) (reporting estimate of $1.5 million in damages). On June 3, the TULSA WORLD told of the Public Welfare Board's efforts to begin assessment of the losses. *To Appraise All Loss By Negroes*, TULSA WORLD 1 (June 3, 1921). The property appraisal form was printed in the paper at page 8.

37. *City Not Liable for Riot Damage*, TULSA WORLD 1, 2 (August 7, 1921) ("Approximately $5,000,000 in claims have been made of the city by negroes for damage alleged to have been sustained as a result of the riot. This included both real and personal property, all of these claims have been refused by the city"); *Not Liable for Damages*, TULSA WORLD 14 (June 8, 1921) ("[T]he Committee stated its belief that from a moral standpoint Tulsa is responsible for the loss and damage"); *City is Not Liable, Says Legal Board*, TULSA TRIBUNE 1 (June 7, 1921).

38. *To Appraise All Loss By Negroes*, TULSA WORLD 1 (June 3, 1921).

39. *See Burned District in Fire Limits*, TULSA WORLD 2 (June 8, 1921) (urging that plan would be "found desirable, in causing a wider separation between negroes and whites").

40. *Plan to Move Negroes into New District*, TULSA TRIBUNE 1 (June 3, 1921). Outside Tulsa, the interpretations in white papers were (somewhat) more balanced. For summaries, see *Mob Fury and Race Hatred as a National Danger*, LITERARY DIGEST 9 (June 18, 1921); *Press Still Lectures Us for Outbreak*, TULSA TRIBUNE 3 (June 6, 1921); *Tulsa Still Target for Editors' Ire*, TULSA TRIBUNE 8 (June 7, 1921); *Editors Keep Pouring Hot Shot at Tulsa*, TULSA TRIBUNE 12 (June 10, 1921); *Taft Places Blame Mostly on Whites*, TULSA TRIBUNE 3 (June 13, 1921).

41. *See Negro Section Abolished by City's Order*, TULSA TRIBUNE 1 (June 7, 1921).

42. *Action on Union Station Project: Reconstruction Committee to Induce Railroads to Accept Plan*, TULSA WORLD 14 (June 21, 1921); *The Tulsa Union Station*, TULSA TRIBUNE 4 (June 12, 1921) (editorial urging relocation of Greenwood); *Union Station is Endorsed [by] Realty Dealers*, TULSA TRIBUNE 9 (June 16, 1921); *Ask Tramway Terminal in Burned Area*, TULSA TRIBUNE 1 (June 19, 1921) (reporting statement by Tulsa county commissioner that Greenwood residents should not receive any reparations from the city, but should "make up their losses by the increased valuation of their property for industrial purposes and by buying cheaper lots elsewhere"); *Want Wholesale Houses in Tulsa*, TULSA WORLD 2 (June 15, 1921) ("Through the reconstruction committee appointed by the mayor and city commissioners Tuesday, Tulsa extends a welcoming hand to wholesale houses and industrial plants, which are to be located on the trackage property in Little Africa swept by fire and which is now within the city fire limits, restricted to the erection of fire-resisting buildings").

43. *Give Furniture to Needy Blacks*, TULSA WORLD 16 (June 23, 1921); *Water Mains on Lansing Avenue: City Begins Improvement of New Negro District North of City*, TULSA WORLD 2 (July 16, 1921).

To secure the conversion of the burned area, one Tulsa lawyer urged that the city purchase the property. The city was too cheap to do even that. Instead, they relied upon the fire ordinance as a way of limiting the use of property. That position ended up legally indefensible. *Humphrey Urges Union Station*, TULSA WORLD 2 (June 24, 1921). *See also Rebuilding Riot Zone Real Task*, TULSA WORLD 16 (June 24, 1921); *Winter's Approach Worries Red Cross Chief; Haste Urged*, TULSA WORLD 3 (June 24, 1921).

44. *Unbroken Faith Shown in Re-habilitation Program*, BLACK DISPATCH 1 (June 24, 1921).

45. *Id.; False Rumor Starts Second Exodus . . . Building Permits Allowed in Black Belt*, BLACK DISPATCH 1 (July 8, 1921) ("The Welfare Board during the past week has issued permits for the Negroes to build temporary shacks on the old home sites, giving as their reason that some preparations should be allowed the Negro home owners to make preparation for the winter months that are soon to come").

46. *See Police Attempt to Block Reconstruction: Blacks Seek Injunction Against Illegal Ordinance*, BLACK DISPATCH (August 19, 1921) (reprinting petition challenging zoning ordinance that made rebuilding of Greenwood prohibitively expensive). Earlier in the summer the BLACK DISPATCH urged filing a lawsuit to challenge the ordinance. *See Invoke the Due Process Clause*, BLACK DISPATCH 4 (July 1, 1921) (urging federal lawsuit to overturn zoning ordinance).

47. *See Petition in Lockard v. Evans, et al.*, Tulsa County District Court, Case 15,780 paragraphs 6–7 (August 12, 1921).

48. *Winter's Arrival Worries Red Cross Chief; Haste Urged*, TULSA WORLD 3 (June 24, 1921). *See also Action Urged on Union Station Project*, TULSA WORLD 14 (June 24, 1921) (Red Cross executive Maurice Willows expressed the need to obtain permanent housing for Greenwood residents); *Relief Committee is Hard-Pressed: Many Aged Blacks to Suffer During Winter Months*, BLACK DISPATCH 1 (October 6, 1921); *First Wintry Blast Speeds up Darkeytown*, TULSA TRIBUNE 9B (October 2, 1921).

49. *Negro Sues to Rebuild Waste Area*, TULSA WORLD (August 13, 1921); *Three Judges Hear Evidence in Negro Suit*, TULSA WORLD 1 (August 25, 1921).

50. *See Can Reconstruct Restricted Area, District Judges Grant Restraining Order to Negroes*, TULSA WORLD 1 (August 26, 1921); *Negroes Can Rebuild in Stricken City*, BLACK DISPATCH 1 (August 26, 1921).

51. *City Will Fight Rebuilding Plan: Commissioners Re-Pass Ordinance Concerning Little Africa*, TULSA WORLD 1 (August 28, 1921).

52. *Digging Justice Out of Chaos and Cowardice*, BLACK DISPATCH 4 (August 26, 1921).

53. *Upright Men Shall be Astonished*, BLACK DISPATCH 4 (September 8, 1921) ("The Negroes of Tulsa are in court trying to find out what moral, and we will go farther to use the term 'legal,' grounds the city stands upon in denying them the right to rebuild their homes upon property which they acquired through sweat and toil and by [what] legal processes that other men acquired their property, and are still permitted to hold").

54. *See Rescind Action on Burned Area*, TULSA WORLD 3 (July 29, 1921) (announcing Real Estate Exchange's rescission of its proposal to convert Greenwood into industrial district); *New Building Law Disobeyed in Riot Area*, TULSA TRIBUNE 4 (July 21, 1921) (reporting that some Greenwood residents were rebuilding and that already forty-four new frame buildings had been constructed in the restricted area). The article reported that 289 homes (some multifamily dwellings) had been destroyed in the restricted area.

55. *The Reconstruction Committee*, TULSA WORLD 4 (July 12, 1921); *The Opinion of the Tulsa World on Petition for Restraining Order*, BLACK DISPATCH 1 (August 19, 1921) (reprinting *Repeal the Fire Ordinance*, TULSA WORLD 4 [August 15, 1921]). *See also A Sound Precedent*, TULSA WORLD 4 (August 27, 1921) (praising judges for striking ordinance).

56. *See Cannot Enforce Fire Ordinance, Court holds unconstitutional act against the burned district*, TULSA WORLD 1 (September 2, 1921); *New Ordinance Passed by City: Three Judges to Make Final Ruling*, TULSA TRIBUNE 1 (September 1, 1921). The judges' opinion has been lost. It remains unclear how the case was resolved; it was apparently appealed to the Oklahoma Supreme Court in November 1921, but the Oklahoma Supreme Court Clerk's office can find no record of the case. The docket sheet in the Tulsa County District Court indicates there was a hearing in the case as late as 1925.

The Tulsa district court's decision in *Lockard* opens a revealing window on Progressive legal thought. *See generally* Morton J. Horwitz, THE TRANSFORMATION OF AMERICAN LAW, 1870–1960 (1992); Barry Cushman, RETHINKING THE NEW DEAL COURT: THE STRUCTURE OF A CONSTITUTIONAL REVOLUTION 47–65 (1998) (discussing public regulation in context of minimum wage); William G. Ross, FORGING NEW FREEDOMS: NATIVISM, EDUCATION, AND THE CONSTITUTION, 1917–1927 (1994) (employing controversy over constitutional rights to education to view Progressive-era jurisprudence); Herbert Hovenkamp, *The Mind and Heart of Progressive Legal Thought*, 81 IOWA L. REV. 149–60 (1995).

57. *Kill Ordinance!* BLACK DISPATCH 1 (September 8, 1921) (reporting that Mayor Evans would not appeal the decision and the city would begin issuing building permits). *See also Attempt to Evade Court's Mandate, Hits*

N.A.A.C.P., BLACK DISPATCH 1 (September 1, 1921) (reporting that zoning ordinance was invalidated by "friendly action brought by residents of the district to determine their rights," rather than the NAACP).

58. *New Dreamland Theater in Tulsa, Oklahoma*, BLACK DISPATCH 8 (September 14, 1922).

59. *See Smitherman is Dead*, BUFFALO CRITERION 1 (June 24, 1961). *Oklahoma Clears Black in Deadly 1921 Race Riot*, NEW YORK TIMES, sec. 1, at 8 (October 26, 1996).

60. *See* A.J. Smitherman, *Aftermath of the Tulsa Race Riot*, BLACK DISPATCH 2 (January 26, 1922); *see also Tulsa Will?* BLACK DISPATCH 1 (August 28, 1921).

61. *See Insurance Men Say Policies Won't be Paid*, TULSA TRIBUNE 4 (June 2, 1921).

62. *City Purse Safe from Riot Claim*, TULSA TRIBUNE 1 (August 7, 1921) (citing *Wallace v. Norman*, 60 P. 108 (1900)); *City is Not Liable, Says Legal Board*, TULSA TRIBUNE 1 (June 7, 1921); *White Victims of Riot to Sue for $500,000*, TULSA WORLD 9 (August 8, 1921); *City Not Liable for Riot Damage*, TULSA WORLD 1, 2 (August 7, 1921); *Not Liable for Damages*, TULSA WORLD 14 (June 8, 1921).

63. *See, e.g., Insurance Men Say Policies Won't be Paid*, TULSA TRIBUNE 4 (June 2, 1921). The Oklahoma law on recovery for race riots was against victims. The Oklahoma Supreme Court had refused to allow recovery against the city of Norman when Norman officials attacked and severely injured a black man. *See Wallace v. Norman*, 60 P. 108 (1900) (limiting city of Norman's liability for April 1898 riot).

64. *City Not Liable for Riot Damage*, TULSA WORLD 1 (August 7, 1921).

65. *$60,000 for Relief*, TULSA WORLD 1 (June 15, 1921); *Excise Board Votes $60,000 for Riot Relief*, TULSA TRIBUNE 2 (June 17, 1921); *Claims City Has Paid Riot Bills*, TULSA WORLD 3 (August 11, 1921). The city and county ultimately contributed $200,000 to relief. *See* Maurice Willows, REPORT OF THE RED CROSS in ANGELS OF MERCY 115 (Bob Hower, ed., 1998). *See also* Tulsa City Council Minutes (September 30, 1921) (approving payment of $2,151.02 to Joe Magee for "arms and ammunition").

66. *Fight it out in the Courts*, BLACK DISPATCH 4 (June 17, 1921).

67. *Id.*

68. *Invoke the Due Process Clause*, BLACK DISPATCH 4 (July 1, 1921).

69. Ellsworth reports 1,400 suits were filed. *See* Scott Ellsworth, DEATH IN A PROMISED LAND: THE TULSA RACE RIOT OF 1921 70 (1982). I have not been able to verify anywhere near that number of suits. Ellsworth probably means 1,400 claims were filed with the city. *See Rebuilding Tulsa*, BLACK DISPATCH 5 (August 5, 1921) (reporting 1,400 claims made by Greenwood residents with the city).

70. *See Wallace v. City of Norman,* 60 P. 108 (Okla. 1900).

71. *See Allen v. Tulsa,* Tulsa County Dist. Court, Case No. 16,013.

72. *See* John Nowak, *The Gang of Five and the Second Coming of the Anti-Reconstruction Supreme Court,* 75 NOTRE DAME LAW REVIEW 1091, 1105–9 (2000) (discussing impact of post–Civil War decisions limiting federal power to protect civil rights). The *Cruikshank* opinion, 83 U.S. 542 (1874), which arose from the prosecution of rioters in New Orleans in which perhaps 130 people were killed, illustrates the Supreme Court's unwillingness to protect against violence, even when it was perpetrated by local government officials. There were extensive congressional hearings into the "deconstruction" of Louisiana's reconstruction. Those hearings now form the basis for calls for reparations in Louisiana, as communities throughout the south and southwest, like Elaine County, Arkansas, are examining their treatment of minorities from the days of slavery through the Great Depression. *See* Claudia Kolker, *A Painful Present as Historians Confront a Nation's Bloody Past; Scholars And Heirs Search For Documentation of The Destruction of Black Communities Decades Ago,* LOS ANGELES TIMES A5 (February 22, 2000) (discussing Elaine, Arkansas, massacre as well questions about reparations).

73. *See Hutchins v. City of Tulsa,* Case 3798, U.S. Dist. Ct., Eastern Dist. Okla. (1922). I am indebted to Beryl Ford, who alerted me to this case, and to Robert Norris, who tracked it down at the National Archives. *See Sues City of Tulsa,* TULSA WORLD (April 28, 1922).

74. *Compare id.* at 34 (testimony of William Redfearn) with Brief for Defendant in Error, *Redfearn v. Am. Cent. Ins. Co.,* 243 P. 929 (Okla. 1926) at 112 (testimony of Green E. Smith).

75. *See Expose Redfearn in Tulsa Riot Probe,* BLACK DISPATCH 1, 5 (April 24, 1924) (discussing Redfearn's suits and his crossing the race boundary between black and white Tulsa).

76. The clause provided:

> This company shall not be liable for loss caused directly or indirectly by invasion, insurrection, riot, civil war or commotion, or military or usurped power, or by order of any civil authority; or by theft; or by neglect of the insured to use all reasonable means to save and preserve the property at and after a fire or when the property is endangered by fire in neighboring premises; or (unless fire insures, and, in that event, for the damage by fire only) by explosion of any kind or lightning; but liability for direct damage by lightning may be assumed by specific agreement hereon.

Brief for Plaintiff in Error, *Redfearn v. Am. Cent. Ins. Co.,* No. 15,851, 243 P. 929 (Okla. 1926) at 1–2.

77. 140 S.W. 148 (1911).

78. Redfearn had to be careful in arguing that police caused the damage, however, because there was also a clause in the insurance contract exempting damage caused "by order of any civil authority." Brief for Plaintiff, *supra* note 77, at 2–3. Here Redfearn had to argue that the damage was by police, but not by order of civil authority.

79. Brief for Plaintiff, *supra* note 77, at 107–8. Redfearn also cited two California decisions interpreting clauses excluding coverage for fires resulting from earthquakes. *Id.* at 107–9 (citing *Pacific Union Club v. Commercial Union Assurance Co.*, 107 Pac. 728 (1910); *Pacific Heating & Ventilating Co. v. Williamsburgh City Fire Ins. Co.*, 111 Pac. 4, 5–6 (1910)). Those cases, when read in conjunction with *Stearns Lumber*, present a credible case for coverage of Redfearn's loss. *Pacific Union Club* held an insurance company liable for a fire that spread following the San Francisco earthquake of 1906. Even though the insurance policy excluded liability for all loss "caused directly or indirectly by . . . earthquake," the California Supreme Court found liability when a fire broke out the next day, which could not be extinguished because the water pipes had been broken by the earthquake. *Pacific Union* deals with a chain of causation that is more remote than the one Redfearn faced, so it may be relatively unhelpful in drawing a line of liability in his case. *Pacific Heating and Ventilating* may be more probative. It held that if a remote cause of a fire was an earthquake—that is, if the earthquake started a fire, which then spread to the insured's property—the insurance company was liable. Such narrow constructions of exclusions make Redfearn's case stronger. He could reasonably argue that the clause denying coverage for damage indirectly caused by riot should be construed narrowly, so that there has to be almost a direct connection between the riot and the loss, and that there was an insufficiently strong connection between the riot and the fire. Moreover, the clause exempted only acts caused by rioters, not by police. They hold that earthquake fire exclusion clauses apply to fires started as a direct result by earthquake.

80. *See* Brief for Plaintiff, *supra* note 77, at 93–94 (discussing issues on appeal); *id.* at 100–1 ("[A]ll of the witnesses who had been able to give any information concerning the destruction of the buildings, claim that the circumstances were such as to indicate certain men who were acting as peace officers, destroyed these buildings by fire").

81. Commissioners acted as special masters for the Oklahoma Supreme Court; their opinions could then be adopted by the Court, as happened in *Redfearn*.

82. The Court described the scene:

From that time until about 9 or 10 o'clock the following day there was a great deal of shooting, especially in the negro section of the city, and

> a number of men were killed. Beginning about 2 o'clock in the morning of June 1st, fires began to break cut in the negro section of the city. The fire department, in attempting to respond to calls coming in from the negro section, found the streets full of armed white men, who, with pointed guns, refused to permit the firemen to connect the hose, and forced them to return to the fire stations without rendering any service in extinguishing the fires. After a few attempts to reach the fire the chief of the fire department directed the men to respond to no more calls until morning.

242 P. at 929.

83. *Id.* at 928–30.

84. *Id.* at 931.

Stearns held that a fire started (wrongfully and without authority) to arrest rioters was not caused (even indirect) by the riot. The Oklahoma Supreme Court, however, thought that a fire started by deputies after the people inside the buildings were arrested was caused at least indirectly by the riot. Comparing the two cases, one reaches the conclusion that if law enforcement officials burn a building to end a riot, the insured receives compensation, but if officials burn the building for their own malicious purposes, without trying to effect an arrest, then the insured receives no compensation. 140 S.W. at 199 ("The marshal's posse, acting under his orders, were not rioters").

85. 242 P. at 931.

86. *See* 153 P. 1160 (1915). *See also* Barbara Holden-Smith, *Lynching, Federalism, and the Intersection of Race and Gender in the Progressive Era,* 8 YALE J. LAW AND FEMINISM 31–73-74 (1996) (locating prize fight films in context of racial violence in the Progressive era).

87. *See St. Louis, Iron Mountain & Southern Ry. v. Freeland,* 134 P. 47 (1913).

88. *Collins v. Oklahoma State Hosp.,* 184 P. 946 (1916).

89. 215 P. 419 (Okla. 1923).

90. So too in the minds of those responding to the Tulsa riot. An editorial reprinted in the CHICAGO DEFENDER alluded to slavery. *See* William B. Smith, *Tulsa's Race Problem,* CHICAGO DEFENDER (July 9, 1921) ("White adventurers trapped him in his native jungle only a few years ago; shipped him in chains to serve the white man in other lands; a stroke of political fortune makes him free and 'equal' to the white man in our country, and he has the consummate gall and impudence to want a place at the council board of the white man's civilization").

91. *Cofield v. Fannelly,* 134 P. 407 (1913) (upholding Oklahoma's grandfather clause in denying right to vote to Theodore Cofield). In *Snyder v.*

Blake, 129 P. 34, 37 (1912), the Oklahoma Supreme Court told of the tests certain election officials imposed on blacks seeking to vote. At one precinct, "no negro was permitted to vote unless he could immediately memorize a section of the Constitution selected and read to him by the election instructor and write the same from memory." *Id.* Such conduct, the Court acknowledged, "can find no justification in the law." Nevertheless, the Court refused relief because the plaintiff failed to established that enough voters were prevented from voting to make a difference in the election. *See also Atwater v. Hassett*, 111 P. 802 (1910) (upholding constitutionality of grandfather clause). It was the United States Supreme Court that struck down Oklahoma's grandfather clause. *See Guinn v. United States*, 238 U.S. 347 (1915); *cf. Allen v. Wildman*, 134 P. 1102 (1913) (refusing to overturn election in which blacks voted).

92. *Miller v. Price*, 33 P. 2d 624 (1934).

93. *Oklahoma City v. Page*, 6 P. 2d 1033, 1035 (1931) (arguing that nuisance was permanent because the area is occupied "by colored people living in huts").

94. *Bixby v. Cravens*, 156 P. 1184, 1186 (1916) (refusing injunction of alleged spite fence, because the fence served to block defendant's view of blacks walking near his window).

95. *Hall v. Russell*, 178 P. 679 (1919); *First National Bank of Watonga v. Wade*, 111 P. 205 (1913); *Hill v. Hawkins*, 149 P. 213 (1915). Or, the Court might note a party's race in passing. *Commercial Casualty Ins. v. Warner*, 16 P. 2d 118, 119 (1932) (plaintiff was "a student in the colored high school at Ardmore").

96. 169 P. 904 (1917).

97. *St. Louis-San Francisco Railway Co. v. Loftus*, 234 P. 607 (1925). Ralph Ellison's account of a ride on a segregated railroad car between Oklahoma City and McAlister details the meaning segregated cars had for riders. *See* Ralph Ellison, *Boy on a Train*, in Ralph Ellison, FLYING HOME AND OTHER STORIES 12–21 (John F. Callahan, ed., 1996).

98. *Id.* at 609–10. *See also Henderson v. Galveston, H. & San Antonio Ry.*, 38 S.W. 1136, 1137 (Tex. Civ. App. 1896) (providing for liability when railroad failed to provide bathroom facilities for blacks traveling in segregated car).

99. *See St. Louis, Iron Mountain & Southern Ry. Co. v. Lewis*, 136 P. 396 (1913). In *Lewis*, a black woman who had sat in an unheated waiting room for a train that was more than an hour late sued for damages. The railroad company argued that Lewis was contributorily negligent because she declined an offer to wait in the railroad station's office. There was no evidence when the offer to sit by a hot stove in the station's office was made, and Lewis would have had to pass through the white waiting room to get

there. The Court cautiously added that "we cannot say . . . that she was duty bound to do so." *Id.* at 399. A few years later, Reverend J.G. Gilmore, a black man, waited outside for at least half an hour for a train at Greenfield station. The door to the unheated waiting room, which doubled as a storage shed for potatoes, could not be opened and the station manager refused to admit him to the white waiting room. He caught cold as a result of the exposure. Chicago, *R.I. & P. Ry. Co. v. Gilmore,* 152 P. 1096 (1915).

100. *See Shawnee National Bank v. Perry,* 276 P. 230 (1929).

101. *See* Larry O'Dell, *Riot Property Loss,* in TULSA RACE RIOT: A REPORT BY THE OKLAHOMA COMMISSION TO STUDY THE TULSA RACE RIOT OF 1921, 143, 145 (2001).

102. An article in the TULSA WORLD two days before the riot, for instance, urged that Oklahoma hire a press agent to tell the rest of the United States about the "intimate details" of the state's growth and possibilities. Such an agent would "forcibly inform" outsiders that Oklahoma "is a state of wealth and happiness, where people are civilized and refined, where the Indians have no more desire for the scalps of palefaces, where the cowboy is the farmer-business man, where a majority of politicians are moral, where there are metropolitan cities with miles of paved streets and many towering skyscrapers, . . . and where IWW's anarchists are tarred and feathered whenever they become obstreperous." *Still Think This is Land of Cowboys and Indians,* TULSA WORLD 6 (May 29, 1921).

103. *See The End of Argonaut Days,* TULSA TRIBUNE (June 5, 1921) ("Tulsa is the capital of an El Dorado. It boasts of its wealth. But Tulsa is better than a city of millionaires: it is a city of generally distributed wealth and has the highest per capita wealth of any city in the world").

104. *See* Ellsworth, *supra* note 102, at 76–77, 83–84.

105. *Tulsa Will?* BLACK DISPATCH 1 (August 28, 1921) ("When Tulsa published to the world that 'Tulsa will restore,' did she mean to deceive the world or has something happened to bring about a change of heart? We wonder if the author of 'Tulsa Will' meant Tulsa will dodge").

Epilogue

1. Edmund Andrews, *Germans Sign Agreement to Pay Forced Laborers of Nazi Era,* NEW YORK TIMES 3 (July 18, 2000); Edmund Andrews, *Germany Accepts $5.1 Billion Accord to End Claims of Nazi Slave Workers,* NEW YORK TIMES A10 (December 18, 1999); *Swiss Banks Reach Accord,* NEW YORK TIMES sec. 4 at 2 (August 16, 1998); Howard W. French, *The World: The Atlantic Slave Trade; On Both Sides, Reason for Remorse,* NEW YORK TIMES sec. 4, 1 (April 5, 1998) (discussing Clinton's apology); Kenneth Gosselin, *Profits Made at The Cost of Freedom; Beyond Aetna, Others*

Reaped Benefits From Slavery in U.S., HARTFORD COURANT 1A (March 10, 2001); Jesse Leavenworth and Kevin Canfield, *Courant Complicity in an Old Wrong; Newspaper's Founder Published Ads in Support of the Sale and Capture of Slaves*, HARTFORD COURANT 1A (July 4, 2000). *See generally* Martha Minow, BETWEEN VENGEANCE AND FORGIVENESS (1998); Eric Yamamoto, INTERRACIAL JUSTICE: CONFLICT AND RECONCILIATION IN POST-CIVIL RIGHTS AMERICA (1999).

2. Boris I. Bittker, THE CASE FOR BLACK REPARATIONS (1973).

3. *See, e.g.*, Steve Subrin, Martha Minow, Mark Brodin, et al., CIVIL PROCEDURE: DOCTRINE, PRACTICE, AND CONTEXT 191 (2000) (discussing statutes of limitation).

4. Ralph Ellison, JUNETEENTH 19–20 (1999).

5. Peter Irons, JUSTICE AT WAR (1983).

6. *See* Linda Gordon, THE GREAT ARIZONA ORPHAN ABDUCTION (1999).

7. *See Not Liable for Damages*, TULSA WORLD 14 (June 8, 1921) ("[T]he Committee stated its belief that from a moral standpoint Tulsa is responsible for the loss and damage").

8. *Where the Responsibility Lies*, BLACK DISPATCH 4 (June 17, 1921) (quoting *Emporia Gazette*).

9. *See, e.g.*, Robert Westley, *Many Billions Gone: Is It Time To Reconsider the Case for Black Reparations?* 40 BOSTON COLLEGE LAW REVIEW 429–76 (1998).

10. *See J.A. Croson v. Richmond*, 488 U.S. 469, 508 (1989) (requiring that affirmative action programs be "narrowly tailored to remedy the effects of prior discrimination"). In 1995 in *Adarand Contractors v. Pena*, 515 U.S. 200, 223 (1995), the Supreme Court reannounced that one of the guiding principles for race-based programs is skepticism: that "any preference based on racial or ethnic criteria must necessarily receive a most searching examination." It remains quite unclear what race-based programs will pass muster, but certainly the case for a race-based program to repair specific discrimination in the Greenwood community is about as compelling as could exist.

11. *Tulsa*, THE NATION (June 15, 1921).

12. Slavery may, indeed, meet those criteria, for there are, in quite real ways, people alive who suffered debt peonage and state-sponsored segregation. These people are in very real ways living victims of institutions born of slavery.

13. *See, e.g.*, William Glaberson, *Who Is a Seminole, and Who Gets to Decide?* NEW YORK TIMES A1 (January 29, 2001); *Davis v. United States*, 192 F.3d 951 (10th Cir. 1999). The payment was made pursuant to a judgment under the Indian Claims Acts, although there is substantial question over who is entitled to recover. The controversy revolves around the question whether descendants of slaves of the Seminole are entitled to a share of

the award and whether African Americans were part of the tribe in 1823, when the dispossession took place.

14. *See, e.g.,* "Act to Suppress Mob Violence," Illinois, Hurd's Revised Statutes, 1915–16 chap. 38, section 256a.

15. *See, e.g., City of Chicago v. Sturigs*, 222 U.S. 323 (1908) (upholding constitutionality of Illinois statute imposing liability on cities for three-quarters value of mob damage, regardless of fault); *Arnold v. City of Centralia*, 197 Ill. App. 73 (1915) (imposing liability without negligence under Illinois statute, Hurd's Revised Statutes, 1915–16 chap. 38, section 256a, on city that failed to protect citizens against mob); *Barnes v. City of Chicago*, 323 Ill. 203 (1926) (interpreting same statute and concluding that police officer was not "lynched"); *Easter v. City of El Dorado*, 177 P. 538 (Kan. 1919) (construing General Statute sec. 3822 [1915] broadly to provide cause of action against city when mob that assembled in city caused damage outside the city); *Moore v. City of Wichita*, 189 P. 372 (Kan. 1920); *Butte Miners Union v. City of Butte*, 194 P. 149 (1920) (applying Montana's act); *Yalenezia v. City of Boston*, 131 N.E. 220 (Mass. 1921) (Revised Law c. 211, section 8); *Cantey v. Clarendon County*, 85 S.E. 228 (SC 1915) (interpreting South Carolina statute providing for liability for failure to protect from lynching); *Wells Fargo & Co. v. Jersey City*, 207 F. 871, aff'd, 219 F. 699 (C.C.A., NJ 1915) and cases cited in Centennial Digest, Counties, sec. 213.

16. *See* Minutes of the Chicago City Council (January 2, 1923) (listing claims settlements). I would like to thank Doug Bukowski, who shared his research on the Chicago lawsuits with me. Dr. Bukowski also shared his extensive knowledge of Chicago courts.

17. *Paying the Piper*, Black Dispatch 4 (July 15, 1921) ("Recent press stories chronicle the fact that during this month the city of East St. Louis pays out $454,000 in liquidation of the damage claims growing out of the race riot occurring there four years ago").

18. *City Not Liable for Riot Damage*, Tulsa World 1 (August 7, 1921).

19. *See* William Tuttle, Riot: Chicago 1919 (1972); Chicago Commission on Race Relations, The Negro in Chicago: A Study of Race Relations and a Race Riot (1922) (reprinted 1968).

20. *See* 62 Congressional Record 1793 (67th Cong., 2nd Sess.) (January 26, 1922) (reporting suits asking for nearly $1 million in claims against Kansas City and $37,000 against Independence, Kansas). *Id.* at 1924 (reprinting article, *Kick on Kansas Mob Law*, Kansas City Star [January 26, 1922]).

21. *See* Black Dispatch (March 19, 1919) (discussing bill in Oklahoma legislature to provide aid to victims of attack).

22. *See generally* Joseph Singer, Entitlement: The Paradoxes of Property 179–196 (2000) (exploring the chief elements of reparations: restitu-

tion of property, payments of money to compensate for damage done, and truth commissions).

23. 50 U.S.C. sec. 1989. In 1992, the funding for the act was increased from $1.25 billion to $1.65 billion. *Id. See also* COMMISSION ON WARTIME RELOCATION AND INTERNMENT OF CIVILIANS: PERSONAL JUSTICE DENIED, REPRINTED IN HOUSE COMM. ON INTERIOR AND INSULAR AFFAIRS, 102nd Cong., 2nd Sess., PERSONAL JUSTICE DENIED (1992).

24. Saul Levmore, *Changes, Anticipations, and Reparations*, 99 COLUMBIA L. REV. 1657 (1999).

25. 25 U.S.C. sec. 70a. *See* Nell Jessup Newton, *Compensation, Reparations, and Restitution: Indian Property Claims in the United States*, 28 GEORGIA LAW REVIEW 453, 468–72 (1994).

26. 348 U.S. 272 (1955). Occasionally, tribes prevail before the Claims Commission. The Seminole tribe, for example, was able to win an award of $16 million in 1976 for land they lost in 1823 in Florida. By 1990, when Congress authorized a payment plan developed by the Seminole tribe, interest had increased that award to $56 million. *See Davis v. United States*, 192 F.3d 951 (10th Cir. 1999).

27. 43 U.S.C. sec. 1601–29. *See* Newton, *supra* note 25, at 476–77. *See also* Carter D. Frantz, *Getting Back What Was Theirs? Reparation Mechanisms for the Land Rights Claims of the Maori and the Navajo*, 16 DICKINSON INTERNATIONAL LAW JOURNAL 489–521 (1998); Jennifer M.L. Chock, *One Hundred Years of Illegitimacy: International Legal Analysis of the Illegal Overthrow of the Hawai'ian Monarchy, Hawaii's Annexation, and Possible Reparations*, 17 UNIVERSITY OF HAWAII LAW REVIEW 463, 494–509 (1995) (discussing modes of reparation).

28. *See* 25 U.S.C. sec. 3007. *See also* Rik Espinosa, TULSA WORLD (September 20, 1999).

29. *See, e.g.,* Randall Robinson, THE DEBT: WHAT AMERICA OWES TO BLACKS (2000); Boris Bitker, THE CASE FOR BLACK REPARATIONS (1973); Robert Westley, *Many Billions Gone: Is It Time To Reconsider the Case for Black Reparations?* 40 BOSTON COLLEGE LAW REVIEW 429–76 (1998).

30. *See Cato v. United States*, 70 F.3d 1103 (9th Cir. 1995) (denying pro se claim for reparations for slavery).

31. *See, e.g.,* Rhonda V. Magee, *The Master's Tools, From the Bottom Up: Responses to African-American Reparations Theory in Mainstream and Outsider Remedies Discourse*, 79 VA. L. REV. 863 (1993); Vincene Verdun, *If the Shoe Fits, Wear It: An Analysis of Reparations to African Americans*, 67 TULANE LAW REVIEW 597 (1993); Mari J. Matsuda, *Looking to the Bottom: Critical Legal Studies and Reparations*, 22 HARV. C.R.-C.L. L. REV. 323, 362–97 (1987); Tuneen E. Chisholm, *Sweep Around Your Own Front*

Door: Examining the Argument for Legislative African American Reparations, 147 UNIVERSITY OF PENNSYLVANIA LAW REVIEW 677 (1999).

32. *See* Robert Westley, *supra* note 30; Eric Yamamoto, *Racial Reparations: Japanese American Redress and African American Claims*, 40 BOSTON COLLEGE L. J. 477 (1998). Similarly, Helen Jenkins made a creative argument for reparations for descendants of illegitimate children of slave owners, relying entirely upon well-tested doctrines from estate law. *See* Helen Jenkins, *A Study of the Intersection of DNA Technology, Exhumation and Heirship Determination as It Relates to Modern-Day Descendants of Slaves in America*, 50 ALA. L. REV. 39 (1998).

33. *See* H.R. 1684, 102nd Cong., 1st Sess. (1991).

34. *See City Aldermen Endorse Study of Reparations for Effects of Slavery*, ST. LOUIS POST DISPATCH 8 (June 17, 2000); *Aldermen Back Resolution on Slavery Reparations*, CHICAGO TRIBUNE 1 Metro (May 17, 2000).

35. Peter Edelman, *Poverty Law Policy: Getting Beyond the Silver Bullet*, 81 GEO. L.J. 1697 (1995) (discussing reawakening of national conscience in the aftermath of the Watts riot of 1965 and other riots and discussing the national programs established in response); Robert E. Tranquada and Peter A. Glassman, *Providing Health Care for the Uninsured and Underinsured in Los Angeles County*, in URBAN AMERICA: POLICY CHOICES FOR LOS ANGELES AND THE NATION 307, 312 (James B. Steinberg, David W. Lyon, and Mary E. Vaiana, eds., 1992).

36. Urban Development Action Grants, New Towns Demonstration Program for Emergency Relief of Los Angeles, 42 U.S.C. sec. 5318 (1998).

37. *See* Rosewood Massacre—1994 Florida Sess. Law Serv. Ch. 94–359 (C.S.H.B. 591), available on Westlaw, FL-LEGIS-OLD file.

38. *Warning Against Further Trouble*, TULSA WORLD 1 (June 4, 1921) ("We are in a measure no more responsible for this outbreak than we would be if a cyclone had visited the city").

39. Arnold Hamilton, *A Year Later, Tornados Still Changing Lives*, DALLAS MORNING NEWS 1A (April 30, 2000) ("So far, officials said, federal, state and local governments have spent more than $218 million on the disaster, including more than $40 million through the Army Corps of Engineers and Natural Resource Conservation Service for debris removal and soil stabilization. The Oklahoma Department of Civil Emergency Management also reported $17.1 million spent for hazardous materials cleanup, $43.5 million in public assistance, $ 67 million in Small Business Administration home loans, $6.8 million in SBA business loans, $2 million in SBA economic injury loans, $5.4 million in individual family grants and $29.1 million federal emergency response").

40. Ralph Waldo Ellison, JUNETEENTH 19–20 (1999).

41. OKLAHOMA GUIDE 4 (June 9, 1921).

42. Representative Bill Graves, speaking on "Democracy Now," Pacifica Radio, February 8, 2000. The program is available in the archives section of the "Democracy Now" web page: http//www.webactive.com/pacifica/demnow.htm.

43. *See* Minow, *supra* note 1.

44. *In Name Only*, BLACK DISPATCH 4 (July 8, 1921). Oklahoma House Bill 1178, signed by Governor Frank Keating on June 2, 2001, provides an alternative history of the riot. It also established a memorial commission and set up a mechanism for providing (privately funded) scholarships for descendants of riot victims and (again privately funded) economic development for Greenwood. *See* House Bill 1178.

45. *An Appeal to Reason*, TULSA WORLD 4 (June 3, 1921) ("The wretched mob spirit still smolders. . . . Standing high above every recognizable fact is this tremendous unsurmountable truth: these people have a right to life, to the pursuit of happiness and to their earthly possessions. To deny them those rights is to set aside the basic law of the land and deliberately take a keystone from the arch of the government in this country").

46. *Digging Justice Out of Chaos and Cowardice*, BLACK DISPATCH 4 (August 26, 1921).

47. The scholar's report to the Tulsa Riot Commission has already demonstrated the culpability of the city and the state. John Hope Franklin and Scott Ellsworth, HISTORY KNOWS NO FENCES in TULSA RACE RIOT: A REPORT BY THE OKLAHOMA COMMISSION TO STUDY THE TULSA RACE RIOT 1921 21–36 (2001), in *id.*, at 1–20. Available at http://www.ok-history.mus.ok.us/trrc/freport.htm. The Riot Commission's report, which was designed to evaluate the scholar's report and present the Commission's understanding is, however, remarkably vague. *See* Danney Goble, *Final Report of the Oklahoma Commission to Study the Tulsa Race Riot of 1921.*

48. *See, e.g.*, Minow, *supra* note 1, at 52–90. *See also* Elizabeth Latif, *Apologetic Justice: Evaluating Apologies Tailored Toward Legal Solutions*, 81 BOSTON UNIV. L. REV. 289 (2001).

49. *See, e.g., Swann v. Charlotte-Mecklenberg Bd. Ed.*, 402 U.S. 1 (1970) (school desegregation); *Rogers v. Lodge*, 458 U.S. 613 (1982) (upholding at-large system of voting to enhance minority voting rights).

50. 488 U.S. 469 (1989).

51. *Croson* invalidated the Richmond, Virginia, minority set-aside program, which required that prime contractors had to subcontract at least 30 percent of the dollar value of the contract to minority-owned businesses. *Id.* at 477–78. The Supreme Court found the requirement unconstitutional because there were only generalized findings of discrimination in the Richmond construction industry. Such vague allegations of "societal discrimination" offered no "logical stopping point." *Id.* at 498 (quoting *Wygant v.*

Jackson Board of Education, 476 U.S. 267, 276, 275 [1986] [plurality]). Given the prima facie case of unconstitutional discrimination in housing in Tulsa, there is adequate basis for race-based set-asides in housing projects. *Cf. id.* at 500 (noting lack of prima facie case of unconstitutional discrimination in Richmond construction industry). *See also Adarand Contractors v. Pena*, 515 U.S. 200, 237 (1995) ("When race-based action is necessary to further a compelling interest, such action is within constitutional constraints if it satisfies the 'narrow tailoring' test this Court has set out in previous cases").

52. *See New Dreamland Theater at Tulsa, Oklahoma*, BLACK DISPATCH 8 (September 14, 1922). *See also* BLACK DISPATCH 3 (August 5, 1921) (reprinting picture of Dreamland before the riot and asking, "This above picture is the once beautiful Dreamland Theater, which was destroyed at Tulsa, in the riots, June 1st. Does it look like a shack?"). The BLACK DISPATCH was responding to the argument that Greenwood had been a shantytown before the riot.

53. *The Disgrace of Tulsa*, TULSA WORLD 4 (June 2, 1921).

54. *See* 1921 Tulse Ract Riot Reconciliation Act of 2001, Ok. H. 3. 1178 (signed Jun 1, 2001), OKTEXT Lexis. Many survivors were understandably disappointed with that result. See Ben Fenwick, *Oklahoma rejects any reparations in deadly 1921 Tulsa race riot; up to 500 killed, 100 survivors left,* SAN DIEGO UNION-TRIBUNE A-12 (May 26, 2001). That result came as no surprise to those of us who had followed the debate, however. For, legislators had run from the issue of reparations. *See* Lois Romano, *No Vow to Make Amends for Tulsa; Legislator's Sidestepping Disappoints Survivors of 1921 Race Riot*, WASHINGTON POST A3 (March 1, 2001); Bill Hanna, *Riot Panel Calls for Reparations; How Oklahoma Legislators will respond uncertain,* FORT WORTH STAR-TELEGRAM 4 (March 2, 2001).

55. House Concurrent Resolution 1044 (March 27, 2001), OKTEXT Lexis.

56. Even David Horowitz, one of the most virulent opponents of reparations for slavery, concedes that reparations are due to Tulsa riot victims. *See* Oralandar Brand-Williams, *WSU anti-reparation ad draws few complaints,* DETROIT NEWS METRO 1 (April 12, 2001).

57. *See generally* Saul Levmore, *Changes, Anticipations, and Reparations,* 99 COLUM. L. REV. 1657 (1999). Professor Randall Kennedy suggested the danger that the precedent of Tulsa may limit, more than aid, the case for reparations for large-scale, nationwide discrimination. Or it may, as Professor Robert Westerly warns, appear more like a case for government largesse than a debt owed to victims of government-sactioned violence.

58. THE IDEOLOGY OF SLAVERY: PROSLAVERY THOUGHT IN THE ANTE-BELLUM SOUTH, 1830–1860, 21, 24 (Drew Faust, ed., 1980).

59. *See* Michael Vorenberg, FINAL FREEDOM: THE CIVIL WAR, THE ABOLITION OF SLAVERY, AND THE THIRTEENTH AMENDMENT 26–27, 108–9, 168–69 (2001).

60. Ralph Ellison, *Going to the Territory*, in THE COLLECTED ESSAYS OF RALPH ELLISON 595 (John F. Callahan, ed., 1995).

Bibliographic Essay

The story of the Tulsa riot is as much about the conflicting interpretations of whites and blacks as it is about what actually happened. And while the white story has been dominant, those conflicting interpretations have been there since the riot began. Those conflicting stories are best represented in the grand jury report, printed on June 26, 1921, in the *Tulsa World*, which blamed Greenwood residents for rioting, and in the poem written by A.J. Smitherman, printed and distributed widely by Smitherman at the end of 1921. It is available in the NAACP papers at the Library of Congress, in the A.J. Smitherman file.

To recover those competing visions, one ought to look at the white and black newspapers in the years leading up to the riot. We have been fortunate to have a nearly complete run of the *Oklahoma City Black Dispatch* from its inception in 1917 through the riot at the Oklahoma Historical Society. The *Black Dispatch*, edited by Roscoe Dunjee, developed sophisticated arguments about the importance of the equal protection of the law in protecting the black community and allowing it to prosper. Much of the evidence in the first chapter comes from the *Black Dispatch*. After the riot, the *Black Dispatch* was the only black newspaper in Oklahoma. It is central to understanding the black interpretation of the riot as the breakdown of the rule of law, for it explicitly challenged the grand jury's report and the *Tulsa Tribune*'s story about Dick Rowland's alleged attack on Sarah Page. It discusses the challenge to the zoning ordinance, which was designed to prevent rebuilding in Greenwood.

Two other black Oklahoma newspapers are particularly important: the *Muskogee Cimeter* and the *Tulsa Star*. The Oklahoma Historical Society has many issues of the *Cimeter*, founded by A.J. Smitherman around 1911, and the *Tulsa Star*, founded by Smitherman after he moved in Tulsa in 1913. Both portray the concerns of the black community in such areas as lynching, housing segregation, discriminatory treatment on railroads, and unequal funding of schools. There are no issues of the *Star* after January 1921, so one must infer from other papers and other records the ideas on the minds of Greenwood residents in the months leading up to the riot.

Together the *Black Dispatch* and *Tulsa Star* contain important data on attitudes toward law and the importance of self-help in the black community to uphold that law and protect against violence and other forms of discrimination. The issues of both papers in September 1920, which present the lynchings of Claude Chandler and Roy Belton, are central to understanding the riot, because they discuss the threats that blacks (and whites) faced of lynching. They also discuss the appropriate response. One editorial in particular, "The Facts Remain the Same," which appeared in the *Tulsa Star* on September 8, 1920, represents well the attitude that led Greenwood veterans to march to the courthouse on the night of May 31, 1921. The Oklahoma Attorney General Investigations of both the Chandler and Belton lynchings, available at the Oklahoma State Archives, are indispensable for understanding the culpability of local officials in the lynchings. From those investigations, one can understand the well-founded fear that Greenwood residents had that Rowland would be turned over to a mob.

Periodicals published outside Oklahoma, like the NAACP's *The Crisis*, published monthly in New York, and the weekly *Chicago Defender*, give a fuller sense of the centrality of appeals to law—and the use of self-help to protect against violence. They also place the rising aspirations of black Americans into the context of World War I and the jazz age.

For the white perspective, the two daily Tulsa papers, the *Tulsa World* and the *Tulsa Tribune*, are indispensable. They often discuss events in Greenwood. They focus on vice there, such as alcohol, prostitution, and jazz. Their perspective is skewed (as one would expect given that Greenwood is frequently referred to as "Niggertown"). But when one reads the papers as texts to divine attitudes, rather than for the truth of the matter asserted, they are valuable. For they tell the story of how whites feared Greenwood—how they feared the breakdown of social hierarchy in Greenwood, the "race mixing," and the vice, as well as the economic and social progress of Greenwood residents. A few other white newspapers, primarily the *Chicago Tribune* and the *St. Louis Post-Dispatch*, have useful and balanced coverage of the riot. White Oklahoma newspapers, like the *Muskogee Times-Democrat* and the *Daily Oklahoman*, are more willing to criticize Tulsa than are the *Tulsa World* and *Tulsa Tribune*.

Beyond newspapers and periodicals, which contain much valuable information on attitudes related to the riot and the aftermath, the key details of the riot are preserved in several court cases. While there were several hundred suits filed, only two (so far as I can determine) ever went to trial. They were the suits filed by Mabel Allen, *Allen v. Tulsa*, Tulsa County Dist. Court, Case No. 16,013, and William Redfearn, *Redfearn v. American Central Insurance Company*, 243 P 929 (Okla. 1926). The trial court records for Tulsa in the 1920s have long since been discarded, so the trial testimony in both Allen's and Redfearn's cases has been lost. However, Redfearn appealed his case to the Oklahoma Supreme Court. Hundreds of pages of testimony are preserved in the briefs filed with the court. The briefs are available on my web site, *www.law.ua.edu/abrophy*, and in the Oklahoma State Archives in Oklahoma City.

One other case, filed by J.B. Stradford after he fled to Chicago to escape prosecution for inciting riot, contains important details about the origins and unfolding of the riot. None of Stradford's testimony is recorded, for the case was dismissed before trial, but there is deposition testimony from Sheriff W.M. McCullough and Police Chief John Gustafson, *Stradford v. American Central Ins. Co.*, Superior Court of Cook County, No. 370,274 (1921). The case is available from the Cook County Court Archives.

Little remains of the other cases arising out of the riot, such as the criminal prosecution of Dick Rowland, which was dropped in September 1921; the prosecutions of Greenwood residents for inciting riot; the prosecution of Police Chief John Gustafson; and the challenge to the zoning ordinance. On the criminal prosecutions, the docket sheet for Rowland is available at the Tulsa County Court Archives, case no. 2188. Gustafson's trial is covered extensively in the Tulsa papers in July 1921. Most of what we know about the successful challenge to the zoning ordinance comes from articles in the *Tulsa World*, *Tulsa Tribune*, and *Black Dispatch* from mid-August through early September. There are some suggestive hints in the petition in *Lockard v. Evans, et al.*, Tulsa County District Court, Case 15,780 (August 12, 1921).

While the Tulsa Court records are sparse, there is some useful material in the attorney general's papers on the riot at the Oklahoma State Archives in Oklahoma City. There are several boxes of papers, containing notes on witnesses and limited trial testimony, apparently from the Gustafson case. Those records also contain the after-action reports of the local units of the National Guard.

There are yet a few other court records that are particularly helpful in understanding race in Progressive-era Oklahoma. The United States Supreme Court decisions in *Guinn v. United States*, 238 U.S. 347 (1915); *McCabe v. Atchison, Topeka,* and *Santa Fe Ry.*, 235 U.S. 151, 163 (1914); and the Oklahoma Supreme Court case of *Stradford v. Midland Valley Railroad Co.*, 128 P. 98 (Okla. 1912). In a number of other cases the Oklahoma Supreme Court, in conjunction with the legislature, created a legal system that governed the separate worlds of black and white Oklahoma, ranging from separate schools to railroad segregation, to voting rights, to criminal prosecution. That world of white "law" and the clash with the black vision of what the world *should* look like is central to understanding the riot.

In more recent times, there have been several important histories of the riot. Scott Ellsworth's *Death in a Promised Land*, published in 1982, is the most comprehensive and serious account of the riot to date. He also co-authored with John Hope Franklin the majority of the scholars' report to the Tulsa Riot Commission and co-edited the remaining sections. The scholars' report contains the most up-to-date information available on the riot. It has been reprinted as part of the Riot Commission's final report, *Tulsa Race Riot: A Report by the Oklahoma Commission to Study the Tulsa Race Riot of 1921* (2001). The entire report is available on the Oklahoma Historical Society's website at: *http://www.ok-history.mus.ok.us/trrc/trrc.htm*. This book represents an expansion of the themes in my section of the report, on legal issues related to the riot.

There have been several other fine studies. Mary Jones Parrish's book, printed just after the riot, presents rich detail about the riot, from the perspective of a riot victim. It is now available in a modern edition. In the early 1970s, two studies opened the riot to serious study: Ed Wheeler's "It Happened in Tulsa," printed in *Impact Magazine* (June–July 1971) and available at *www.TulsaToday.com/*

racewar.htm, and R. Halliburton, "The Tulsa Race War of 1921," which appeared in the *Journal of Black Studies* 2 (1972): 333–57.

Bob Hower's *Angels of Mercy*, published in 1994, is a history of the Red Cross's assistance after the riot. It is an important study on the role of a private institution in rebuilding; it also has reprints of many key riot documents. Hannibal Johnson's *Black Wallstreet*, published in 1998, portrays well the culture of Greenwood, as well as the riot. Brent Staples' article in the *New York Times Magazine* on December 20, 1999, connects the most recent research on the culpability of the city to the city's current struggle to understand the riot and what should be done now. It is a stark portrait of the divisions that stretch across the generations, as will be James Hirsch's *Riot and Remembrance*. Jewell Parker Rhodes' novel *Magic City* (1998) is set around the story of Dick Rowland and Sarah Page.

The photographs, which are so important in understanding the riot, are available in several locations. The University of Tulsa special collections has the largest collection; the Tulsa Historical Society has some of the most important photographs and several panoramic pictures; the western history collections at the University of Oklahoma have some photographs not available anywhere else; and the Oklahoma Historical Society in Oklahoma City has many of the same photographs. The Oklahoma Historical Society also has photocopies of many of the riot documents. Photographs are conveniently available in several places. The University of Tulsa's Special Collections Library's web site has many of them. Bob Hower's *Angels of Mercy* reprints many photographs. The *Tulsa Race Riot: A Report by the Oklahoma Commission to Study the Tulsa Race Riot of 1921* (2001), availabl at the Oklahoma Historical Society's website: *http://www.okhistory.mus.ok.us/trrc/trrc.htm*, has many rare riot photographs.

Suggestions for Further Reading

I drew on many other historians' studies of race, riots, and law in the Progressive era. The host of books, which explore other riots, were helpful in understanding what was common to riots in the era and what was unique to Tulsa. The most useful were: Eliot Rudwick, *Race Riot at East St. Louis, July 2, 1917* (1966); Roberta Senechal, *The*

Sociogenesis of a Race Riot: Springfield, Illinois, in 1908 (1990); William M. Tuttle, *Race Riot : Chicago in the Red Summer of 1919* (1972).

Lynching, which has received substantial attention from historians in recent years, is central to the riot. Lynching as a social phenomenon is treated in such books as Leon Litwack, *Trouble in Mind: Black Southerners in the Age of Jim Crow* (1998); James Allen, *Without Sanctuary: Lynching Photography in America* (2000); *Under Sentence of Death: Lynching in the South* (W. Fitzhugh Brundage ed., 1997); William Fitzhugh Brundage, *Lynching in the New South: Georgia and Virginia, 1880–1930* (1988); Daniel F. Littlefield, *Seminole Burning : A Story of Racial Vengeance* (1996). Lynching's relationship to law is treated in James Harmon Chadbourn, *Lynching and the Law* (1933); Emma Coleman Jordan, "Crossing The River of Blood Between Us: Lynching, Violence, Beauty, And The Paradox of Feminist History," 3 *J. Gender, Race, and Law* 545 (2000).

Several studies detail the development of legal thought, particularly about race, in the Progressive era, including Alexander Bickel and Benno C. Schmidt, *The Judiciary and Responsible Government, 1910–21* (1984) and Kenneth W. Mack, "Law, Society, Identity, and the Making of the Jim Crow South: Travel and Segregation on Tennessee Railroads, 1875–1905," 24 *Law and Social Inquiry* 377–409 (1999). The political and intellectual context more generally appears in Glenda Gilmore, *Gender and Jim Crow: Woman and the Politics of White Supremacy in North Carolina, 1896–1920* (1996); C. Van Woodward, *The Strange Career of Jim Crow* (1957); and Eric J. Sundquist, *To Wake the Nations: Race in the Making of American Literature* (1993). It also appears in anthologies, such as David Levering Lewis, ed., *The Portable Harlem Renaissance Reader* (1994), and in biographies, such as David Levering Lewis, *W.E.B. Du Bois: The Fight for Equality and the American Century, 1919–1963* (2000) and David Levering Lewis, *W.E.B. DuBois—Biography of a Race, 1868–1919* (1993).

The reparations movement is inspired by, and related to, larger problems of race, racial discrimination, and law in America. One interested in those issues might begin with Randall Kennedy, *Race, Crime, and the Law* (1997). The starting point for reparations discussion right now is Randall Robinson's *The Debt: What America Owes to Blacks* (2000). Robinson's book rests, in turn, on the legal arguments advanced in Robert Westley, "Many Billions Gone: Is it Time to Reconsider the Case for Black Reparations," 49 *Boston College Law Review* 429–76 (1998). Boris Bittker's 1973 book, *The Case for Black Reparations*, uses civil rights law as a framework to analyze reparations claims for slavery, much as I do in the epilogue. Martha Minow's *Between Vengeance and Forgiveness: Facing History After Genocide and Mass Violence* (1998) places reparations claims in an international context.

Index

CPSIA information can be obtained
at www.ICGtesting.com
Printed in the USA
BVHW070439180719
553742BV00005B/69/P

9 780195 161038